BRITAIN
A VIEW FROM WESTMINSTER

EDITED BY
Julian Critchley

BRITAIN
A VIEW FROM WESTMINSTER

BLANDFORD PRESS
POOLE · NEW YORK · SYDNEY

First published in the UK 1986 by Blandford Press
Link House, West Street, Poole, Dorset BH15 1LL

Copyright © 1986 Blandford Press Ltd

Distributed in the United States by
Sterling Publishing Co., Inc.,
2 Park Avenue, New York, NY 10016

Distributed in Australia by
Capricorn Link (Australia) Pty Ltd
PO Box 665, Lane Cove, NSW 2066

British Library Cataloguing in Publication Data

Britain: a view from Westminster.
  1. Great Britain—Social conditions
  —1945—
  I. Critchley, Julian
  941.085'8   HN385.5

ISBN 07137 1679 7

Typeset by Furlonger Phototext Ltd., Bournemouth, Dorset.

Printed in Great Britain by Mackays of Chatham, Kent.

Contents

Introduction

Written by sixteen Parliamentarians, this book reflects the background and conditions of life in those parts of the United Kingdom which they represent, or have represented, in the House of Commons.

In order to present a unique collection of views, there is deliberately no uniformity of style in these contributions — each having been left free to treat the subject in his own way. Some are evidently more historically-minded than others; some see in the physical features of the counties of their region an important influence on contemporary life; some treat in more detail than others the social consequences of the changing industrial conditions of the recent past and of today.

This very diversity of approach to their subject by the authors, who represent the different political parties of Britain, illustrates clearly one main fact which emerges. This overriding aspect is, that despite the sameness of external life and topics of public interest portrayed by the media, and so displayed to the rest of the world, Britain today is a place of infinite variety.

The past is alive in most of us. It still survives most evidently, no doubt, in Scotland, Wales, Northern Ireland, the West Country and the North East; much less so in the mixed population of Greater London. The new technology is transforming life, and particularly in southern England, where it radiates from the capital along the motorways. Yet you will find its impact absent from articles on other regions. In London, and in several other cities in which there is a concentration of descendants of black and Asian immigrants, certain aspects of racial tension are emerging as a major cause of disorder; yet in most chapters of this book you will find no reference to the subject. The unemployment, which stemmed from the eclipse of the labour-intensive industries, remains acute in the North, Northern Ireland and the Midlands, whereas a growing affluence is the prevailing picture elsewhere.

This same disparity is to be seen in the impact of the Nuclear Disarmament Movement, which loomed so large in the media between 1981 and 1984. In fact, its only mention is the account of the problems of the Thames Valley Police at Greenham Common and contained in my own essay. However, this is not surprising, for one looks in vain for any overall popular interest in foreign affairs. They may indeed be a lively concern of the activists of the political parties and at the universities, but just how far they can affect the electorate and its deliberations is anybody's guess.

I have no doubt that there is an underlying foundation of national sentiment and also of moral principle within the United Kingdom but which does not come to the surface at first examination. Indeed, there is no suggestion that such a collection of regional essays could give an exhaustive description of life and ideas in Britain today but the very diversity of this testimony is a tribute to the reality of our freedom.

Julian Critchley, M.P.
Farnham, November 1984

THE HIGHLANDS AND ISLANDS
Lord Grimond

Baron Grimond of Firth was, as Jo Grimond, twice leader of the Liberal party and M.P. for Orkney and Shetland from 1950 until 1974. He is a former Rector of Edinburgh and Aberdeen Universities and Chancellor of the University of Kent.

Lord Grimond is a distinguished writer whose journalism is a delight, and whose autobiography is among the best to have been written since the end of the Second World War.

I n spite of all that industry, planners, trippers and modern architects can do, it is impossible to come to the Highlands and Islands except by routes of great beauty. You might approach across the Atlantic to meet the stark and lonely stacks of St Kilda, or from Norway to see the Muckle Flugga rising from an ever threshing sea. You could sail past the Mull of Kintyre or breach the Highland hills through the Trossachs or past the Ochils. Or you could drive up into the glens from Angus, the Mearns, Aberdeenshire or beyond, past stubble and plough, yellow oil rape and the changing colour of the woods. For me the best parts of the Highlands are where the fields run into the moors and the hills look down on the sea.

*   *   *   *

We will start our travels from the north, skirting Muckle Flugga and landing at Baltasound, in Unst, in Shetland. We are on the latitude of Leningrad. Our nearest railway station is Bergen and we are as far from the tip of mainland Scotland as Darlington is from London. Baltasound was once the largest herring port in the world. The voe, or sea-loch, on which it stands was once encircled by herring stations and in the Summer its waters were blanketed by herring boats and its shores by girls, mostly

Irish, who came to gut and pack the herring. Among the boats lay the steamers, Klondykers, which carried the herring to the Baltic and Germany. Here we notice the first peculiarities of the Highlands and Islands. In some ways, they are the most insular because they are the most remote part of Britain; in others they are international. The sea is not a barrier, it has been the great thoroughfare of history. After the herring fishing declined many Shetlanders went into the Royal Navy, the Merchant Navy or Salvesen's antarctic whaling fleet. Even in the 1950s you could find quite a few Shetlanders who knew Yokahama and New York but had never been to Edinburgh; who had visited Capetown and Buenos Aires, but had never seen a railway train.

Unst is for the most part barren. Thin and stony soil and a long straight road running to the South across a tundra, or at least what I imagine a tundra to be like. However, it is a great place for ponies. Yell, the next island, is a deep cushion of peat. But we must push on. From the jagged moorlands of Shetland we pass to the green and pleasant land of Orkney. Nowhere in the north do you find the dense lush growth, the brambles and hedgerows of Devon, but Orkney cattle browse on good grass throughout the long summer days and the Orkney landscape is as hospitable as Somerset. So, crossing the Pentland Firth, a fierce piece of water through which the tides race, we come to Caithness. But Caithness is very different from Perthshire or Argyll.

Meeting Sinclairs, Gunns and Mackays, we are now in the Clan country where although the Norse influence remains, the outward signs of Celtdom are to be encountered − kilts and Gaelic. But Caithness also has swathes of farmland fringing the moors to the east. Much of it is flat. Its seas heave below that steely light which is the hallmark of the north.

From Wick or Thurso you can take the railway south, or travel by a road of great beauty, but apt to be made somewhat murderous by heavy lorries. Or you can wander in and out down the West Coast. On the East you can find some of my favourite country, woods, hills, lochs and rivers penetrated and mixed with prosperous looking farms. Spring in Scotland is apt to be snowy, but to drive down to Inverness on a fine autumn day is pure bliss. On the West the landscape is very different. Romantics love the West. To me it is rather surprising and not wholly a pleasant surprise. For the hills are often as green as a billiard cloth. The bonny purple heather is steadily in retreat and with it the grouse. Grouse are now rare birds down the West of Scotland. The West too is very depopulated causing me some pain, for I do not admire deserts.

Then we come to Inverness which claims to be the capital of the Celtic highlands. I am a lover of small Scottish towns, having been born and brought up in St Andrews, the pearl of them all. But they have suffered grievously. Many towns and cities sit on positions as fine as any in Europe. Dundee, Aberdeen, Inverness, and of course Edinburgh, have marvellous sites. Their use of them makes one weep. The banks of the Ness at Inverness are pleasant enough; you may even watch a man fishing. But on the whole it is a disappointing town, making little attempt at beauty or ingenuity. However, it is filled with decent people and the sort of shops you find everywhere, from Penzance to Perth and beyond. Yet like all of Scotland, indeed all of Britain, it has its share of the blight cast by modern architects and planners. This blight is particularly bleak and depressing in the Highlands, where the concrete matchbox streaked with rain, its paint peeling, is an outrage to the landscape. Furthermore, Scotland had a tradition of small stone houses, well-made, unpretentious, sheltering and fitting snugly with their background and one another. They had too their individual quirks and character. Many have been destroyed, few have been copied.

However, Invernessshire had for a time after the last War a county architect whose legacy shines like a good deed in the hidden grey and sad world of council housing. You may spot his work throughout the county, plain white houses with well-set windows and a welcoming air. I believe, possibly wrongly, that he was originally not an architect at all, but a soldier. I have always admired military education. And while we are on the subject of soldiers it is worth slipping down the coast to look at Fort George. Until I saw it I thought that 17th and 18th century fortifications were built only in Europe: Vauban fortresses in Northern France or Vienna in the days of the Turkish menace. Fort George is an interesting reminder of how recently the Highlands were regarded as wild and insubordinate, a scarcely pacified colony. The Romans in Gaul must have felt rather like the English regiments at Fort George.

*   *   *   *

The cleft of the great glen running across from Inverness to Fort William is the most obvious mark on the map. But it is not a very significant division in reality. Having left the Norse lands behind, the chief division is between east and west. Indeed, this division runs through Scotland. At one time, separate kingdoms ran from North Wales to the Clyde, and from Edinburgh through Northumberland. Historically, had things gone only a little differently, we might have had five kingdoms: southern England, West Wales, two more running side by side up what used to be the East and West coast railways from York and Crewe to Glasgow on the one coast and Aberdeen on the other and a Norse kingdom beyond them.

Whether that would have been better than the present arrangement I do not know. But what is certain is that Britain has become a highly centralised country dominated by London. This has damaged the outlying regions, particularly Scotland.

The Highlands and Islands have suffered peculiarly severely from this centralisation. For they are a region within a region. Whether the Central and Western Highlands and the Hebrides could have been a sixth kingdom is doubtful. The history of Ireland shows how fissiparous and feckless are the Gaels. But if the Norse, whether Scandinavian or Norman, could have kept their hands off them the Highlanders, then Gaels, might have developed a civilisation of their own. The battles of Stamford Bridge and Hastings appear to me to have been disasters. The English way of life, or failing that the Scandinavian way of life, and the Celtic church seem to me to have been much preferable to the grim Normans and the rule of Rome.

*   *   *   *

If we continue down the West we pass through the country of Mackenzies and MacDonalds into the land of the Campbells. Here we have the mini-history of fierce clan disputes in a wet and mountainous country falling into the Atlantic ocean. Sentimentally, Scotland is against the Campbells. They were Whigs and magnates choosing the winning side when all Scottish heroes except Bruce were losers. Practically, the divergence from their neighbours and the dominance of the Campbells has left little mark. But their chieftains, the Dukes of Argyll, have left us a delightful small town − Inverary, white, well-planned and well built. Straight south from Inverness over Slochd summit and down into the valley of the Garry and Tummel, the hills are drier and carry more heather while the river valleys are somewhat more fertile. But the way of life of the Macphersons and Murrays did not until the '45 differ greatly from that of their Western neighbours. Since then, however, the Central Highlands have been rather more prosperous than the West: they give a feeling of having come to better terms with modern life.

Further east still, if you take the Aberdeen road out of Inverness, the countryside is lowland. You may be a hundred and twenty miles north of Fife divided from it by the Grampians, but the farmlands of Moray, Nairn, Banff, Aberdeenshire, the Mearns and Angus are of the same stock as their southern neighbours; farm lands, market towns, large arable holdings. Indeed, as I have noted, this belt of good farm land continues, sometimes only as a narrow passage between the hills and the sea, but nevertheless unlike any area of the Western Highlands right up to Caithness and Wick.

Nevertheless, though the land and climate of the eastern seaboard differ from the west, the life of the upper classes was in many ways similar to that of their neighbours in the hills. The Gordons, though essentially a great family of the European kind, from the borders of Scotland and England, wore the kilt — and no doubt up to the 18th century their leaders, Marquesses of Huntly and the like, would have spoken Gaelic. But the life of the ordinary man and woman in the north east has been no more like that of the Highlands proper than the life, say, of Galloway, or the moors of Ayrshire and Lanarkshire. There have been, therefore, not only the geographical distinctions, which mark one part of the Highlands and Islands from another, but also class ramifications. As always, the upper classes mingled with their equals south or north of the Highland line, east or west of the road from Perth to Inverness. But in the north, there was added to differences of accent, occupations and amusements, peculiarities of dress. The wearing of the kilt was proscribed after the '45. The crofter and labourer seem never to have reverted to it with any great enthusiasm. It was the lairds who blossomed out with plaids and skean dhus. It is true that some of the general run of inhabitants march at the Highland Games. But the Games themselves were the invention and plaything of the gentry. It is they who led the gathering with bonnets and eagles feathers, pipers and shepherds crooks. As the successors to those who had cleared the glens they were not universally popular in their own country but with the cult of Walter Scott and Balmoral the Highland revival attracted followers far beyond those who either by blood or residence were part of the North. When efforts began to be made to stir political conscientiousness it was to the language that non-aristocratic highlanders turned. The poor continued to speak Gaelic long after the rich had lost it. Indeed, the efforts made to suppress it were not instigated by any feeling that it was a symbol of revolt, but because it was thought that boys and girls who spoke Gaelic would be branded as inferior.

*   *   *   *

Both in the west and in the east we are now looking over the Highland Line at Industrial Scotland as exhibited in Glasgow, Aberdeen, Dundee and, to a lesser extent, Perth and Stirling. Before considering the present situation of this area, which I have sketchily described, it is worth commenting on some aspects of its history, because they are relevant to any consideration of its present and future.

Apart from its diversity the history of the Highlands and Islands has some features not normally recognised. Orkney and Shetland have never been Celtic. No kilts were worn, no Gaelic spoken. Until the 15th century,

Orkney was one of the earldoms of the great Norse empire. It became part of Scotland not by conquest but, together with Shetland, as the forfeited surety for the dowry of a Danish princess. The Norse influence ran down the west as far as Dublin. On the other hand, the Normans crept up the fertile east coast. Until the 18th century the Gaelic clans prevailed over the centre and west of the area.

After the Synod of Whitby, the Roman prevailed over the Celtic rite in the church. But among the hills feudalism never prevailed. The conventional view is that the clan system was finally broken at Culloden, and that brutal Hanoverian repression then devastated the Highlands.

There is some truth in this view. The English and lowland Scottish establishment got a severe fright from the '45 and vented their terror on the Highlanders. But after the rebellions of 1715 and 1745, serious efforts were made to improve the living standards in the north. I am rather surprised that more attention has not been paid to their efforts, for in some ways they preceded by two centuries the efforts made to resuscitate the depressed areas after the Second World War. New towns were founded. The government intervened to assist fishing and agriculture. What would now be called conservation was introduced and small industries encouraged. General Wade set about building roads and attempts were made to guarantee safe passage to men and goods. Large caravans of cattle moved south to the lowland markets.

Nevertheless the economy of the Highlands and Islands remained at best precarious and their people impoverished. The experiments were too small, too far ahead of their time perhaps, but above all they could not make headway against the political and social customs. Politics, as we understand them, were virtually unknown. As the old patriarchial clan system disintegrated, the landowners, whether native or incoming, treated their estates as sources of income from which to support a style of life which took them increasingly to London or Edinburgh. Sheep paid better than men − so we had the clearances. The Crofting Acts at the end of the last century were entirely justified in their time. They gave the surviving Highlanders some security of tenure. But they forged the pattern of land-ownership over much of the area into a mosaic of small crofts backed by common grazings.

As the standard of life rose the arable land of the crofts became too small to support it. Meanwhile, it was in no one's individual interest to improve the common grazings. So as with the 18th century experiments the Crofting Acts by themselves failed to remedy the Highland economy.

The industry which should have done far more for the Highlands and Islands population was fishing. Where, for instance, in certain Shetland islands it took root, the population held. Unfortunately, and rather perversely, considering their long seaboard and many islands, the West Highlanders did not prove very keen or enterprising fishermen. Despite the foundation of new towns, such as Kyle of Lochalsh, the West Highland fisheries were, and still are, largely exploited by fishermen from the east coast of Scotland. These fishermen have certainly maintained their economy, not only from the string of towns and villages from Aberdeenshire round tò Inverness but also by setting up fishing centres on the Minch, such as Kinlochbervie. I use the rather neutral phrase 'maintained their economy' for while fishing does maintain the population where it survives, it is only lately that inshore fishermen have made much money. The industry which has, of course, made a lot of money is whisky distilling. Unfortunately, it employs few people and many of them indeed from the comparatively prosperous coasts and farm lands of the north east.

For the last hundred and forty years or so recreation has been a main feature of the central, north and west mainland in the Highland area. Stalking, shooting, salmon and trout fishing, walking and now ski-ing and bird watching have yielded a considerable income to native Highlanders as well as pleasure to incomers. They have indeed 'opened up' the hills and the lochs. The 'opening up' took longer than we are apt to realise. In spite of General Wade, Highland roads long remained pot-holed in summer and like river beds in winter. Even Queen Victoria was 'couped' into the ditch, though that may have been partly due to drunken driving. When other grandees followed the example of Balmoral, their great baronial mansions were the centre of a village of bakers, brewers and carpenters as well as domestic servants, keepers and ghillies, for communications were poor even to such shops as existed. Now all this is gone and tourism means more and more the car-driver and hiker.

But here we come up against the weather. The north of Scotland is a wet, windy and comparatively sunless area, growing ever more stern as you move towards the Arctic. It was all very well for the 19th century potentate. He handed his soaking clothes to his valet to be dried in the cavernous drying-rooms — a feature of every lodge. He then after a hot bath, regaled by whisky, settled down to a five course dinner with full butler service. Or perhaps, if the day was too bad, he would while it away with billiards and bridge. A week's bad weather was annoying but he was usually in residence for two months or more, so that a few fine days were a certainty. Now the bed and breakfaster begrudges every rainstorm out of his meagre fortnight. However kind the landlady — and they are very kind — it is a much less luxurious holiday. But here again things are not quite as many expect. In many parts of the west and north the climate if wet and windy is far from Siberian. Fuchsia flourishes in Orkney, and in sheltered gardens of the west are to be found trees and shrubs which would shrivel in the frosts of Kent.

*   *   *   *

As I have said, the fabric of life in the Highland area proper — the hills and glens of the centre and west — the Inner and Outer Hebrides broke up with the disintegration of the clan system in the 18th century. The old religion, Roman Catholicism, also largely disappeared except in the southern islands of the Outer Hebrides and a few other pockets. Its place was taken by Presbyterianism — and largely by the 'Free' Presbyterian Kirk. I cannot go into the numerous splits in the Presbyterian church. But the great and significant one was when whole congregations with their ministers rejected the patronage system. As with 18th century development the rise and fall of the Free Kirk seems to me too little known. Anyone who has read Osgood Mackenzie's *A Hundred Years in the Highlands* must be struck by his description of the great gatherings which came together in the middle of the last century to celebrate communion. Hundreds of people, after tramping to the trysting place, would camp there for several days while communion was celebrated and sermons preached.

The Kirk was the most important social as well as religious factor in the lives of ordinary people. And unlike so much else in the area it was at its prime ubiquitous. It was the great institution from the north of Shetland to Perth, from Peterhead to Stornoway (its last stronghold). Cousins of mine were farmers and small mill owners at Blairgowrie. Until the last of the family died in the 1950s their lives were dominated by the Free Kirk. On Sunday no travel by vehicle was permitted. Their clocks took no notice of Summer time. They read and were guided by the Bible. They were amongst the happiest people that I have ever met — partly because they were never racked by uncertainty. They knew exactly how to behave. They accepted this world and were sure of their place in the next.

At the other end of the Highlands and Islands, I used to go out on a fishing boat from Burra Isle in Shetland. The local boats had been fairly recently equipped with radio which enabled them to chat agreeably and usefully among themselves, but at a certain time every evening all boats fell silent so that a fisherman could sing a hymn to his family. Incidentally, one result of the materialism which has withered religion is that the old and easy going ways of the sea have also been shed. At one time different nations fished for different catches, no one grudging each their speciality. A small Swedish fleet came every year to Shetland, their boats were white, their prey was ling, they had their own chapel and pastor. The Belgians came for mackerel, the Spanish for hake. Now much richer fishermen all over Europe fight like cats for their quotas and subsidies.

It is not only therefore that the old clan relationships were destroyed. The way of life which to some extent succeeded it has also decayed. This way of life permeated by religion, in some places owed something to the lingering sense of clan kinship. But in others, for instance, those islands which had never known the clan system, or those small towns whose roots were quite different from those of the clans there was a considerable degree of cohesion. The crofters helped each other, as a matter of course, in spring and at harvest time. Serviceable ploughs came quite late to Shetland. Before that a line of men would dig the in-bye land with spades. The scattalds or common grazings were of course held in common.

At a wedding on a Shetland island the whole population would attend. Eating and dancing would go on for two or even three days with intervals for sleep. As their parents would be there, so too would babes in arms. Though there might be one or two castles in the neighbourhood, many islands and districts were virtually classless with no extremes of wealth. Fishing boats were, and still are, owned by their crews — share fishermen as they are called.

The impact of machinery, wireless, communications and rising standards led to new habits — and to new demands from those remaining in the Highlands and adjacent areas. But many had left. The stream of emigration continued through the 19th century and from many parts of the area continues today. Aberdeen, Dundee and Glasgow were the nearest destinations. There, at least until the First World War, there was a substantial demand for labour. The Industrial Revolution hardly touched the Highlands directly, but it overwhelmed many Highlanders. They and the Irish were the infantry of the factory system. They were swallowed into the urban proletariat which maintained the engineering and textile industries.

The stream also continued to flow to the dominions and North America. When I visited New Zealand in the 1950s, I was entertained by the Orkney and Shetland Society of Wellington which had a membership of over 800. Many of these members took *The Orcadian* and the *Shetland Times* and were as well up in the local news as I was. It is difficult to judge what the effect was, or is, upon the north of the feed-back from the Highlanders and Islanders gone from their native land. But two things are certain. First the connection with the cities to the south and lands overseas made it easy for Highlanders to leave. And to leave not only for the cities; Aberdeenshire has many Orkney farmers. Secondly, comparisons were certainly made between the old life and the new one in new surroundings.

*   *   *   *

The civilisation of the Celts has left few visible signs. Some crosses and ornaments are about all that have survived. About the language I am not qualified to speak. A few people still write in it. But the tradition was best maintained by such people as John Campbell of Canna who recorded the songs and folk-stories. The bagpipes are still taken seriously and new music written for them. As far as piping is concerned the Scottish regiments have played an important part. Shetlanders still play the fiddle. Indeed there has been an extraordinary growth of playing in Shetland which owes much to the teaching of Tom Anderson and the wider known and more commercial playing of Aly Bain. In general, the schools encouraged a great many children to play instruments and to paint.

But taken as a whole the north was more famous for its professors than its artists – and would-be professors had to emigrate, at least as far as Aberdeen and Glasgow. I can think of no well-known painter from the Highlands, though many have worked in the Highlands. Graham Sutherland and D. Y. Cameron presumably come from Highland families but can hardly be counted as Highlanders. As for writers, Edwin Muir and Eric Linklater came from Orkney and Neil Gunn from Caithness – all beyond, or nearly beyond, the Celtic area.

Scottish Nationalism made no general appeal in its political or literary form. Such nationalists as were successful owed their success as much to their personal abilities and services to their local communities as to any widespread desire for Scottish Independence. Indeed, despite the Hebrideans devotion to their Member, Donald Stewart, many in the north look to Edinburgh with an even colder eye than they do on London. Such writers as Grimble and Prebble produced admirable works on the history of the North, but it cannot be said that there was any great upsurge of art, nor any artist to give shape to the aspirations of the northerners. No Abbey Theatre sprang to life in Inverness.

*   *   *   *

Looking back at the inter-war period I see it in general as a period when the tides within the area stood still. The main livelihoods remained agriculture and fishing. Tourism was still the tourism of shooting and fishing. The area remained poor, its population declining, with little or no industry. But it escaped the degradation of the worst of the industrial, urban squalor and it appeared, and indeed in many respects was, a pleasant enough place in which to live. Questions, however, were being asked about its past treatment and future prospects. The Second World War chrystallised this feeling of unease. Planning became fashionable. It was accepted on all sides that governments had a positive part to play in seeing that employment was available, that the social services were extended to all and that, if politicians could not guarantee a land fit for heroes to live in, at least they should ensure that the land was not only fit for impoverished colonial serfs. To describe the northern inhabitants as such would be a gross exaggeration. But the more radical of those interested in the area could justifiably point to periods of neglect, even if the periods of active oppression were long past.

In a country enthused by the Beveridge Plan the level of unemployment in some districts was not to be tolerated. In Lewis, the rate of unemployment regularly ran at over 20 percent and many crofters were in serious need. How far the statistics were to be trusted as a guide to the number genuinely seeking work could be disputed. But that something was wrong could not. But what exactly was wrong. Or rather, what exactly could be done to put it right beyond programmes of public works and a decent rate of unemployment pay. As I have mentioned, the public authorities even in the 18th century had attempted what for those days was a quite remarkable programme of development. Ever since then there had been schemes for road-building and such like. But they had failed to establish a new more prosperous and variegated type of economy.

Although it was generally agreed that depopulation was a major affliction yet the existence of 'congested districts' Acts showed that in some places the population was bigger than the land could sustain. Further, there was the dilemma that schemes for raising the standard of living for crofters inevitably meant bigger holdings and fewer workers — a tendency accentuated of course by the steady increase of machinery.

What was the opinion of the natives. In answering this question we must remember the diversity of the area. It should also be borne in mind that subordination to the Establishment of Lairds, officials, etc. was considered by most people to be the best guarantee of a quiet life. There was no tradition of political agitation on the scale of that in Ireland. The memories of the clearances and the hearings before the Crofters Commission indeed incensed such public opinion as was interested. There had, in the later years of the 19th century, been a riot in the island of Sanday in Orkney, but a remarkably mild one considering the provocation. In the 1950s a wall on the by then uninhabited island of North Fara was pointed out to me as the place where a crofting family sheltered after their landlord had burnt their house over their heads.

Such was the power of the Laird that the neighbours had to wait until darkness to rescue them. And this was in Orkney where the rule of the Lairds was mild compared with some other places. Such leaders of revolt as existed were usually 'Wee Free' ministers. Outside the lowland fringes political activity was desultory. In Shetland, there were no voters up to the 1830s because no Shetlander had enough money or property to qualify.

Up to the end of the century the Lairds controlled politics. There were indeed curious quirks such as the election of Charles James Fox for Orkney — but as he never visited the islands and was in any event a member for another constituency, his election was not of much significance. After the Crofting Acts of Gladstone's government and the reforms of the Franchise, the Liberals dominated the scene. Such indeed was the gratitude for security of tenure and for the old age pension that the old Liberalism survived longer in the North than in most of Britain. The memory of Gladstone who personified something of the old religious fervour lasted long among the older folks. They had indeed reason to be grateful for what his party, in alliance with the more radical ministers of religion, had been able to achieve. My Tory opponent told me that during the 1950 General Election, an old woman who was his friend and neighbour, had promised to vote for him. After polling day she confessed that having put on her bonnet she was about to do so when she looked up and saw a plate with Gladstone's face upon it. 'I could not do it, Sir Basil, I could not do it'.

In any case the Highlands and Islands, even their lowland fringes and small towns, were naturally well disposed towards the Liberal Party. While they had no reason to love the Tory Lairds, crofters and fishermen had little in common with the Labour Party. They were independent men, if poor. The crofter now owned his own house. He was secure in his few acres. The fishermen owned their boats. The trades allied to farming and fishing were also carried on by men who were their own masters. Apart from some retired seamen and dockers in a few harbours the Trades Unions were weak. Labour appeared as a southern- based party of the cities.

Nevertheless, by the 1930s it was apparent that the Liberal Party was regarded more and more as a party of the past. Radical, professional men, such as schoolmasters, doctors and now Ministers of the church turned to Labour. Politics became fluid. In the 1945 General Election there were at least two Highland candidates elected in spite of some doubt, even in their own minds, as to where their allegiance lay. Personal impact counted far more than in most of Britain. In Caithness, parties ran neck and neck. Sir David Robertson ultimately supplanted Sir Archibald

Sinclair the then Liberal leader. But he was a maverick Tory who eventually sat as an Independent, as did Sir William Duthie, the much respected Member for Banff. In the meantime, the Western Isles went Labour, as did Caithness after a brief return to Liberalism. The southern constituencies in the area went Conservative but their Members put a heavy emphasis on local issues.

From this fluidity there emerged something of a coalition of Highland Members. We met on the Highland Panel with others nominated to it for their interest in Highland affairs. There we discussed, at one time under the chairmanship of a judge of the Court of Session, matters of local interest such as transport, roads, agriculture, fishing etc. The high cost of freight became a dominant issue. There was a widespread feeling that our constituents were penalised by exorbitant transport costs. We agreed upon the need, while supporting farming and fishing, the basic industries, for new forms of employment. None of this was very remarkable or controversial. We were, after all, a government-appointed, all-party body. It would be a mistake to suppose that anything like a Highland Party emerged. We remained members of Conservative, Liberal, Labour and National Liberal parties.

At General Elections, unlike the old days when some seats were not contested by all parties, all Highland and Island seats were fought by at least three parties each, and soon the Scottish Nationalists also joined in every contest, eventually capturing the Western Isles from the Labour Party. The South of Perthshire (the constituency called West Perth and Kinross) was later represented by a man who for a short time was Prime Minister: Sir Alec Douglas-Home, as he then was. In these circumstances there could be no agreement on radical departures in the Highlands agreed upon by a majority of M.P.s from the area owing allegiance only to the area.

The most notable departure was perhaps the creation of a Highlands and Islands Development Board. Believing that the area was starved of capital and industrial expertise I, and no doubt others, had recommended the creation of such a board in the late forties. A Labour government set it up in Inverness with access to fairly small funds for new businesses. The Liberals who in the 1964 General Election captured all the seats from Inverness north (Inverness, Ross & Cromarty, Caithness and Sutherland, Orkney and Shetland) tried to formulate a plan for the Highlands. But the party did not of course command many Members at Westminster. Incidently, one of the Liberal M.P.s, Alistair Mackenzie, was one of the first, if not the first, M.P. from the area who had actually earned his living as a worker in one of its own occupations — he had been a shepherd — and spoke Gaelic fluently (he was not the first Member of the Commons to do that). It may seem odd that in an area which complained of neglect where the 'upper classes' had such a bad historical reputation that there had been so little of a working class movement. But then, as I have said, 'the working class' in the north is very different from the urban industrial working class of the south and lacked the nationalist loyalty of the Irish.

*　　*　　*　　*

Meanwhile, outside politics, the 'Highland Problem' continued to be discussed. Some practical efforts were made to improve the economy, for instance a 'Highland Fund' was set up largely on the initiative of Mr Rollo. It lent small sums for the purpose of implements, equipment, etc. With limited resources it did good work. It is worth remembering that it had very few bad debts. Fishing and agriculture with a few ups and downs prospered after the war. Apart from the statistics showing improved earnings and profits, you had only to look at the houses in the fishing communities to see how well things were going. Additions, fresh paint, cars, television, deep freezes and sometimes neatly kept gardens were evidence of surplus resources unknown to the grandparents of the mid-century fishermen. Different types of agriculture too enjoyed booms. Sometimes, as in the case of small farmers, these booms were modest; sometimes, and for a time in the case of the big 'ranch' owners such as Lord Lovet and Mr Hobbes, these were substantial. In spite of taxation there were still very large estates. Indeed it might be true to say 'because of taxation' for land was a good investment for the very rich. This led to some complaint from radicals. However, the question remained 'what more can be done?' The Forestry Commission acquired a large acreage. That too led to some complaints. A paper mill was set up near Fort William — but that had to close when the depression came. A tourist and ski- ing centre was established at Aviemore. The climate however, at least in my view, limits the appeal of Scotland against the Costa Brava in Summer and Switzerland in Winter. Whisky retained its grip on the affections of many all over the world. A large new distillery was established in the Black Isle. The trade did not escape the fashion for take-over, though at Perth, Messrs Bell and others maintained a vigorous independence (though Bell have recently succumbed). Radical socialists had found it difficult to persuade Highlanders that state enterprise was the hope for the future, some of the same Highlanders ambivalent in their reaction to new departures and new owners. In the last century Lord Leverhulme had been driven away when he tried to help the fishing industry in Lewis. Some of the old suspicions lingered on — not without reason. For the people who relied upon their small incomes for a day to day survival had already been bitten by abandoning them for new enterprises and were shy of trying again. A favourite of the developers was the woollen industry. It had long been the mainstay of Lewis. There it was indeed operated in a somewhat eccentric way. Imported yarn was spun in Stornoway and then sent out to be woven on hand-looms. The resulting tweed had become a prestige product but too heavy for modern taste. However, any attempt to modernize the industry was seen as killing its main purpose – that of giving work to the crofters.

But there were many failures by too enthusiastic newcomers. Further, the trade had great difficulty in dealing with sudden increases in demand. In Shetland, for instance, it was still largely in the hands of local merchants who had neither the staff, nor capital, nor wish, to be tycoons.

One I knew well looked forward with dread to a visit to England by his American agent 'with his telephones, ulcers, and demands for 10,000 garments by return of post'. There were few factories outside Stornoway and those which existed employed comparatively few people – textiles were still in much of the region a cottage industry. The only spinning mills outside the Hebrides were at Brora in the north east Lowlands.

*   *   *   *

While the question of how employment could be increased was being debated the region was engulfed by the bureaucratic revolution. Although the onset of bureaucracy took many years and was singularly unbloody, it is justifiable to describe it as a revolution. It had been coming a long time, but the bureaucratic attitude really took hold in the war. It was then that officials proliferated. I have never seen the figures of the ratio of officials to fighting soldiers in Britain during the Second World War, but including staff officers as officials it must have been high. After the War, the British looked more and more to public authorities to run their affairs. Bureaucrats bred bureaucrats (not only in the civil service). They became a powerful interest on their own. Soon not only was it assumed that whatever the future held for the North it must remain increasingly dependent on government and local authority aid and regulation but the public authorities became the biggest single employer over most of the Highlands. The Development Board itself kept some 300 officials in Inverness.

The bureaucratic revolution led to by far the greatest changes in the area. Changes which were all pervading. Changes which could be visibly seen all over the landscape. Roads were as far as possible replicas of southern roads with their accompanying 'furniture' – sodium lighting, kerbs, and the useless straightening of corners, whether the traffic made it necessary or not. No architect evolved a new house from the old crofts. The housing estates got bleaker and more urban, planning laws suitable to London or Edinburgh were enforced up the glen and over the island. And then little box-like Kremlins appeared in the larger towns to house the officials. Finally, new tiers of government led to career structures and marvellous new jobs (such as 'the shell fish industry co-ordinator' in Orkney). Enquiries, reports from consultants, position papers, seminars, multiplied. At least the transport services greatly benefited from the number of councillors and officials continually in transit. But the area was in danger of becoming one vast begging bowl held out to London.

I began to wonder what was the purpose of Highland Development. If it was to establish life as near possible to that led in the small and on the whole dreary industrial towns of southern Scotland or Lancashire, why not encourage the inhabitants to emigrate to such places. But if it was thought worth-while to 'develop' the north, and if people wanted to stay and work there, then surely we must break the bonds of centralised conformist thinking. This would never be done by bureaucrats in or out of the public service. Of course there are other factors working for bureaucracy and uniformity: television now covers almost the whole area and in most places four channels are available. For some reason too the tourist bureaucrats believe that their clients demand uniformity as do those who look after travelling businessmen. So every hotel is trying to be as faceless as possible – a poor relation of Hiltons and Holiday Inns. And finally oil.

*   *   *   *

The impact of oil has been great in some ways, but not as great as you might think. It is largely confined to certain localities. The biggest impact has been made in Aberdeen. There you can see the offices of the international companies and hear of American schools and clubs. The harbour is busy with supply vessels (as are some other harbours in the north). Aberdeen looks a prosperous city and its unemployment rate is less than that of other parts of Britain. But even in Aberdeen it seems to me doubtful whether oil has done more than accelerate and magnify changes which were coming anyway. Even the prosperity it has brought is limited and many who look to oil for their future have been wafted away to other oil centres.

In the rest of the north, oil has changed a few localities out of all recognition. But most of the Highlands and Islands are untouched by it. The construction period gave much highly paid employment to certain areas where rigs were to be built or where pipe lines were to come ashore. At one time four thousand workers were toiling away at Sullom in Shetland, mostly imported Irish and living in relatively luxurious camps.

Shetland boys out of school could earn as much in a week as their fathers had in a year. But the work was unskilled.

The boys were apt to acquire expensive tastes which can probably not be accommodated in Shetland. Once the construction period was over, a certain amount of extra local employment has been generated (the population of both Shetland and Orkney has risen – in the case of Shetland quite substantially): and a few skilled immigrants – pilots and engineers – have been imported. There are, of course, still one or two sites where rigs and platforms are built or assembled. But most of the upper management continues to live in the South (or America) and fly in and out by jet. Nor has there been as much 'spin-off' as was hoped. Airfields have been expanded. Taxis, hotels and pubs have burgeoned. One or two strip-tease clubs have blossomed in Aberdeenshire. But outside the consumer supply industries, the results are fairly small. Glaxo at Montrose is still the chief science-based industry in the North. Aberdeen University has attempted to cater for the needs of oil. But taking the area as a whole and looking to new outlets for the young the long-term effect is I think unlikely to be as great as once supposed though the North Sea Oil seems to have a fairly long future. Certainly the general public have not benefited. Petrol is one of the commodities which is more expensive in the North. Hotel prices have soared.

* * * *

So we come back to transport and communications. The North should gain enormously from the advance of transport and information technology. So far it has not because the air industry is tuned to Atlantic travel and rigid bureaucratic methods. It is much cheaper to fly from London to New York than from London to Kirkwall. People should soon be able to live in Buckie or Kyle of Lochalsh and conduct a business world-wide. So first let us free transport from its shackles – if necessary assist its expansion and subsidise its cheapening. Then let us have done with centralisation. If people want to live in the north they must give up demanding southern standards. Let us try at any rate to break the British habit of never reforming what is wrong but applying palliatives, never take the simple solution, but always prefer complication. The easiest and most effective help to the North would be to reduce taxation. Let everyone north of the Highland Line pay a lower rate of income tax. And if local authorities were wise they would aim to make it a low-rate area. Then encourage people to help themselves and put their savings (which are quite substantial) into local industry. It is a great pity that the Savings Banks have not been turned into channels to direct local money into local investments.

But these simple and obvious reforms are unlikely to catch on in to-day's Britain. In the meantime, the north survives with a marvellous range of beauty, a peculiar climate (to say the least of it) and in spite of efforts to debauch them an agreeable and varied population. I can't think of a single beautiful building erected since the War; the landscape has been scarred by new roads and here and there some monstrosity affronts but on the whole the plough lands of the North, East, and the hills of the North West, the strange calm of islands on a windless day and the fury of the sea under a gale still give great pleasure. And you can occasionally avert your eyes from the sodium lamps and see the Northern Lights hanging like silver hair in the sky.

LOWLAND SCOTLAND
John Smith

The Rt. Hon. John Smith shows the Lowlands of Scotland with a history so different from that of the clans of the Highlands, to be the birthplace of the Scottish Kingdom in its chronic contention with England and so, in the course of time, the essential partner in the Union of the two countries.

John Smith was born in 1938 and was educated at Dunoon Grammar School and Glasgow University. He is an advocate (barrister), and has held important posts in the Labour Party since he entered the electoral lists in the 1960s. He was M.P. for North Lanark from 1970 to 1983 and is now the Member for Monklands East. He has been Minister of State in the Department of Energy, Minister of State in the Privy Council Office and then Secretary of State for Trade. He is a member of the Shadow Cabinet and has been Opposition Spokesman on Energy since 1982.

The truly low lying part of southern Scotland is the broad strip of land between the Forth and the Clyde. To the south, much of the Lowlands are not lowland at all. North of the English border, a great tract of land running right across from the Solway Firth to the North Sea is high, wild, and hilly. But it is so different in character from the Highlands that it has not seemed inappropriate to think of the whole of Scotland to the south as the Lowlands. While the Highlands are set in the dramatic outlines of hard and weather resisting volcanic rock, the Lowland hills have been weathered into gradual slopes and undulating valleys. The colours of the Highlands – and its 'rocks and heather' scenery – tend to be browns, greys, and blues – while even in the highest part of the Lowland hills a grassy greeness predominates.

It is in this low lying part that the population has accumulated. In a fairly narrow corridor across the 'waist' of Scotland are located most of its industries, its urban communities, and the preponderant majority of its people. It was in this central belt that most of the history of Scotland unfolded, and the greater part of the character of modern Scotland — and of the Scots — was formed.

*   *   *   *

The War of Independence was fought over lowland Scotland, and by lowland Scots like Wallace and Bruce. The establishment of an independent Scottish state was essentially a lowland achievement as was its defence from continual English harassment. Lowland Scotland was open to influences from the Continent through political alliance with the French and trade, mostly through its east coast ports, with the Low Countries. Scots lawyers learned the Roman law at Leyden and Utrecht and founded at home an independent and still surviving jurisprudence. A merchant class grew in importance and prosperity in the burghs of lowland Scotland and became an important reason for the success of the Reformation in the 16th century when the new ideas from the Continent were spread so successfully by the lowlander John Knox. The Highlands remained largely unaffected by the Reformation which was to have such a profound effect on the Lowlands, and Scotland as a whole. While the reformation in England was political in character, in Scoland it was essentially ideological as the passion of the Covenanters was later to display. For centuries after the spirit of Calvin was to have a major effect on Scottish life and manners.

When the Highlanders rallied to the Jacobite cause in 1715 and 1745, the Lowlands did not join. In the years which followed Culloden, the Highlands were kept in subjection, but lowland Scotland began to find a new dynamic in the Industrial Revolution. Already a prospering agriculture was being advanced in the fertile plains, but it was the discovery and exploitation of the large deposits of coal and iron in lowland Scotland which fostered the greatest economic and social changes in its history. So began the growth of the industrial towns of the central belt and the prominence of Glasgow and its industrial hinterland. The contribution to the Highlands was to send its population, driven out of their native glens by poverty and clearances, to swell the burgeoning population of Glasgow.

From across the Irish Sea came the Irish to man the ironworks, the coal mines, and the new factories. One of the major results was to change the social character of the West of Scotland. The large influx from Ireland was largely, although not exclusively, Catholic, and for the first time since the Reformation, a substantial Catholic presence existed in lowland Scotland. For many years, rivalry persisted between Green and Orange, and in times of competition for employment dissension on religious grounds became acute. Fortunately, in recent times, ecumenical influences have overcome much of the legacy of the past, and the fifth or sixth generation to follow the original immigrants are much more conscious of their Scottish heritage than their original Irish origin. Much of the extrovert ebullience of the West of Scotland lowlander, as opposed to his more canny and reserved eastern counterpart, stems from the mix of lowland, highland, and Irish influences.

The celebrated Scottish intellectual activity of the eighteenth and early nineteenth centuries was a lowland phenomenon. Allan Ramsay's verse was later to influence Robert Fergusson and the genius Burns who drew his inspiration almost entirely from his lowland surroundings. Sir Walter Scott, Scotland's supreme publicist to the outside world, was very much an eastern lowlander, although he drew on a wider Scottish tradition for his extensive literary output. Adam Smith of Glasgow University, and David Hume of Edinburgh, were the most outstanding of Scotland's intellectual pioneers. And, perhaps most of all, the dour determined practical character of most of the Scots is shaped by their lowland background.

*　　*　　*　　*

The most direct link between Scotland's past and present is the capital city of Edinburgh. The mediaeval town grew along the ridge which ran from the Castle rock down to the Abbey of Holyrood. For a time, growth was restricted by a city wall built in 1450 by James II, but it soon expanded until, in 1513, the Flodden Wall was built as a result of the panic following Scotland's defeat at the Battle of Flodden. For 250 years thereafter Edinburgh was confined within its walls and in restricted space built upwards to create the characteristic 'lands' or tenements which were often eight, ten, or even twelve storeys high. In its crowded streets and closes, living almost literally on top of each other, old Edinburgh's nobles, merchants, and artisans lived through troubled times like the Reformation. It was the home of the Parliament until 1707, but it was also a rumbustious city, torn by the civil and religious disputes of the times. Often short of water, it was distinctly unsanitary, a problem compounded by the habits of the citizenry who emptied chamber pots from its tenements with the warning cry 'Gardyloo' − a corruption of the French Gare l'eau.

Following the Act of Union, Edinburgh entered a new phase. There was less concern for security and more for trade. To secure its expansion to the north, the Nor Loch (now Princes Street Gardens) was drained in 1760 and the North Bridge built across it in 1772. The way was opened to the building of the New Town. James Craig won the competition for its design and the basic plan of the squares and terraces was his. It was, fortunately for Edinburgh, a brilliant period of Georgian architecture, of which the elegant New Town is such a splendid example. The spirit of the early period of the New Town is evocatively displayed today in the Georgian House in Charlotte Square, where the National Trust for Scotland has restored the home of an early 19th century Senator of the College of Justice. Next door is Bute House, also recently restored to become the official home of the Secretary of State for Scotland.

In the same period, Edinburgh entered upon what has been described as its Golden Age when it became such a centre of learning, wit and wisdom that it was known as 'The Athens of the North'. Recalled in Cockburn's lively Memorials, it was the city of Hume, of Bothwell, Walter Scott, Robert Burns, the painter Raeburn, and Telford the engineer.

The New Town today has more offices and hotels than residences, although the Scottish legal profession — which migrated almost en bloc from the Old Town when it was the fashion so to do — still has a tenacious grip on the Advocate's Quarter where the brass plates on many a door indicate their presence.

Modern Edinburgh is proud and self-assured, conscious not only of being the nation's capital, but also of its status as one of the celebrated cities of Europe. When, in late August and early September each year, the Edinburgh Festival of Music and Drama (and the ever expanding Festival Fringe) bring thousands of visitors to the City, the languages of most of Europe are heard in Princes Street, the Royal Mile and the Bridges. Edinburgh takes such international attention in its stride in much the same way as it has been the stage for so much of the turbulent history of Scotland.

It is a visitor's delight. The Castle dominates from the ridge and looks over the constantly varying skyline of a city built on Crags. Down the Lawnmarket and the Royal Mile, past St Giles and at the foot of the Canongate, is the Palace of Holyroodhouse, scene of the murder of David Rizzio, secretary and friend of Mary Queen of Scots in 1566, and now the home of the Queen when she visits Edinburgh. In the middle of the Royal Mile is the High Kirk of St Giles, which was at the very heart of the Reformation struggle, while tucked behind it is the Parliament House, once the meeting place of the Scottish Estates, and now the busy centre of the Scottish Courts, where advocates still walk the floor of Parliament Hall beneath its magnificent wooden roof. The Old Town is the more romantic, but no visitor should neglect the contrasting cool and mannered elegance of the New Town, or the splendid galleries and museums, such as the Scottish National Gallery at the foot of the Mound, or the new Scottish Gallery of Modern Art in the West End. Perhaps the greatest charm of Edinburgh to the visitor is the opportunity it affords to those who explore it on foot to discover the picturesque and historic surprises round almost every corner.

*　　*　　*　　*

Stirling was also at the hub of Scotland's history, partly because it is geographically in the centre of Scotland. Strategically the castle, on its volcanic rock rising sharply from the carse land of the Upper Forth Valley, has dominated the routes to the North and the Western Highlands since the Middle Ages and before. Little of the mediaeval castle now remains, but much of the royal castle built by the Stewart kings still survives. Near the castle gate is the 15th century Church of the Holy Rood where the infant Mary Queen of Scots was crowned in 1543.

Earlier, during the War of Independence, the castle changed hands no less than seven times. Wallace won it from the English at the battle of Stirling Bridge, but Edward I recovered it and held it until the day after the crucial Scottish victory at Bannockburn. The decisive victory of Robert the Bruce is now commemorated by a National Trust rotunda and an equestrian statue of the warrior king at the field of the battle. The other champion of independence has, for a long time past, been celebrated by the pinnacled tower of the Wallace Monument which looks down over the plain from Abbey Craig. On the nearby Arithrey Estate, the modern University of Stirling has found a strikingly attractive home.

From Stirling one looks north to the Perthshire hills and east to the western shoulder of the Ochils. In the Ochil foothills along the Vale of Devon, are the quiet towns of Alva, Tillicoultry and Dollar which are often missed by tourists heading north from Stirling. To the south, the scene changes to that of the industrial belt. Falkirk has been an important industrial centre since the Carron Ironworks were founded in 1760 and the flarings from the modern oil refineries at nearby Grangemouth light up the sky over the Firth of Forth.

*　　*　　*　　*

At the western end of the new Lothian Region, is the former county town and ancient royal burgh of Linlithgow. Its royal palace is set on a knoll above the lovely town loch, almost like a chateau on the Loire. It was a favourite palace of the Stewart kings who regularly settled it on their wives, and it was here that Mary Queen of Scots was born and spent her early years. Burned - perhaps accidentally — by Cumberland's troops in 1746, it is now a roofless ruin, but its splendid setting and remarkable internal sculpture still command attention. Beside the palace, is the ancient parish church of St Michael, one of the finest churches in Scotland. Its contemporary golden spire in the symbolic shape of a crown is a well known landmark for rail travellers between Glasgow and Edinburgh.

Along the shores of the Forth, and nearer to Queensferry and the Forth Bridges, is the most spectacular mansion in Scotland. Hopetoun House was started by Sir William Bruce, but the wings were designed by William Adam, father of the more famous Robert who, in turn, completed much of the interior work. The severely classical building is situated in parkland with formal gardens in the style of Versailles surrounding the house.

South of Linlithgow are the industrial towns of the western Lothians. Bathgate still suffers from the decline of the post war vehicle industry, but the new town of Livingston, in the manner of the Scottish new towns, is in the forefront of electronics. The landscape is dominated by the not unattractive shale heaps which rise up from the flat lands like red hills − a reminder that here Paraffin Young developed petroleum.

The Lothian Region now also incorporates the former counties of Midlothian and East Lothian to the south and east of Edinburgh. The gentle rolling Pentland Hills dominate the southern aspect right up the edges of the city and overlook the coal mining area around Dalkeith to the east. Mining is now very much an east of Scotland industry, and there are collieries in East Lothian although most of the sunny area between the Lammermuir Hills and the Forth is richly productive farmland. From Musselburgh − the soi-disant 'Honest Town' − at the mouth of the Esk, the coastal line runs through Aberlady, with a nature reserve nearby, to Gullane, where the Honourable Company of Edinburgh Golfers founded the oldest golf club in the world at Muirfield in 1744. North Berwick on the northern promontory, and Dunbar further round the coast, are both popular east coast resorts. Near North Berwick is the former Douglas stronghold of Tantallon Castle, protected on three sides by precipitous cliffs, and Dunbar Castle, now in ruins, was a very temporary residence of the peripatetic Mary Queen of Scots in 1567. Inland is the gracious town of Haddington. The well proportioned Town House was the work of William Adam and the 15th century St Mary's Church was known as 'The Lamp of Lothian' on account of a lantern which once hung in its tower as a guide to travellers.

*   *   *   *

North of the Forth is the Kingdom of Fife. In 1973, the planners of the Scottish Office sought to divide it between the Lothian and Tayside regions, but Fife fought back hard and preserved its status as one of the new regions. It is rich in contrast and diversity – a mix of coal mining and farming, of industrial towns and fishing villages, of older traditional industries and new electronics on the frontiers of high technology. The new town of Glenrothes has been developed in the western heart of Fife in counterpoint to the well established Kirkcaldy and Dunfermline to the south. From the Lomond Hills in the west, the countryside dips through the rolling farmlands of the Howe of Fife to the rocky coastline of the East Neuk. Roughly speaking, the west is industrial, the east agricultural.

On the eastern coast St Andrews looks out over the North Sea as if it were not part of Fife. Nor truly is it. Despite its importance in the history of Scotland, St Andrews has always been curiously isolated. Almost as if to emphasise this feature, the rail traveller has to change to the bus at Leuchars Junction. Yet St Andrews is both the home of the world's most famous golf courses, and the seat of Scotland's oldest University. It was here that Cardinal Beaton, the pre-Reformation Archbishop of St Andrews had the Protestant martyr, George Wishart, burned at the stake only to be murdered himself in his own Palace a few months later in an act of swift retaliation. Today, St Andrews lives in less troubled circumstances, but the relics of its eventful history combine with the green sward of four great golf courses and the Scottish domestic architecture of Southgate, Marketgate, and Northgate to make a strikingly attractive town.

To the south, along the coast, are the unique fishing villages of Crail, Anstruther, Pittenweem and St Monans where distinctive vernacular buildings have been cleverly adapted to modern living, and where the box-like harbours at their centre provide refuge from the relentless North Sea. Inland from the coast, is the comfortable countryside of the Howe, given over to prosperous farming, and set out in colourful and well tended fields, and quiet places like Ceres, Pitlessie, Springfield and the market town of Cupar. On the edge of the Howe, and the foot of East Lomond, is the 16th century Palace of Falkland, built by James IV and improved by his son, James V. The Renaissance style Italianate south wing survives (another wing having been destroyed by Cromwell's army) together with Scotland's only 'real tennis' court as a reminder of its brilliant royal past.

Of the larger towns, Dumfermline has the most interesting history. The great Abbey Church was founded by Malcolm Canmore and Queen Margaret and both are buried there with five early Scottish kings and Robert the Bruce. Dumfermline's royal associations persisted to later years when, as a result of being a favoured residence of James VI and Queen Anne of Denmark, it became the birthplace of ill-fated Charles I.

*   *   *   *

High in the Southern Uplands, and not many miles apart, the two arterial rivers of southern Scotland, the Clyde and the Tweed begin their course. For a distance, they proceed almost parallel until the Tweed twists to the east to become the river of the Borders and reaches the sea at Berwick. The Clyde keeps on north through Clydesdale, Lanark, the industrial towns, and Glasgow and then on to the opening Firth and sea on the west. At the start, the Clyde passes through the high and featureless country where lead, and even gold, were once mined. Then it drops through an attractive farming landscape — near Biggar, Symington, Coulter and Lamington — until it reaches Lanark, well placed on a strategic bend where the river bank deepens into a gorge.

Pleasant though Lanark is, there is today more interest in New Lanark, a few miles to the south. There the model industrial town of David Dale and his son-in-law Robert Owen has been restored and rebuilt to make a fascinating exposition of their unique social experiment. Near Lanark too is the fruit growing area. On the fertile, and often steep slopes of the river, and in the nearby lands, there flourishes a prosperous horticulture of soft fruits, Scotch tomatoes and early vegetables. Going further north, the Clyde flows between Hamilton and Motherwell and enters right into the heart of industrial Lanarkshire. The giant steel complex of Ravenscraig is the dominating presence, but nearby is the very attractive and modern Strathclyde Country Park.

Industrial Lanarkshire is based on four towns, Hamilton and Motherwell to the south of the M8 motorway, and Airdrie and Coatbridge to the north. Within and near the quadrilateral which they form, occurred one of the most prominent of the industrial revolutions based on the local deposits of coal and iron. Today, the scene has changed. Steel, for example, is still an important industry, but it is much reduced in size and the last of the Lanarkshire coal mines has closed. The emphasis is now much more on new industries, with an electrical and electronics base as in East Kilbride, one of the earliest Scottish new towns which has grown quickly, but has also matured well. Hamilton, the former county town of Lanarkshire, is set, for an industrial town, in an attractive landscape, and Airdrie to the north still shows signs of its market town past. Coatbridge and Motherwell are more directly the product of the industries which caused their growth and drew in a new population from as far afield as Poland and Lithuania. Their descendants are now well settled in lively communities which, despite having to cope with the difficult problems of industrial change, are a vigorous part of the Greater Glasgow conurbation. The Monklands District — which incorporates Airdrie,

Coatbridge and their satellite villages — is named after a much earlier period when the monks of Newbattle Abbey were given a royal charter to work for coal, centuries before the Industrial Revolution.

* * * *

Glasgow's rise to prominence as Scotland's largest city — and for a time 'Second City in the Empire' — was very much a matter of trade and industry. As the simple and severe cathedral of St Mungo in the heart of old Glasgow reminds us, it was in mediaeval times, a Bishop's seat — a place of some political importance in pre-Reformation Scotland, but with a small population and an undeveloped commerce. As in the rest of lowland Scotland, the Reformation stimulated major changes in society and in atitudes which led to a quickening of the commercial spirit, but it was the Treaty of Union in 1707 which laid the foundation of Glasgow's prosperity. The way was opened to trade with the American colonies, and a fortunate Glasgow and its River Clyde faced in the right direction. Throughout the 18th century, Glasgow grew to become the largest centre of the tobacco trade in Europe. Although the American War of Independence disrupted the tobacco trade, Glasgow found itself in the late 18th century and early 19th century, well placed to profit from the Industrial Revolution. It expanded rapidly as a port and a major industrial centre, and its population grew relentlessly. So was formed Victorian Glasgow, a city proud and prosperous as the splendid buildings of the commercial centre display to this day. It was also the city where the new working classes were huddled together in the characteristic tenements which, when the prosperity later faltered, too often declined into notorious slums of the black years of the inter-War depression.

Glasgow is now much smaller in population, having in post-War years, dispersed its people to new towns in the central belt. The heavy industries — steel, shipbuilding, large scale engineering — which were the basis of its wealth, its employment and its bustle — have largely disappeared, and for a time it seemed as if Glasgow was set on a course of irreversible decline. But Glasgow has, in recent years, begun a remarkable renaissance. The urban decay of the east end has been reversed by a remarkable rebuilding project, and imaginative renovation schemes have saved the best of the Victorian and Edwardian sandstone buildings for a new generation of occupants.

While Edinburgh anguished over, and petitioned for, a new opera house, Glasgow rescued the Theatre Royal from television studios and refurbished it as the stylish home of Scottish Opera. The fabulous Burrell Collection is now permanently displayed in a splendid modern building on Pollock Estate and draws thousands of new visitors to a city already well endowed with the richest municipal art collection in Britain at Kelvingrove Art Gallery and Museum. In the delightful Hunterian gallery, the University displays a unique collection of Whistler, the Scottish colourists and the works of Charles Rennie Mackintosh whose legacy is found throughout the city, most notably, of course, in the art nouveau College of Art on a hill behind Sauchiehall Street. A new exhibition centre under construction on a former dockland site on Clydeside is a further demonstration of the life of the new Glasgow. Once again, the visitor quickly notices the vigour and liveliness of the city as well as that of its warm hearted, witty, and fiercely proud populace.

As the Clyde moves in from Glasgow, it soon reaches Clydebank in whose shipyards the famous Queens were built. Now the product is oilrigs. The town, like many on Clydeside, has had to face the painful transition from dependence on traditional industries like Singers sewing machines (once sold through the Empire) to newer trades. Further on, the river is spanned by the modern Erskine Bridge, a suspension bridge which provides speedy access over the river and on its southern side leads to the new town of Erskine, one of the smaller of the Glasgow overspill towns. It is close to Paisley, famous for its threadmaking and its Abbey, a Cluniac foundation whose nave is still in use as the parish church. The town's museum and art gallery houses a notable collection of the famous Paisley shawls whose motif came from Kashmir in the eighteenth century. The patron saint St Mirren, is remembered not only by a chapel in the Abbey, but in the name of Paisley's football team.

In its lower reaches, the Clyde is dominated on the north by Dumbarton Rock which commands its approaches. On the rock was built a royal castle which, in its time, was another of the temporary halts for Mary Queen of Scots. Between Dumbarton and Clydebank, the Forth and Clyde canal − once a major communications artery across Scotland − joins the river, and nearby at Bowling, is the western end of the Antonine Wall, built in 140 AD by Antoninus Pius to keep the warring Picts at bay.

On the south of the river, Greenock founded its prosperity by importing sugar in ships whose propulsion was designed by James Watt, the Greenockian founder of the steam engine. During the Second World War, the river at Greenock where it ends at 'The Tail of the Bank' was crowded with the ships of Atlantic convoys and above the town is a unique war memorial in the shape of a hugh cross of Lorraine which commemorates the Free French sailors who died in the Battle of the Atlantic. Gourock, on one side, is a pleasant seaside resort and yachting centre for the Firth of Clyde, and on the other is Port Glasgow which, as its name implies, was once the port for the city before the Clyde was deepened.

*   *   *   *

Round 'The Tail of the Bank' and stretching south as far as Galloway, is the long Ayrshire coast. It is sheltered by hills to the east and by Arran, Bute and Kintyre to the west, and its pleasant fresh climate – together with its proximity – made it a traditional holiday ground for the Clydeside industrial communities when they went on their annual summer pilgrimage 'Doon the Watter' to Saltcoats, Large and Ardrossan. In parts, the coastline is rocky, but in others it opens out in wide sandy bays which are often fringed with a springy natural turf ideal for golf as at the famous courses at Turnberry, Troon and Prestwick.

The old county town of Ayr, 'Wham ne'er a toon surpasses, for honest men and bonnie lasses', is a natural centre for exploring the coast, the countryside, and of course, 'the land o' Burns'.

Born at nearby Alloway on 25th January 1759 – a date of annual and ritual significance to lowland Scots at home and abroad – the poet not only immortalised his native landscape, but laid the foundation of a flourishing modern tourist trade based on souvenirs of his life and work. So did the world come to know of Mauchline, of Kirkoswald, and of Tarbolton.

The inland part of Ayrshire is rather like Fife, an intermixed combination of agriculture and industry, although the prevalence of dairy farming gives a much greener aspect to the countryside. At Cumnock – where the young Keir Hardie was a miners' federation official – is coalmining, and further north, Kilmarnock, the largest town, is an important whisky bottling centre.

Along the River Irvine, is an older industry of lacemaking in the villages of Newmilns, Darvel and Galston, where Dutch Huguenot refugees settled in the seventeenth century. Sadly, steel is no longer made in the Garnock valley, but explosives are still manufactured at Ardeer in a factory founded by Alfred Nobel in 1873. The new town of Irvine attracts modern industries, and Prestwick is now a freeport as well as an international airport.

On the southern coast, the herring fishing villages of Dunure, Maidens and Ballantrae, and the pleasant resort of Girvan, face outwards to the high rock of Ailsa Craig. Also overlooking the Firth, on a clifftop in the south, is Culzean Castle begun in 1772 by Robert Adam and now in the care of the National Trust of Scotland.

*   *   *   *

When Daniel Defoe visited Drumlanrig, the Nithsdale seat of the Queensberry family, he compared it to 'an equestrian statue set up in a barn' because it was 'environ'd with mountains and that of the wildest and most hideous aspect in all the South of Scotland'. Later generations, fortunately, do not share this aversion of Defoe's time to the close proximity of high hills, and find a special attraction in the wide and empty spaces of the green grassed uplands of the interior of Galloway.

The human settlements in the Dumfries and Galloway Region are along the coast or in the river valleys which penetrate deep into the hills. Dumfries, itself, the major town and administrative centre, is some miles inland where the River Nith is crossed by a mediaeval bridge said to have been built originally by Devorguila, the widowed mother of John de Balliol, briefly King of Scotland under the English in the 13th century. Of more recent date is the tomb of Robert Burns who died at an early age at his house in the town.

Along the Solway Firth, where the River Dee joins the sea, is the picturesque town of Kirkcudbright, where the local light and colour have long attracted artists who became best known in the late nineteenth century as 'The Kirkcudbright School'. The name − pronounced 'Kirkoobry' − means the church of St Cuthbert, a saint of the early church. Across Wigtown Bay at Whithorn, are more relics of early Christian activity. Here Saint Ninian, son of a British tribal chieftan who went to Rome and returned as a missionary, founded his church in the late 4th century. It was succeeded by a Priory of which impressive relics remain. For centuries later, Whithorn was a special place of Christian pilgrimage. It was at Whithorn that James IV resolved as a penance to wear an iron girdle round his waist, which he did until his death at Flodden.

At the western extremity of Galloway and facing Ulster across the North Channel, is the hammerhead peninsula of the Rhinns of Galloway. It is blessed by the warm waters of the Gulf Stream and the mild climate permits half tropical gardens to flourish as at Port Logan on the Atlantic side. The major town is Stranraer, at the land locked end of Loch Ryan, a busy port and the Scottish end of the ferry route from Larne in Northern Ireland.

Like the Borders, Galloway is a country of castles and abbeys. The castles were made necessary by the raiding armies from England who often chose a route north through Annandale. They were also fortifications of powerful local chieftans like Archibald the Grim, whose castle at Threave, near Castle Douglas, built on an island in the River Dee, was the symbol of a fierce authority in the 15th century. The abbeys are a happier memory of the remarkable spread of monasticism into the border lands of Scotland. Sweetheart Abbey, near Dumfries, at one time a community of 500 monks, and Glenluce Abbey, at the head of Luce Bay, were both Cistercian foundations, while the beautiful ruins of Lincluden in Nithsdale were once an abbey of Benedictine nuns.

The glory of the Borders is the four great 12th century abbeys, now ruined but enchanting reminders of the monastic movement. The monks were men of the land as well as of the Rule, as the prosperous farmlands near their foundations still bear witness. But it is the buildings, or what remains of them, which now attract attention, as at the Melrose Abbey of St Mary, at Jedburgh, at Dryburgh (the burial place of Sir Walter Scott), and at Kelso, where the ruins still display the Romanesque arches of this distinctive Border Abbey.

*   *   *   *

Today, the social life of the Borders is conditioned by the happy circumstance that none of the many small towns is large enough to dominate the area. This may explain the strong survival and perpetuation of local pride and tradition. In Hawick, the largest town and a woollen manufacturing centre, they ride the Marches in the Common Riding each June. In Galashiels, another tweed and woollen town, they enact in June a pageant of the town's history at the Braw Lad's Gathering. In Jedburgh, a former royal burgh, the 'Uppies', those born above the Mercat Cross, play the 'Doonies', born below it, in an ancient game of handball on Shrove Tuesday. Pride of custom is only seriously challenged by the passion for rugby in the Border towns, each with its own team in which, unlike other parts of Scotland, the whole community takes part in the sport. It is not uncommon for the larger part of Scotland's international rugby side to be Borderers.

The River Tweed, joined down the river valley by the Teviot, the Yarrow, and the Jed, flows through the heart of the Borders and through Melrose, the small town in the shelter of the Eildon Hills, which is the centre of Walter Scott country. His home at nearby Abbotsford, a Scottish baronial pile, preserves his memory in the countryside from which he drew so much of his inspiration.

To the west, also on the Tweed, is Peebles, a salmon fishing centre as well as a tweed and knitwear town. Nearby Neidpath Castle, on a hill overlooking the river, was battered into submission by Cromwell's artillery, though later restored and sold to the Queensberry family. The spendthrift fourth Duke felled the trees on the estate to earn the prim Wordsworthian rebuke 'Degenerate Douglas, Oh the unworthy Lord'.

From Selkirk, home of the 'souters' or shoemakers who captured an English flag at Flodden and yet another tweed town, can be explored the lovely Ettrick and Yarrow valleys.

The river valleys, the woodlands, the rolling countryside, the castles, the abbeys, and the smart and well tended towns of the Borders, are perhaps best seen when they are displayed to special effect in the colours of autumn. Then, or indeed at any other time, they are a pleasing introduction to the traveller from the south to the Lowlands of Scotland.

NORTHERN IRELAND
Enoch Powell

The Rt. Hon. Enoch Powell, one of the classic figures of British Politics for more than thirty-five years, was Member for Wolverhampton South-West from 1950 to 1974 and was a candidate for leadership of the Conservative Party in 1965. Since 1974 he has been Member for the Northern Ireland constituency of Down South, which he won as a Unionist by a small majority over his SDLP opponent, Mr McGrady.

His contribution deals fairly with the problem of a permanently divided population.

Enoch Powell was born in 1912. He is a classical scholar who, after his training in King Edward's School at Birmingham and Trinity College, Cambridge was Professor of Greek at Sydney University for two years before the Second World War. He served in the Army throughout the War, rising from private to brigadier, and, after the end of his military service, began to take an active part in politics.

He was Financial Secretary to the Treasury in 1957-58 and was Minister of Health from 1960 to 1963. He was dismissed as spokesman for Defence in the Opposition by Edward Heath in 1968, because of his speech strongly opposing large-scale immigration into the United Kingdom of coloured people from Commonwealth countries.

I am a lucky man. I represent in the House of Commons one of the most beautiful, if not the most beautiful, constituencies in the United Kingdom. The Mountains of Mourne 'sweep down to the sea' in the middle of my coastline, between two marvellously scenic but contrasting sea loughs, Carlingford and Strangford.

When I fly in to Belfast's Aldergrove Airport and set off to my constituency through the Ulster countryside, never does the first hour pass without my drawing a deep breath unawares and saying to myself 'How much better I am feeling!'. There is something indefinably exhilarating, physically and spiritually, in the air of that wonderful province.

I went there in 1974, not of my own volition, but because those who have subsequently three times elected me asked me to 'come over and help them'. In my constituency, where my majority in 1983 (after major redistribution) was only a few hundred, I go everywhere freely and often unaccompanied, enveloped by the natural courtesy, kindness and good humour of those I represent.

Although I had supported throughout the parliament of 1970-74 what I believed, and believe, to be the true cause of Ulster, I had much to learn about the country and its history. The knowledge I needed came slowly and piecemeal and not without some diligent search. In what follows, I have tried to set down in my own way and in my own order of presentation what, after eleven years, I find to be the facts most necessary to understand about Northern Ireland.

*   *   *   *

Of the 650 constituencies represented in the House of Commons seventeen are in Northern Ireland. Fifteen of those seventeen constituencies at present return Members to sit in Parliament because, by varying majorities, their electorates wish Northern Ireland to remain an integral part of the United Kingdom. The electors of the remaining two constituencies, likewise by a majority, return Members who either stay away or only come in order to say they do not wish to belong.

How did this come about. The answer can be as short or as long as one likes, and any starting-point is arbitrary and to some extent unsatisfactory.

Until 1800 the island of Ireland had a parliament of its own, as Scotland did until 1707. In 1800 this was amalgamated with the Parliament of Great Britain to make the Parliament of the United Kingdom of Great Britain and Ireland (the 'Union'). As the 19th century proceeded and the franchise was extended, a large and growing number of Irish constituencies returned Members to the House of Commons to demand some form of self-government or independence from the United Kingdom. These Members (Irish 'Nationalists'), especially as Ireland was numerically over-represented in Parliament, could hold the balance whenever the government of the day had a less than overwhelming majority. Virtually none of them, however, came from the north-eastern part of the island, which remained almost totally attached to the Union. Consequently, when governments dependent on Nationalist votes — the Liberal governments of 1885-6, 1892-5 and 1910-16 — proposed to confer far-reaching self government ('home rule') upon the island, they encountered the natural objection and the stubborn resistance of the people of the north-east.

Notwithstanding this, 'home rule' for the whole island, passed by the House of Commons in 1912, would have come into effect, with uncalculable consequences, in 1914 but for the outbreak of the First World War. At the first General Election after the armistice in 1918 (the 'Khaki election') the old pattern re-emerged unaltered. Seventy-three of the 105 Irish seats returned Sinn Fein (Gaelic: 'Ourselves alone') members to refuse to sit in Parliament and to repudiate the Union and all its works; but only three of these came from the six counties in the north-east of the island.

Britain then took a paradoxical and fateful decision, the consequences of which continue to be felt to the present time. Instead of accepting that the greater part of Ireland had seceded *de facto* from the Union, and acknowledging this *de jure* by recognising that territory as a new, independent nation state, Britain resorted to pretence and chicanery and enacted separate 'home rule' for the north-east (which did not want it) and for the rest of the island (which wanted complete independence) within a framework that was designed to facilitate the anticipated subsequent coalescence of Northern Ireland and Southern Ireland. Thus Northern Ireland − the expression came into official use for the first time at this juncture − was to some extent hived off from the United Kingdom, with reduced representation in Parliament and a home rule parliament and government of its own. Northern Ireland accepted this reluctantly as the best of a bad job; but the rest of Ireland broke into an insurrection, at the end of which Britain was fain to recognise the 'Irish Free State' as (so it pretended) 'a dominion like Canada'.

Why did Britain behave in this extraordinary and illogical fashion. Britain believed that it was essential, for strategic and political reasons, to try to keep the island of Ireland within the Empire and Commonwealth − at best friendly, at worst benevolently neutral. As the only price at which that outcome was to be obtained was the absorption of Northern Ireland into an all-Ireland State, that became the objective of British policy from that time down to the present.

The only change over the years has been that after the Second World War, the strategic interest in question became that of the Western Alliance, and the American factor, always present to some extent, became dominant. The Northern Ireland 'home rule' set-up (known popularly as Stormont, after the seat of government) fell in 1972 − or was it pushed. − and Westminster resumed 'direct rule' over the province. Yet the old objective of British policy has been pursued with redoubled vigour through a series of political contrivances designed to create the mechanism for transferring Northern Ireland from the United Kingdom into an all-Ireland, preferably confederal, state. Nothing on the other hand has lessened the separateness of the north-east of the island or the pertinacity of its peoples self-identification with Britain. The electoral verdict in 1983 was unmistakably the same as it had been in 1974 — or in 1918 — or in 1885.

* * * *

What then is this entity, that so obstinately belongs not to Ireland but to the United Kingdom and which is officially called Northern Ireland (at bottom a propaganda phrase) but whose own people call it 'Ulster' and themselves 'Ulstermen' and 'Ulsterwomen'.

A word, first, about the name. When Ireland was shired in the 16th-17th centuries, the thirty-two counties into which it was divided were grouped in four provinces. To three of these — Ulster, Munster and Leinster — were given names of Viking origin, as the '-ster' termination betrays. Out of the nine counties of Ulster, three (Cavan, Monaghan and Donegal) went along with the secession of the rest of Ireland. It was to the remaining six (Antrim, Armagh, Down, Fermanagh, Londonderry and Tyrone), which remained in the United Kingdom, that the ancient name of Ulster has been popularly, if arbitrarily, restricted.

There is nothing arbitrary, however, about the distinctness of the north-eastern part of the island of Ireland from the rest or about its special link with the adjacent island of Great Britain, from which no more than 12 miles of sea separate it at the closest point. This distinctness was a fact of geography and ethnology long before it became a fact of political history.

Geographically, the greater part of Ulster is a system on its own, a basin draining into a central depression occupied by the largest sheet of inland water in the British Isles, Lough Neagh. It has often been remarked that the traveller heading northwards from Dublin is conscious on entering Ulster that he is crossing a genuine barrier into a different region. From this central plain, the deeply marked natural outlets are sea loughs or fjords, which point towards the north, north-east or east — clockwise, Lough Foyle, Belfast Lough, Strangford Lough and Carlingford Lough.

It was in these directions that in legendary times exchanges of population with the adjacent mainland took place, so that the Scots looked to Ulster for their origin no less than the people of Ulster looked to Scotland and the Isles. The geological bridge of basalt, between the Giant's Causeway in Co. Antrim and the islands of Skye and Staffa, lies along the line of the interchanges of goods, of culture and of people which linked Ulster with the mainland since before the beginning of historical record. This orientation of Ulster towards the north-east was in later periods to have economic and other consequences which differentiated it still further from the rest of Ireland.

* * * *

The Ireland in which Henry II, armed with the Papal Bull *Laudabiliter*, landed in 1171, more in order to avoid his vassals establishing themselves there than in order to create a new dominion, was an Ireland in which no single or central authority existed. Local chiefs in the different regions, including Ulster, recognised no practical overlordship and lived in a condition of mutual hostility and aggression. They were no match for Norman military technique. On the other hand Anglo-Norman control was dependent upon bases along the coast to keep open the sea communications for supply and reinforcements.

A characteristic figure, who anticipated many typical traits of the Ulster experience, was one John de Courcy who in 1176 left Dublin with a body of knights, crossed Carlingford Lough into my constituency and worked his way up the east coast, establishing depots and mottes as he went, until he reached Downpatrick. He made it his headquarters, refounded the cathedral on Norman lines and settled down as effectively the Earl of East Ulster, a position from which the Scottish Bruces were more successful than King John in ultimately dislodging his successors. The map of Ulster is to this day characterised by the network of roads, travelling straight as arrows from fortified ports to the inland towns and strategic river crossings, and testifying to a military penetration which remained anchored to the bridgeheads.

Not even the determination of the Tudors and their strategic interest in denying France or Spain a foothold on the island could enable them to bind the allegiance of the leading Irish chiefs, especially after the process of assimilation was blocked by the Anglican Reformation, logically but impractically applied to Henry VIII's other 'kingdom' (as it then became) of Ireland. Irish rebellion headed by Ulster chiefs was 'unfinished business' which Elizabeth bequeathed to James I. What did not then happen is as important as what did happen for the making of Ulster.

In legend and in theory, massive forfeitures in all but three of the nine Ulster counties made possible a sweeping 'plantation' with English and Scottish colonists. The reality was that in an area where there had already been substantial but gradual immigration from Great Britain, the bulk of the existing population remained, but within a new economic and agricultural regime. A census taken twenty years after the 'plantation' found only seven thousand adult males from Great Britain. They must have been outnumbered, if not swamped, by the pre-existing population, which, contrary to royal intention, supplied both labour and families. More significant numerically and in other ways than the 'plantation' was what took place during the War of the Three Kingdoms, 1641-48, when a general Irish rising of great ferocity was countered by Parliamentary forces, which succeeded in holding the situation in Ulster with troops from Scotland until under Cromwell the Commonwealth in 1649 proceeded to the re-conquest and pacification of the rest of the island. It was these events and the forfeitures which followed under the Commonwealth and the Restoration that set the decisively English and even more Scottish stamp, in religion as well as the language and outlook, upon Ulster.

The generation after the Civil War, and even more the generation after the Siege of Londonderry and the Battle of the Boyne in 1689-90, decided forever that Ireland would not be a separate Jacobite kingdom. This was a period of reconstruction and vigorous growth in Ulster. The Presbyterians established themselves, bringing their own internal divisions, in the counties adjacent to the Scottish homeland; and their congregations swelled and produced offshoots as the population grew. The Church of Ireland rebuilt its parish churches on fresh, though mostly adjacent, sites in a characteristically solid neo-classical style, its incumbencies and dioceses staffed by clergy of often considerable dedication. The celebrated divine Jeremy Taylor was Bishop of Dromore, Co. Down, where, in the eighteenth century, an intellectual group was to gather around Bishop Percy — him of *Percy's Reliques*. Large landlords set out to restore agriculture provided in elaborate detail for cultivation, fencing and tree-planting.

The 18th century was an age of growing affluence and increasing population in the whole of Ireland; and in this Ulster fully shared. It is rarely remembered that at the end of the 18th and in the early part of the 19th centuries Ulster contributed disproportionately to Irish emigration, especially to the New World. The Ulster input was later to be most marked in Canada; but no fewer than eleven of the Presidents of the United States could trace their origin to Ulster homesteads. Studies have shown that emigration was typically of single individuals, male or female, and drawn fairly evenly from all parts of the province, so that the family structure and the tenures at home remained substantially unaltered.

*   *   *   *

Economically, however, Ulster set off on a distinctive course, with profoundly important consequences. Flax-growing and the complex stages of the manufacture of linen printed an indelible pattern on the Ulster countryside. Almost everywhere ingenuity created sources of water power for the mechanised processes, and a large part of the rural population became, in respect of their main source of livelihood, industrial. Their land holdings — for the Ulsterman remained throughout tenacious of his land — thus became supplemental to a cash crop and manual earnings. One notable result was that in the 19th century the repeated failures of the subsistence crop, the potato, which culminated in the great famine of 1845-46, left Ulster largely unscathed. In addition to this quasi-industrial character of the Ulster peasantry, the traditional form of land tenure in Ulster, known as 'Ulster tenant right', gave to them a degree of independence which spared Ulster almost completely from the evictions and 'land wars' that were so characteristic of the rest of Ireland in the 19th century.

The impressive engineering skill which enabled the water-driven machinery to exploit the water resources and the terrain of most of Ulster must also have contributed to make the opportunities of the later industrial revolution attractive and congenial to the province and its people. It is worth recording that Ulster boasts the first hydrographically engineered canal in Europe – the Newry Canal, opened in 1742 – which carried coal from Lough Neagh to the port of Newry and goods, including salt, from the port of Newry to the hinterland.

Interestingly, the current revival of flax growing in Ulster, rendered economic again by new chemical crop treatments, has helped to stimulate the rediscovery and restoration of the industrial archaeology of the province, which is admirably documented and will certainly form one of the items of attraction exploited by the province's growing tourist industry.

But I have jumped ahead from the nineteenth to the twentieth century.

The dispersed industrialisation which waterpower ordained for Ulster gave its population a distinctive economic strength and resilience which was not shared with the rest of the island. It was not unrelated to the peculiar settlement pattern of the countryside which so surprises an observer from Great Britain. The village pattern familiar in England is almost non-existent in Ulster. Towns there are, large and small, usually originating from markets at natural communication points; but outside the towns the holdings and habitations are scattered as if at random over a landscape exhibiting fascinating field-patterns. Enclosure came to Ulster some sixty years after its culmination on the mainland and took the form of the allocation of lands thitherto cultivated or grazed in common among the families of often internally interrelated communities, which then proceeded to enclose their respective holdings and provide each with a dwelling house. Consolidation of holdings and amalgamation of plots followed only slowly and gradually and is still far from having reached its natural limits. Combined with the small size of the province and the relative shortness of distances, this dispersal pattern of the population has had two continuing effects: one is that light, small industry can find a labour force available almost anywhere in the province; the other is that the divorce between the land and an industrialised people so typical of

English experience never really took place in Ulster, which remained and remains at one and the same time urban and rural, with a natural and enduring linkage between the two cultures.

No advantages, however, are ever without their corresponding drawbacks. The rural industrialisation of Ulster exposed it to a special impact when water power was replaced by steam power and domestic production by mass factory output. In weaving, admittedly, domestic 'homework' only died out within living memory. Indeed, a proportion of the standard 'labourers' cottages' which were erected in large numbers in the early 1900s and are still in high demand for conversion and modernisation, were built with a shorter or longer annex projecting to the rear at right angles which contained one or two looms that provided a welcome supplement to the income of the occupier.

Steam, however, in the early processes of manufacture proved irresistible, and a number of factors combined: the eastern ports received the coal from the coalfields of Lancashire and Cumberland across the short sea passage and the railways distributed it up the valleys with their processions of 'mill towns'. Linen in Ulster had scored a decisive triumph over cotton well before the American Civil War gave the linen market a boost by cutting off Lancashire's supplies of raw cotton.

The new steam-driven mills were as greedy of manpower as of raw materials and coal; and since the existing skilled labour was locally dispersed, the concentration of labour economically necessary could only be secured by importation from the rest of Ireland. This was the story of Belfast, where Belfast Lough with its excellent port and its canal and river communications drew in the fuel and sent out the goods, and where the population changed so rapidly that in the first half of the 19th century the proportion of Roman Catholics rose from one tenth to one quarter in a single generation. On a smaller scale, the steam mill created similar phenomena across the province.

The linen story was but one aspect of the integration of Ulster into the British economy: shipping and shipbuilding − here again the admirable physical properties of Belfast Lough came into play − engineering and finance, all made Belfast, whose population reached two-fifths of the total population of Ulster, into one of the leading industrial and business centres of the United Kingdom, feeling itself part and parcel of the British phenomenon and benefiting from the Atlantic-ward orientation of British trade. Was it not in Belfast that Brunel's *Great Britain* was fitted out and Cunard's *Titanic* built. Glasgow on the Clyde and Belfast on the Lough were like twins, and Scottish and Ulster families would commute for their annual holidays and retirement as well as business one way or the other across the North Channel. Thus, Ulster's immemorial orientation eastwards was clinched decisively by the economics of the nineteenth and early twentieth centuries.

*   *   *   *

Yet there was another Ulster characteristic which survived all the pressures and changes of the rise of modern industry and business, its astonishing variety within so relatively small a compass. Belfast is important, very important, for understanding 'Ulster', but Belfast is not Ulster, nor is Ulster Belfast. The beginning of wisdom for the student of Ulster is when he learns that there are two places: one is Belfast and the other is not. What is more, no two counties have so much in common that what is true of one can be automatically assumed about the other. The texture of place and people, the different admixtures of people and their different interaction with their physical environments make Ulster a patchwork of endless variety. Some of the pieces are very small indeed. The so-called Kingdom of Mourne in Co. Down extends only from the crest of the Mountains of Mourne to the sea, and yet the Men of Mourne recognise themselves and are recognisable by others as distinctive in speech, habits and outlook, as they are in origins and in way of life. Or again, cross from South Down into neighbouring Co. Armagh and at once you find yourself in a different countryside, orchards and fruitgrowing brought originally from Worcestershire and Herefordshire. The unity which is Ulster is, by reason of its eventful past, a unity of variety, a coalition of contrasts.

*   *   *   *

Returning from such a story and such a picture to the political scene it is not difficult to understand why the secession which brought a separate nation into existence in the rest of Ireland left Ulster part of the British Nation, attached to Great Britain and represented in the Parliament of the Union. It explains also something of the stresses which have been created by Britain's attempts to ignore or to reverse that political event. The imposition of 'home rule' upon Ulster in 1920 created an inherently unnatural situation, which was summed up classically by Edward Carson, the Dubliner and British cabinet minister whom the Ulster majority chose to represent them, when, in resisting Ulster 'home rule', he declared to the House of Commons, 'I do not want Protestants to rule Catholics or Catholics to rule Protestants; I want both to be ruled by this house'.

The formula which Carson used is a reminder both of the inherently unnatural character of the form of 'home rule' established in a part of the United Kingdom by the Government of Ireland Act 1919 and also of the unique role played by religion in political identification in Ulster.

The Government and Parliament of Northern Ireland which were created in 1919 and lasted until 1972 were modelled upon the constitution of a dominion, commonly called 'the Westminster model', of which the essentials are a cabinet government collectively responsible in effect to an elected chamber, taking decisions by majority vote. This majority in the elected chamber is liable in Great Britain to alter according to changes in circumstances and in the opinions of the electorate. Where the majority is for practical purposes unalterable, the system becomes unacceptable and arguably oppressive to a political minority. The circumstances of Northern Ireland from 1919 to 1972 were, from this point of view, peculiar in two respects: the majority political opinion, which was essentially in favour of Ulster remaining part of Britain ('Unionist'), was not likely to change in any forseeable future; and secondly, the main minority political opinion was not in favour of running the province on different policies but of removing the province from the Union altogether. Thus, Britain imposed upon Ulster a 'home rule' which was not only unwanted, but which would not be workable in the spirit of the British constitution itself. To use emotive terms, it was Britain that built the sense of injustice into Northern Ireland.

This was due to the foreseeable permanence of the majority and not to the fact that the principal minority was secessionist. After all, both in Wales and Scotland there are minority political parties which aim at an eventual (if visionary) majority for secession in their respective countries. Yet this does not make the Westminster system unworkable or unacceptable in Wales or Scotland: the electorates of these countries participate in the political process of the whole United Kingdom and devolution has not been forced upon them – indeed in 1979 they refused it when it was offered.

*   *   *   *

If there were an equation between 'Catholic' (which in Ulster means Roman Catholic) and anti-Union and between 'Protestant' (which in Ulster means anything except Roman Catholic) and pro-Union, then that would again imply a fixity of minority and majority which would be self-evidently incompatible with the spirit of the 'Westminster system'. That is no doubt one reason why the equations are so popular, apart from the journalistic convenience of type-casting; but the reality does not conform, refuses to conform, with the stereotype. The religious question which in Ulster is included optionally in the census does not produce absolutely hard results, because of the considerable proportion – 18.5 per cent in

1981 – where no religious affiliation is declared; but the ratio of Roman Catholic to other denominations (28 to 53.5 per cent) would be generally accepted as broadly correct. It does not, however, translate directly into political terms, because there is cross-voting, negligible in the case of non-Roman Catholics voting for anti-Union candidates, but really substantial in the case of Roman Catholics voting for pro-Union candidates. An opinion survey in 1979, promoted (ironically) by the Government of the Irish Republic, which showed the Union as the preferred option of half the Roman Catholic voters in Ulster, agrees with the necessarily impressionistic view of Unionist parliamentary candidates that in marginal seats they benefit significantly by Roman Catholic votes – and abstentions.

If, however, the politico-religious equation is fallacious that does not mean that the religious factor is unimportant in the total picture of Ulster. On the contrary, the culture of the province has a religious dimension totally strange to the tolerant and slipshod self-identification with a national church which the unique form taken by the Reformation in England left as its legacy. In Ulster that relationship between church and state is simply not understood. The Act of Union of 1800 created, logically, a United Church of England and Ireland; but the disestablishment of 1869 and the political secession of 1921 left the Church of Ireland a vigorous and active, though not the largest, Protestant denomination in Ulster. It is rather the largest of the Protestant denominations, the Presbyterian Church of Ireland, which is most typical of Ulster ways of thought. It inherits the essentially covenanting notion of a compact between church and state, whereby the latter in return for civil obedience guarantees freedom of religion and the independent self-government of the Church.

This relationship is the key to understanding the political role of the Orange Institution, with its quasi-military ceremonial so misleading to the casual observer. It is a role which derives logically from the perceived function of the State as guarantor and the consequent need for the guarantee to be jealously policed and supervised. For its members, who have a prescribed obligation 'ever to abstain from all uncharitable words, actions or sentiments towards their Roman Catholic brethren', undertake 'to support and defend the rightful sovereign, the Protestant religion, the laws of the realm and the succession to the throne in the House of Windsor, *being Protestant*'. It could be said that what the reformation settlement and toleration are in England is represented in Ulster by the Bill of Rights and the Act of Succession. When Ulster celebrates in July the Williamite revolution, it is wiser than the onlookers and many of the participants perhaps understand: for that was the phase of the evolution of the United Kingdom with which the Ulster Protestant's philosophy is most at home.

*   *   *   *

Since 1969, and explicitly since 1972, the Government and Parliament of the United Kingdom have exercised directly the authority over Northern Ireland which had always been implicit in its continued recognition as part of the Union. This explicit assumption of responsibilty might appear an event as plain and decisive as the secession of the Irish Free State recognised in 1921. It might also seem the only possible resolution of the constitutional impasse which the enforced 'home rule' of 1921 had created, dissolving in the larger political unity the antitheses insoluble in a purely local context — the same idea indeed which had inspired the Union of 1800.

Parliament itself has been bewildered by the sequel. Every government since 1972 has attempted to re-introduce 'home rule', while in the interim renewing from year to year the power to legislate for Northern Ireland on 'home rule' subjects by ministerial Order in Council and preserving intact the structures of a 'home rule' government, such as a separate financial system and a separate Consolidated Fund. In the attempt, however, to eliminate the drawbacks, demonstrated by experience, of a fixed party majority, a series of 'fancy constitutions' were proposed embodying contrivances designed to put an electoral minority on an equal footing with an electoral majority. Since they were incompatible with the Westminster principles of a government resting o the support of an elected assembly, they either collapsed as soon as they were attempted — as, in 1974, the so-called 'power-sharing executive' — or were laughed out of court as soon as they were proposed.

Side by side with these attempts to square the circle ran the attempt to put back the machinery which the 1919 Act had contained for a gradual coalescence between Ulster and the Irish Republic. That was the 'Council of Ireland', of which acceptance at a conference held at Sunningdale in December 1973 was made the condition precedent to establishing the 'power-sharing executive'. Since then the name Sunningdale has been a by-word and a term of derision in Ulster politics.

The British State, it gradually became clear, had still not relinquished its cherished ambition of reversing the verdict of history and moving Ulster into an all-Ireland state; but it was clear that to succeed it would need to use more refined and subtle methods than heretofore.

The account of these methods will bring our story down to the present day. In 1981, the Council of Ireland was established in a camouflaged form as the Anglo-Irish Council, which would have three tiers, ministerial, official and parliamentary, the last being left temporarily in abeyance. Then in 1982 there was instituted an elected Northern Ireland Assembly, which avoided the 'home rule' conundrum by being destitute of all legislative and executive functions whatsoever, but even so did not escape being shunned by its anti-Union members. The crowning act of the wizard's wand would be to give the assembly real powers on condition that it provided the Ulster component for the missing Anglo-Irish parliamentary tier. At the time of writing that event had been deferred, if not aborted, by prime ministerial intervention; but play continues.

*   *   *   *

So what, ask the electorate and parliamentary representatives of the rest of the United Kingdom, is the 'solution'. The 'problem' of Northern Ireland, they complain, is too 'complex'. The 'problem' and the 'complexity' have consisted in perpetual and deliberate ignoring of the facts, the facts of Ulster and the facts of Ireland, such as this brief view has tried to display them. The 'solution', if the use of the word 'problem' makes it unavoidable to use the term all politicians should eschew, is to stop ignoring these facts, and to accept as historically and politically valid the continuing massive plebiscite of the Ulster electorate for membership of the United Kingdom, the parliament of which is proud enough to believe that it can accord justice and a role even to the most intractable of minorities.

THE NORTH EAST
Austin Mitchell

Austin Mitchell, Member for Great Grimsby since he won a by-election in 1977, is a journalist whose name is known to millions of television viewers, since his work on the news for Yorkshire TV between 1969 and 1977 and as a presenter of the BBC current affairs group in 1972 and 1983.

Newcastle-on-Tyne holds the centre of the stage in his article on North East England, and he might well be himself a Geordie to judge from the vivid way in which he expresses that part of England as God's own Country and its prevailing prejudice against the affluent South.

Austin Mitchell was born in 1934 and went to Woodbolton Council School then to Bingley Grammar School. He was next at Manchester University, then at Oxford.

In Parliament he is a Member of the Select Committee on the Treasury and the Civil Service. He was a history lecturer from 1959 to 1963 at the University of Otago, New Zealand, then Senior Lecturer on Politics at the University of Canterbury at Christchurch. On his return to England he was an Official Fellow of Nuffield College for two years. He is Vice Chairman of the economic and financial group of the Parliamentary Labour Party and a man of many parts.

The Bishop of Durham may deny it, but God is a Geordie. And I suspect He did take it a bit personal when Peter Walker castrated God's own county in 1972. He hit back by extending the title to the whole North East. This is God Zone.

Its boundaries are clear. The British are great line drawers and demarcators. A nation so homogeneous has to become adept at making fine distinctions between people which any decent American would dismiss as merely Caucasian Limeys. In the past this art centred on class. Now, with Marks and Spencerisation of the entire nation, that restless search for boundaries concentrates on geographical lines. It is devoted to dividing real people from the rest. But as Pope put it:

'Ask Where the North. At York 'tis the Tweed
In Scotland at the Orcadese, and there
At Greenland, Zembla or the Lord knows where'.

As England has shrunk, we cling to local identities more tenaciously, particularly in the North, defined as that part of the map where real people live, chip butties are eaten and brass bands play.

On a broad definition, real people begin at Watford. Yet a visit to that suburban migrant camp shows that any line drawn there includes too many lesser breeds without the North. So how about the Trent. Far more useful and covering all those areas marked 'Hic Wasta est' in the Domesday Book. Yet also including miners who neither struck nor joined the Northern Hymn, 'All Hail the power of Arthur's name. Let Coal Boards prostrate fall'. The Yorkshire boundary, wherever it is after Peter Walker's attempts to disorientate the nation by digging up its roots, may be a better prospect. But Yorkshire has become a comedy routine to impress southerners, not a sub-nationalism, and birth there is now merely an admission ticket for that species of white flannelled tag wrestling they call Yorkshire cricket. Out-of-tune versions of *Ilkla Moor*, with some deterioration in the dialect, don't make an identity — and the Yorkshire fetish is pure sentimentalism, out-of-date attitudes to a past that is already dead. In the North east, by contrast, the past is still alive. The area may be an industrial museum, but life is still lived in it more as it was than anywhere else in Britain, even if they no longer go 'Gannin a lang the Scotswood Road, to see the Blaydon Races'.

The boundary is the Tees and God Zone is the land 'twixt Tees and Tweed. Attempts are made to include others, for Britain is melting south. Tyne Tees television and Radio Tees reach down to Leeds in their missionary endeavours. Local government reorganisation has Cleveland straddling the river down to Whitby. Yet no purist can accept this or a claim that we're all Northerners now. Mustn't spoil people in Thatcherite Britain by giving them anything they're not entitled to. So real people (Exclusive Brethren) begin at the Tees. They get more real up to the Tyne. They fade to trainee Scots and wet Liberals on the borders. To the west, the petering-out Pennines and the hills of the Lake District form a border through Cumbria and its isolated coasts, with the declining centres of Worthington and Whitelaw, are also a part of the psychological North East because they are isolated. They look to Newcastle, are linked to it for administration purposes such as hospitals — if only because there is nowhere else to look to. Except Belfast. Further North come the Cheviots, defining long, coasting counties which run eastwards down to the sea in dips and end, where the National Coal Board hasn't ruined it with the most rugged and spectacular part of the whole east coast with its necklace of castles. A land fit for cameras to click in.

*   *   *   *

This is true North, magnetic in the case of Newcastle; a gigantic nature park in which real people live in man's natural habitat: council estates, blocks and terrace houses. Their way of life, dying in the rest of the country, is here perfectly preserved: its own language: a local culture, with a capital *K*: a real warmth and a built in sense of superiority based on a clamorous inferiority complex.

The life style is schizophrenic. They huddle together for warmth in crowded towns, but are surrounded by some of the most magnificent country in Europe. The strongest case for the towns is that they are easy to escape from — to four National Parks and all within easy reach. The life style is fuggy, smokey, fog ridden; the country open, windswept, clean. Working class values dominate, but they claim social superiority. They are effusively friendly, yet resentful of southerners who are immediately assumed to be guilty until proved innocent by not condescending. The light is dazzling, but a substantial proportion of the population work underground or in dark factories with museum piece machines. The culture is rough, even violent, more drunken vomit per acre and more blows *per* (and usually at) *capita* than anywhere else. Yet hearts are of gold, touchable for any good cause. More new roads, fewer cars. Some of Britain's most outdated industries. Yet also some of the newest. This is a land of paradoxes.

Since there is no need for a poet to sing its praises, the British Tourist Authority should use it as a living Disneyland. Already Scandinavians come, for ferries to Norway, Gothenberg and Denmark and regular flights to and from Scandinavian centres bring them over for Geordie Weekends, for football or Christmas shopping sprees which take them back better laden than their Viking ancestors. Why not open up the same benefits to the less privileged tourists taking dollar-laden Americans and camera festooned Japanese by the coachload, not to see castles and embalmed history but folk culture as it is lived. The working men's clubs, miners' institutes, strip clubs and 'Boozahs' offer far more interest than craft centres and nick-nack shops — which are all nick and no nack. A country conscious of commercial realities would take visitors round the council estates, the leek and produce shows, the allotments. It would give them massive dollops of pease pudding and put the natives on the payroll in national uniform of clogs, string below the knees and regulation flat hat. They would give incomprehensible replies to visitors equipped with *Vade Geordicum* books filled with such useful phrases as 'wear's the nitty' (can you direct me to the toilet) or more usefully 'Gizabroon Jack'.

Linger a little. It will become longer. Trouble is most people don't. The North East is good to pass through. Southerners stay away, fearing culture shock and preferring to go abroad in order to find people to patronise. The flood of American and Japanese tourists in search of that part of the British psyche they haven't already bought at auction and exported (f.o.b), plus the wandering Scandinavians, all pass through at speed, courtesy of British Rail, British Airways or the West German motor industry. All they see of the Northern paradise is a blur of slag heaps or, for the really wealthy, the stains on a British Rail table cloth.

* * * *

History is to blame. The North East has been a good country to invade, to march through, or to retreat to. The Romans did it first. Being men of low ambition, and long wine supply lines, they first advanced into Scotland then retreated to build the Geordie Wall — which Hadrian also claimed — across the country to Wallsend, which seemed as good a place as any. Next came the Saxons. Knowing all the Angles, they naturally chose Newcastle as the gateway to England because fares were cheaper. After them, the Vikings. Description of their raids and the ambiguous reaction of the local nuns, provided both news pages and stop press for the *Anglo-Saxon Chronicle*, and they spread across the country from Tweed to Cockermouth and as far south as Norwich, where they naturally lost interest. Their rape, loot and pillage details left an enduring folk memory and certain practical skills. As did the Normans with their national sport of *Jus Primae Noctae*. A long succession of English armies all marched north and then retreated. Scottish armies did the ladies steps in this dance routine — and by the 16th century, the North East was not a region in its own right, but the longest parade ground in Britain.

That claim to fame was fading when Daniel Defoe passed through on his famous *Tour of Great Britain* in the 1730s. Despite Defoe's continuous complaints about the state of the roads and the depth of the ruts, apparently he managed to see out of them in the North East. He didn't like it:

> 'Darlington, a post town, has nothing remarkable but dirt, and a high stone bridge over little or no water'.
> 'Chester in the Street — (before it got *le* delusion of grandeur) — an old dirty throwfare town ....'.
> 'The road to Newcastle gives a view of the inexhausted store of coals and coal pits ...we see the prodigious heaps. I might say mountains of coals which are dug at every pit and how many of these pits there are'.

Of Newcastle:

> 'The situation of the town to the landward is exceedingly unpleasant and the buildings very close and old, standing on the declivity of two exceeding high hills, which together with the smoke of the coals makes it not the pleasantest place in the world to live in'.

Of Berwick on Tweed:

> 'Old decayed and neither populous nor rich'.

Yet amongst all the abuse he did observe the legacy of history:

> 'Taking a guide at Wooler to shew us the road he pointed out distinctly to us the very spot where the engagement was, here he said Earl Percy was killed and there Earl Douglas, here Sir William Worthington fought upon his stumps, here the Englishmen that were slain were buried and there the Scots. A little way off this, north he showed us a field of battle called Flodden Field upon the banks of the hill where James IV King of Scotland, desperately fighting, was killed and his whole army overthrown by the English under the noble and gallant Earl of Surrey, in the reign of King Henry VII upon their perfidiously invading England'.

The limbs and the bodies have been cleared up. The legacy remains of the greatest army exercise yard in history, though now used only by the Sealed Knot Society and armies of football hooligans going to and from Newcastle.

As Defoe wrote, the area was changing. The battleground was being built over with industry. Newcastle was emerging as a great port, never the greatest because the narrowness of the river's gorge constrained development, but still the focus of trade with Europe, shipbuilding, and the coal trade from Newcastle to London and Europe: Newcastle prospered while London burned. An obscure aristocracy (largely created because the best use for greedy roughnecks with delusions of grandeur was to ennoble them for border work) became, in the shape of the Marquesses of Londonderry, the Dukes of Northumberland and the Earls of Durham, coal kings, and commoners jostled with them for wealth. With all this came the railways, taking out the coal: the iron industry round Teeside using Cleveland ore; lead mining round the Tees; glass making in the shape of W.G. Armstrong, pioneer of the hydraulic crane; ship and bridge building, the latter an art which could be readily practised in six bridged Newcastle; and the heavy electrical engineering. It was Geordie, Joseph Swan, who developed the electric light bulb before Edison even thought of it. Finally, chemicals came to Billington under Mond and to Wilton when his conglomerate had become ICI. It was an inventive, exciting two hundred years, a surge of initiative of which Mrs Thatcher would have approved more than she does of its results now, even if she couldn't contribute anything but sermons to help either. Industry shaped the North East and made it unique. The industrial heavy heartland of England, Britain's Ruhr.

With industry came prosperity. William Cobbett, coming to the end of what must have been the most saddlesore literary life in history, wrote of the North East in 1832:

'You see nothing here that is pretty; but everything seems to be abundant in value: and one great thing is, the working people live well. Theirs is not a life of ease to be sure, but it is not a life of hunger. The pitmen have twenty four shillings a week; they live rent free, their fuel costs them nothing, and their doctor costs them nothing. The work is terrible, to be sure, and perhaps they do not have what they ought to have; but an any rate they live well, their houses are good and their furniture good; and though they live not in beautiful scene, they are in the scene where they are born, and their lives seem to be as good as that of the working part of mankind can reasonably expect'.

Areas are shaped by their industries. A British economy which was divided geographically into areas of specialisation: cotton in Lancashire, wool in Yorkshire; coal, iron and heavy engineering in the North East gave each a unique way of life. The pattern of settlement, pit villages, city slums, mill towns, was shaped by industry. The working hours, shifts and holidays patterned lives. Politics reflected its structures and its scale. Even drinking, heavier drinking of stronger beer in mining and heavy engineering, wowserish in textiles, and the diet, stodgier or beefer with heavy work, and health and injury patterns were all reflections of industry. We are, or rather were, what we made and worked at.

So the North East was built tough but community conscious, one industry communities clustered round the shipyard, the coal mine, the engineering plant, more prissy and better trained in the chemical areas. There, more chiefs, fewer indians and the chiefs more widely dispersed. On the Tees all indians; no chiefs on the Tyne. In the towns this was a rough diamond, highly skilled people, jealously acquiring and demarcating their skills, living the hierarchy in their lives, not as one community, the North East, but as a whole series of smaller ones. The life style was urban-rural unlike the urbanised working class of Manchester or Birmingham, because the communities were small and easy to escape from to the coast, the hills (alive with the sound of brass bands) and some of the most beautiful countryside in the world.

*   *   *   *

Industrial life created industrial politics. Mass radicalism in the 19th century, Lib-Labbery towards its end; then Labour, solid, sensible, unradical, of a type the party becomes naturally when it holds power and serves people, not ideology. The intellectual origins were in more sophisticated areas elsewhere. The North East took on its natural role of providing back bone. It is strong, not so much on ideas, as on organisation and achievement. So it was the scene of Labour's first organised and effective presence; its first M.P.; the first county, Durham, to be controlled by Labour. Labour just took over. Within two decades it dominated the area, providing a firm bedrock of sense and seats for a national party ever prone to wander off into intellectual abstractions. It also gave a ballast of common sense, loyalty and right wing politics which sustained that party through follies and periods of achievement. The area was unperturbed even when the local tradition of importing intellectuals — for few were home grown — and then giving them an undemanding seat (which worked well with Dalton) went even sourer with the SDP deserters than it had with Ramsay MacDonald. It quietly exorcised them. Impractical middle class intellectuals who'd let it down. It closed behind them as if they had never been. Which, so far as local impact went, they hadn't.

The North east is Labour's bedrock; Britain's most solidly Labour area. Others talk of Scotland as the last bastion of socialism. The socialist republic of South Yorkshire gets more publicity. Yet the North East is really the Party's foundation stone, if silent, like the species. It always did prefer organisation to ideas, achievement to show-biz politics. The North East's Labour vote never fell below fifty percent until a 1983 low of two fifths; yet still the highest in the country, and well above Scotland. Labour takes ninety percent of the seats and fills them with men with large bottoms, a firm base for the party to rest upon. The party does not deserve the North East — it gets it nonetheless.

In turn, the area has done well from Labour. Socialist politics took root and emotional shape in the sharp class divisions in the North East, a mass working class, concentrating in, for the time, comparatively few units of production with increasingly remote bosses. The coal mines were owned by companies; the engineering works and ship yards concentrated in giant monoliths such as Armstrong-Vickers and Swan-Hunter. ICI and all the predecessors were big and impersonal, pioneering a process of agglomeration which ruined the North East even before it sank our ailing British capitalism. From clogs to conglomerates in three generations. Marx and the early socialists formed their views of capitalism from Lancashire rather than from the small masters of Sheffield or the myriad screw manufacturers of Birmingham. Had they ventured up to the real world they would have found the picture of class and capitalist confrontation deeply etched. And essentially masculine. Where the figures on Lowry's landscapes and in his factories were largely female, the North East workforce needed strong backs and schooled skills, both male monopolies.

This pattern of monoliths was reinforced by Labour. Repaying its dues to the area, it brought help in industrial decline, in the form of public spending. The North East was — is — by far the biggest beneficiary of regional development grants, averaging a third of the total, 17 percent more than Scotland. These grants went mainly to the biggest of the big firms, paying them to set up production outposts in the North East or to expand what they had there already.

Meanwhile, nationalisation concentrated the scattered, declining industries in the NCB, BSC and British Shipbuilders, reinforcing a trend to concentration which is implicit in decline. Simultaneously, depression drove out the smaller, weaker and more vulnerable, so there was no landscape of thriving small firms to please the eye of a passing Friedman. The 'enterprise culture' was merely a working class struggle to get more out of the DHSS.

The North East took on the appearance of a huge game reserve dominated by mastodons and dinosaurs, with few intermediate life forms between them and the human ants.

*   *   *   *

Light years away from the petty pluralism and sheltered self-employment of the South, this breeding ground of monsters still developed a far greater sense of community, of involvement, even fraternity, than the frigid southerner or the materialistic midlander could ever aspire to. Its world of 'them and us' was one of the few 'them', a thin congealed middle class veneer, and many 'us'.

Mateship too, survived in an area with a stable population, three quarters of whom had always lived there as compared to less than half those in the South East. People grew up together and stayed, and the area lost population rather than gained it. Thus there was no disorientating admixture; no incoming tides of black or brown which changed the nature of politics and ownership of the chip shops as in Bradford and the West Midlands; no spread of subversive ideas like that of women's emancipation coming in with itinerant Polytechnic lecturers. Newcastle and the region each have a lower proportion of young people, and a higher proportion of older ones, than the rest of Britain. Both are characteristics of decline and stability. The aspiring junior executives of ICI and the managers of the 'fly by night' factories lured in by regional development grants were either transients who never put down roots, or campers in the isolation ward of the Yorkshire Dales, so much 'neecer' than the real world.

So in terms of real people, the region did nothing but lose. It was a steady drain of ability, skills, brains − to the south, to the oil fields, to West Germany, to the Middle East − all in order to seek not fortunes but skilled jobs and to send money home. This still left community behind. Deportees may not have grown poor, as those that were left grew poor. Yet they widened the Geordie sense of community rather than diluting it.

A working class community which is also isolated breeds resentment: of London, the South, the different. You name it, they'll hate it. Yet it also breeds local pride and a sense of community, greater in the Falklands than Kensington and Chelsea, and warmer in the North East than in Surrey. In all the clamour about Scottish devolution in the 1960s and 1970s and until the Kilbrandon Commission actually went out and asked people, the point was long missed that the North East has as great a sense of isolation and alienation from London, as great a feeling of neglect by central government (and that is not paranoia but a simple recognition of reality) and just as much claim to (though less desire for) its own regional government, as Scotland. Only the Labour tradition of looking for and getting help from the centre kept it in line − and prevented an independence movement developing beyond anything other than bumper sticker slogans.

Only two million fewer than the Scots and with a clearer, simpler and less divided sense of identity, the North East would have been a more natural unit of regional government. Yet unlike the Scots they did not want it. Ever pragmatic, they looked for the benefits of devolution without the theory or the framework. Labour is their separatism, just as it is for the smarter Scots. Taking power at the centre and using it to help Geordieland is far more straightforward, and rather more likely than opting out into secessionist myths and mists.

So when home rule for Scotland produced a devolution bill and a shower of special favours which the North East, equally deserving, had never had, it was the solid, sound and dependable north-eastern M.P.s who rebelled and said 'enough is enough'. They torpedoed the first devolution bill and came near to sinking the second, until they were bought off by a better deal for the North East. By which stage the fickle Scots had lost interest in the business.

*　　*　　*　　*

This sense of regional identity comes from work, isolation, and the slow growth which damps change. It is strengthened by the dominance of a major city, that straddling conurbation called Newcastle but which is really a much wider built-up area giving its character to the region. Rural dwellers are much the same wherever they are; slow, cunning and, these days, rolling in Eurogelt. The North East's are no exception. The tendency Cobbett noted for them to be pastoralists, raising cattle and sheep, rather than arable farmers, remains much the same despite the incentives from the Common Market to turn the whole of Britain into second-rate prairie farms or third-rate rape seed grounds.

There are more small farmers, struggling on poor land and hill country, but the North East rural community is self-sufficient, cut off from the dominant culture and focused on its small country towns of Morpeth, Chester-le-Street, Hexham, Durham and Barnard Castle. These are pinched and straightened islands of southern gentility and Northern Toryism, builded here in Geordie's green and pleasant land, all struggling to get by on bed and breakfast, house lets, commuters to Newcastle and the other devices open to declining gentility.

Equally isolated are the small fishing ports such as Seahouses, and the declining resorts of Redcar, Saltburn, Wearside all bustling and jangle pocketed in Summer, tired and sad in Winter.

*   *   *   *

The real North East is the industrial towns, Middlesborough, Darlington and its now less than ubiquitous railways, the pit village and above all river-ribbon development along the Tyne. Every Geordie pilgrimage ends in dirty, black Newcastle (pronounced New-cassel). With 285,000 people out of two and a half million in the region it is less dominant than most regional capitals. Yet a third of the population live in the built up Tyne and Wear County and that dominates the area. Life, entertainment, careers, and in so far as there are such luxuries, politics, art and culture, all focus on the Newcastle conurbation. Gateshead is a town without a heart, Newcastle across the river a head too big for its body.

The communications focus there too. At one time, Newcastle sat so firmly athwart the roads that it blocked them entirely, choking up the Great North Road with traffic jams reaching back to Durham. Thousands of car-bound southerners were privileged to see the city and absorb something of its atmosphere and rather more of their own exhaust fumes. Those days are gone. The motorways, built here in profusion by guilt ridden southern governments anxious to make amends, speed the motorist through tunnels and underpasses north and south. The only glimpse they get is of the Tyne Bridge they're on, a Sydney Harbour Bridge for beginners, and the flickering view through its girders. Only the more astute − or the breakdowns − see the great black heart of

Newcastle, the archetypal northern industrial city. Which leaves regional communications focused on it, ferrying, now with unimpeded speed, local life into this capital city looking for a country.

Isolation gives Newcastle a clearer sense of identity than those other dying giants which dominate the North. Manchester has been pulled down, Leeds is too cosmopolitan, Glasgow and Liverpool are divided between orange and green and Birmingham is just another Motor City; Nowheresville. Newcastle alone remains largely intact, a better place to live in than any. Local culture is concentrated because the city is smaller. It is do it yourself, except for its 'mini' symphony orchestra, the Northern Symphonia, and the life style is for living, though it still exports well. The local commercial television company is not a network company embalming local life in soap as Granada has done with *Coronation Street*, London's own broadcasting corporation with *East Enders* or Yorkshire with *Emmerdale Farm*. Yet *The Likely Lads, When the Boat Comes In* and *Auf Wiedersehen, Pet* have all filled the gap and done much the same for the North East as *Boys From the Black Stuff* for Liverpool or John Braine for Yorkshire. There is even a flourishing literature. The North East played little part in the kitchen sink literature but has still produced its own; a romantic history in Catherine Cookson, a realism in Pat Baker's *Union Street* drawn from C. P. Taylor and Tom Hadaway, but not much poetry: that breeds in gentler climes. Yet none of this has made the impact on the national consciousness that *Room At the Top* did for Yorkshire. *Close the Coal House Door* was no alternative to the *Price of Coal*, its local literary character, Scott Dobson is a working men's club comic manqué and his Geordie books a local cult, but mystifying elsewhere. Even Alex Glasgow, its bard and folk singer, has gone to Australia. Compensation comes in pop. The great provincial revival of the 1960s and 1970s spawned groups in Liverpool and Manchester, Sheffield and Bradford; and Newcastle provided some of the best with the Animals, Bryan Ferry and Lindisfarne, mostly currently making a new career out of re-unions.

The Liverpool accent became the symbol of the new brutalism. The cockney accent bespoke the shrewd operator, Yorkshire blunt talking was the tongue of the new men of power trying to conceal their duplicity behind bluff, honest exteriors. Yet the Geordie's dulcet tones remain comic, quaintly symbolic of an old backwardness. As if ashamed, the region's T.V. presenters switch it on and off depending on whether they talk down or up. Yet the fact that Newcastle has been merchandised, homogenised and sold to the South doesn't mean that the area doesn't have an identity, a feel, a way of life all its own. Its way is working class culture, in its only pure surviving form. It is not undiluted. Four decades of social change and food snobbery have left their mark, even on

Newcastle – though still, to quote the guides 'a gastronomic desert'. Newcastle is no longer a work town but still defiantly working class. And more so than any city outside Liverpool, more safely, and sanely, more Labour. It has its veneer of middle class pretentiousness, but a thin one indeed. *Newcastle Life* is really a kind of half life, when it isn't just a vehicle for rampant commercialism. There are two middle class islands in the proletarian class stream; Jesmond and Gosforth. Yet neither is as rich as Cheltenham nor as assertive as Alwoodly. They do manage to return a Tory M.P., currently one anxious to be a journalist when he grows up. Yet both are cut off from Geordie culture. To survive in the town those who venture out feel obliged to wear local colour as a disguise.

Local pride, isolation and decades of Labour have produced a strong civic culture which even the combined effects of decline and the Tory government have failed to kill. A better site could have made this a major city. As it is, the Tyne gorge is not so much a development opportunity as a set of cliffs; narrow bottom, steep sides, irregular top, which means higgledy-piggledly growth; Britain's only split level city.

The early wealth of the city shows in Georgian buildings, the magnificent Victorian street developments of Grainger and Dobson, the beautiful curve of Grey Street with its column (statues here are useful people like reformers, not generals and admirals who mainly rose to the top by getting Northerners killed). Most northern cities would have taken this magnificent legacy and knocked it down in the development bonanza of the 1960s, when Britain was built anew and usually badly. Newcastle compromised; it left most of the city standing and moved office buildings in amongst it.

That great rebuilding was initiated by T. Dan Smith, Labour leader, first city boss, first man to appoint a city manager and all-purpose media darling, until he was lured by that whiff of corruption to which the flesh of one-party states is always heir. Under him, development was a home grown, bootstraps operation, motivated by civic pride, rather than bomb damage of which there was little. That background accounts for its triumphs and its tragedies. With the constant need for hucksterism, in order to impress the media and con the reluctant locals, half-baked concepts were floated like 'the new Brasilia' or the 'New Venice' (with motorways instead of canals'), the 'walled city' (with motorways now transmuted into walls – a far more realistic view as anyone who has tried to cross them and lived, could testify).

Despite the grandiose rubbish, Newcastle avoided the planning disasters inflicted on Bradford or the wholesale destruction of Birmingham. The long, ugly Byker Wall, housing 2,500 families, is a magnificent environment, once you penetrate beyond the blank face it presents to the outside world. The University and the Poly bring life and youth to the city centre. The architecture is better than average. The Civic Centre (Cynic's Centre to the humourist) is magnificent. Finally came the Metro, the only one of the several plans for 'out of London Undergrounds' which actually made it from the drawing board – and despite the opposition of central government. Earth has a good deal to show more fair than the view from the Tyne Bridge. It certainly has a good deal to show that's cleaner. Yet Newcastle still provides the environment for a solid, comfortable and easy existence instead of squashing people into suburbs and turning out the lights in city centre deserts.

*   *   *.   *

The North East is more than a city state. It is also a language. Many of its words and some of its pronunciation descend from the original Scandinavian and the natives like to think that modern Scandinavians who throng in for Christmas shopping, which they do in locust fashion, can understand it. But they can't. Defoe noted in the 18th century:

'I must not quit Northumberland without taking notice that the natives in this country of the ancient original race of families are distinguished by a shibboleth upon their tongues, namely a difficulty in pronouncing the letter 'r' which they cannot deliver from their tongues without a hollow jarring in the throat, by which they are plainly known, as a foreigner is, in pronouncing the 'th'. This they call the Northumbrian 'r', and the natives value themselves upon the imperfection because forsooth it shews the antiquity of their blood'.

The same affectation survives today at the 'r's end of every word. Scott Dobson, the chronicler of the Geordie language whose book *Larn Yersel Geordie* triggered a horde of more successful imitators in Liverpool and Yorkshire, advises anointing the tonsil with a mixture of surgical spirit and Madras curry powder before making the sound. He also urges practice of the 'Geordie Diphthong' as in the phrase 'Thor's not a byad Tyab' (these cigarettes are rather good) or 'Me da's byad wi the beyor' (father is indisposed). Some of the vocabulary has reached the outside world as in 'canny', or 'ganning', which most people assume is only done along the Scotswood Road, or the all purpose meditative phrase 'Whyaye'. With a little practice they can be combined into words and phrases such as 'hoositganningathematchwithecanny lads'. This means 'how are our fine fellows progressing in the football game' though it's not advisable to put it that way. Using the phrases will either unleash a flood of conversation, in which case you've made a friend and can pay for a round (remember this is a depressed area), or a taciturn silence. In that case it may be time to move away with the all purpose benediction, 'Yebuggermar'. Practice makes perfect. Or rather its northern counterpart, Geordie.

Language is the verbal side of a dominant working class culture which still survives, almost intact, in the North East. It is insulated, isolated, rough and tough.

This is the most drunken, most violent part of a nation once viewed on the continent as a riot prone collection of thugs. And now, of course, through the goodwill ambassadorships of its soccer hooligans, albeit from another region, having fully resumed that traditional image. Geordie crime, violence, delinquency and wife beating are high. Yet there's less AIDS. 'Poufters' are for beating up, not for consorting with. This is male chauvinist country: the bitter adverts turned into a way of life. Women are a subordinate race and conversation, even chatting up, is reduced to a terse, 'How about it?'. Women may pull wires behind the scenes. As managers they sustain family living standards by their economies the struggles and the pin money jobs. The increasing importance of these supplementary wages, as men lose theirs, may even make them potentially dominant. Yet they've not used this new power or shown any indication of wanting it. Unpolluted by emancipationist thoughts imported from southern sisters they may even agree with the men: a woman's place is on her back.

Southerners find all this unsophisticated. Air passengers landing at Newcastle are invited to put their watches back twenty years and the area has the feel of the 1960s, without their prosperity. Yet it's really had the rough end of every stick. Change and improvement came with growth and consumerism. The North East, last, loneliest, most loyal to the old ethos has had less of all of them. It got the droppings from the multi-national table, the ASDA end of the food trade not the Sainsbury's; Comet and MFI, not their up-market counterparts. Now that the bingo boom is over, the Fiesta has closed, the Meccas are turned into discos, it all looks more tawdry than ever.

Even frightening. Outsiders, if only because some are public school, Oxford educated, can see north-easterners as nasty, brutish and short. John Ardagh, living in Newcastle as part of his anthropological consumer test on five European cities said,

> 'Sometimes in the back streets of slums, amid football crowds, or in a dismal pub, with the beer spilt on the table and workers talking a language I could not follow, I even felt something of that Angst in the presence of an alien, vaguely menacing culture, that I have felt in Muslim lands such as Iran or Algeria, (after all, Geordies treat

their women in an almost Muslim manner)'.

Yet of Toulouse, Stuttgart, Bologna and Ljubljana, Newcastle was the one he liked best.

* * * *

Like the local 19th century capitalists who made no provision for the future, the workers have practised gathering rosebuds, or rather Newcastle broon while ye may for tomorrow — who knows. Money is to be spent. And it was. Fecklessness as Mrs Thatcher may call it. Yet this is a very un-Thatcher area. So they think differently. Place less emphasis on getting on through their own efforts and abilities, more on collective solidarity. Enjoy; together. Much happier than accumulating separately.

The culture was sustained by isolation. Britain is an over centralised country and has become more so. The death of basic industries, the centralisation of the media, career ladders and politics all focusing on the Great Wen and its south-eastern annexes (which live by draining the life out of the rest of the country) has all meant the decline of those provincial centres Liverpool, Manchester, Birmingham, Leeds which once provided a self-sufficient society and a rival focus, with their own politics, their own media, their own economy. Once these were a dominant influence, forcing the effete, imperialistic, bureaucratic South, to free trade. Then having forced it on to provide industrial protection, English provincialism has become a pale shadow of its former self. Independence has been replaced by the begging bowl as a way of civic life. Newcastle alone has maintained a degree — and it is only that — of independence and distinctiveness. It has resisted the pull to London better, mainly because it is further away but also because it is more brutal, less deferential to the South East's pretentions. This comes out in insularity, contempt for the South and better and more vigorous begging bowl techniques: the money is theirs by right. The Ruhr needs reparations for what has been done to it.

So from Newcastle, as from all parts of the North, trains to London are filled with deputations off to whine, and dine, at the hand-out centre, Whitehall. The improvement in communications: Newcastle to London by plane one hour, by train three hours, by motorway four hours dead (on occasion totally literally) merely means that deputations for concessions, grants, aid incentives, benefits receive their refusal that much quicker. Their sole consolation is that the only major town between Newcastle and London is Gateshead, which fact, together with the speed of travel, prevents them from seeing how much better off most of the rest of the country is than themselves. All they see is London, and no one in their right mind likes that.

The North East pioneered the technique with the 1936 Jarrow March. The town had pioneered the technique with the 1934 march to Ramsey MacDonald in Bishop Auckland. Then, in 1936, 200 unemployed — a number determined by the fact that subscriptions raised £800 and the costs were calculated at £4 there and back for each man — set off for London to highlight the plight of a town where the closure of the Palmer shipyards had killed hope, murdered the town (according to its M.P. Ellen Wilkinson), and brought unemployment to 70 percent. J. B. Priestley, a latter day pilgrim to the North East, described its living death:

> 'There is no escape in Jarrow from its prevailing misery, for it is entirely a working class town. One little street may be rather more wretched than another but to the outsider they all look alike. One out of every two shops appeared to be permanently closed. Wherever we went there were men lounging about, not scores of them but hundreds and thousands of them. The whole town looked as if it had entered a perpetual penniless bleak sabbeth. The men wore the drawn masks of prisoners of war'.

Instead of doing that at home, the 200 converged on the capital in a media event before the media existed. They succeeded. The shipyard re-opened, the War brought jobs, its aftermath brought development. Yet today, Jarrow's plight is as bad as ever: more public provision, more culture, better roads, museums and a civic centre; yet no jobs. Still. The local authority is the largest employer, the shipyard is in mothballs, the steel mill is closing, the unemployment rate is 29 per cent. The town has come full circle, to a sadder version of a blight which has settled once again over the whole North East. And all despite the development area policies, the grants, the new industries, Harold Macmillan's affection for the North, Lord Hailsham in his cloth cap, Ted Heath's visits, Labour's efforts and everything else.

The North East has had to run faster, and that not even to stand still, but to slip back. The decline which characterises the whole of Britain is at its most acute in its industrial heartland. Steel, once a dominant industry is now relegated to one massive plant at Redcar. Since that was designed long after Britain had lost the knack for big plants, the furnaces were found to have been designed to burn Japanese coke. To import that coke would have been ridiculous, so they were initially allowed to burn themselves, as smelting plants are prone to unless properly run. Now they are replaced, though one still lies in parts waiting to be assembled like a giant Japanese jigsaw. The steel plants of yesteryear, particularly Consett which was still profitable when closed, are sad and shut: dead hearts in a mouldering body. The number of steel workers is but a third of what it was in the 1960s.

Engineering and shipbuilding numbers are down by a third each. On the Tyne, the yards are shades of their former selves. Only defence work remains at Swan Hunter, nicknamed 'lame swans' after the failure of its attempt to break into supertanker construction. The few successful yards are concentrated on the Wear. Chemicals, booming in the 1950s, have ceased to expand. The ICI giant is transferring its weight to its foreign foot and the oil giants are closing British refinery capacity now that we have British oil. Coal, producing 56 million tons before the First World War dug only sixteen million by 1978. The coal industry has migrated from the West, where pits were closed and villages rated A to D in terms of their ability to survive and with D meaning 'leave to die', to the East to run against the sea. And underneath it. Mining provided 150,000 jobs in the early 1950s, but only 30,000 today. Its great event, the Durham Miners' Gala, that street theatre of socialism, has shrunk to a shadow of its former self. To the horror of traditionalists who remembered the solidarity of 1926 the 1984 drift back to work was faster than either Scotland or Yorkshire. All because the future of local industry was less secure.

Saddest of all, even the new industries from which so much was hoped have proved not to be hardy perennials but more fleet in departing than even they were in coming. What were lured to the North East by the development area strategy as it emerged in the 1960s and 1970s were *not* the knowledge, high skill, high pay industries the area needed to give it an admixture of white collar jobs, technical skills and brains. The Tyne remained a muddy scrap-yard, not a silicon valley. The new industries were food processing, assembly work, components, light electronics, even textiles. They came not through any passionate desire to live in Britain's closest approach to paradise, but simply because grants were higher than they were further south. Some, such as Findus, actually evacuated intermediate or development areas to grasp the money which special development status could offer, and shedding 1300 jobs in Humberside to create 600 at Long Benton.

A cash nexus is not a transplant. The firms put down few roots. Their managers were immigrants, their plants peripheral parts of larger organisations coming for opportunistic reasons and disposable when opportunism pointed in another direction. Boards in London felt no compunction about inflicting more misery on the North East. They were used to it. And too far away to picket the Board Room. Easy come guaranteed easy go – and redundancies in the 1980s have been twice the national average, with painful consequences for the locals whose jobs were dashed as quickly as their hopes had been raised.

*   *   *   *

The North East fell between too many stools. Newcastle was neither big enough nor near enough to the centre of population to be the new Liverpool, as trade shifted from the Atlantic to Europe. The area was too far south to benefit much from North Sea oil, and too north to do anything but land gas, a fairly unprofitable pastime when the jobs go further south. Less lavish in its development lure than Northern Ireland and less effectively organised to attract the new than the Scottish Development Agency, lacking the intellectual capital of the Oxbridge-London triangle, its physical attractions less well known and certainly less heavily promoted than Scotland's, the North East hovers and hovers, clutching at every available straw but with no real prospect of having anything which can replace what is gone. And still going. Redundancies still run at twice the national rate.

The struggle against decline has become the dominant pattern of local life and politics. Overwhelmingly, solidly, instinctively Labour the North East struggles to help itself − despite, rather than with, the Conservative Government. Public spending has become the only answer to its problems because it's the only way to do anything at all. A road doesn't provide many jobs but at least it stays there. Unlike Courtaulds. J. B. Priestley wrote in 1934:

'I never saw a bit of country that was in more urgent need of tidying up … We are all fond of saying that people 'get used to' things but I do not believe anybody can look complacently at a dirty mess of this kind. It must have been depressing folk for years. All around this hideous muddle, where industry had had a dirty black meal and had done no washing up, there must have been schools'.

Only the new depression liberated the money to make a start on clearing up that mess which is − or rather was − the North East. It is not a world built anew, but the roads, the new housing stock, the new towns, each more successful than, say, Lancashire's, the improvement of the environment, with slag heaps carefully landscaped, the coast carefully manicured, have all got better as the industrial situation gets worse. Yet there are limits to preparing for an industry which never comes and in making life better where there is no work. The North East could still become the best groomed wilderness in the world, a museum of industrial archaelogy.

Maybe that would have been the case if the Conservative Government hadn't stopped the grooming. They have cut down regional aid. They demolished the Tyne and Wear Metropolitan County Council, thus ending the valiant effort it has waged for development. The road programme, housing and infrastructure spending are all threatened with economies, despite their importance in sustaining the area. Nor are the

Government's chosen alternatives in the form of bribes and lures of Free Port and Enterprise Zones any real compensation. They have merely initiated a game of industrial musical chairs or attracted supermarkets and distribution, not new industries.

So depression has become a syndrome, a way of life. Gunnar Myrdal remarked that every nation has its 'South'. In Britain it's the North East: a concentration of problems, an institutionalised depression. As Britain has slipped down every available international league table for the standard of living, so the North East, once the great beating boiler room of Empire, building its ships, providing both fuel and the sinews of war, has slipped down the British tables. Now it is left with the detritus of industry: the slag heaps, the pollution, the dying villages and towns. Plus the problems of decline. Unemployment is 30 percent in the inner areas, 20 percent overall. Poverty is worse, earnings are lower, so are living standards. Its towns are high in the Department of the Environment's 'misery index'. In the EEC's latest index of regional disparities, the four counties of the North East came in the bottom twelve of 131 regions. Along with Sicily and Northern Ireland. Depression breeds despair, violence, crime and misery. Its breeding ground is the North East. Only the sense of community holds them in check.

Reduced to humming its own Recessional, perhaps Depressional, the area is living in the past because the present holds out so little and the future seems to have been cancelled. Unable to control its own destinies or pull itself up by its bootstraps, it is refused sufficient help from a centre on whom it has come reluctantly to depend. So it sits impatiently, waiting for change at the centre: a change of heart, a change of government or, either the beginning of the national expansion which alone can kick start the Geordie motor. The North East waits for Godot. And he's none too well.

So a saga which began in hope born of the growth, the expansion, the new industries and local initiatives which transformed this elongated parade ground into a power house of a new economy has come to a dead stop. Now only hope is left − and that the super, slimmed down, lean, hungry version which alone is appropriate to the mean new Britain. A world we haven't quite lost lingers on but without the industrial core to support it. As outdated as a coal fire.

*   *   *   *

The North East is a way of life, a set of attitudes, a syndrome mixing the resentment which betrays doubt and provincialism with a sense of independence and a self-contained working class life, weakened but still there. It is humanity: warm and friendly, quick tempered and insular, particularly when accumulated resentments boil over and expectations, never very high, are betrayed. Again, Disappointment Rules — not O.K.

This is a paradigm for the nation. When Britain sneezes the North East gets flu. Now Britain is mortally sick. The former workshop of the world is entering a straightened retirement living on a pension from the North Sea. Old roles are fading fast. The industrial base of our way of life is undermined. No alternative is either offering or obvious. The rentier lifestyle of the semi-retired, or Dennis Thatcher economy looms ahead, living on revenues from investments stashed abroad at the expense of investment at home by top people — the Tyne industrialists' folly turned into a national characteristic. That may be fine for the well off, or even for southerners whose life's ambition has always been to retire to the South Coast. It is no use at all to wage earners and would-be earners, who don't have financial flab on which to live. Neither is it any use to hardy northerners, whose coastal resorts are too cold to retire to. In any case these are people born, built and conditioned to work. All they need is something to work at, a job, a role, a future.

The North East knows the problem well. It pioneered the role but for it the consequences are more severe than they are for the nation. Britain is abdicating, but the North East was betrayed, let down by the original leaders who made it, the captains of industry who never thought about the future, a usual local trait. They made money, built monoliths and sold out, leaving the land that made them; they to retire, it to rot. THe first depression of the 1930s hit harder than anywhere else in England, then after a recovery as industrial Britain revived, the area was struck down by the sickness of British industry. Now let down by central government, it is left with the consequences of that series of betrayals. Still a good place to live. Too little to live on. Three million people looking for a purpose. Just as fifty five million may be — once the oil runs out.

THE NORTH WEST
Gerald Kaufman

The Rt. Hon. Gerald Kaufman has been active in Labour politics since 1955; he contested Bromley that year at the age of 25, when he was Assistant Secretary of the Fabian Society, and Gillingham four years later. He was then Political Correspondent of The New Statesman *and on the political staff of the* Daily Mirror. *He was the Member for Manchester Ardwick from 1970 till 1983 when he won the Manchester Gorton seat with a very large majority.*

Since 1980 he has been chief Opposition Spokesman for the Environment. He was Minister of State in the Department of Housing from 1975 to 1979 and became a member of the shadow cabinet. He is a prolific journalist and author.

Gerald Kaufman was born in 1930 and was educated at Leeds Grammar School and then went to Queen's College, Oxford.

I was born and brought up in Yorkshire. In fact, to make no bones about it, I am a Yorkshireman. To me as a child in Leeds, Lancashire people were those folk we fought the Wars of the Roses against; growing up a bit, as a Labour supporter I begrudged them their red rose as against our white. Lancashire was also the place of origin of entertainers like George Formby and Gracie Fields. I noticed that these popular singers pronounced their words in a peculiar way, their letter 'r' ostentatiously emphasised where it should have been silent, their diphthong 'ou' (as in 'our house') concave instead of being, as in Yorkshire, sturdily convex. Lancashire was far away, on the other side of the Pennines, separated from us in the West Riding by the almost insuperable barrier of the Backbone of England. The people who lived there, I learned at school, made clothes out of cotton instead of wool.

It was not until I was eleven that I set foot in the North West. I was taken on my holidays (not, in Leeds, 'on holiday') by one of my elder sisters to, of course, Blackpool. Even though the War was on, we had a high old time. We went to the pictures (*Boom Town,* with Clark Gable). We danced in the Tower Ballroom, and went to the top of the Tower itself. We had tea, proper, Northern high Tea, in the Woolworths on the front. It was so much bigger than the Woolworths on Briggate in Leeds and which, daringly, was also open on Sunday. We rode the trams – at that time nothing special, since Leeds had an excellent tram fleet of its own, including, like Blackpool's, some vehicles with sections open to the sky. We went to the Pleasure Beach, on the South Shore, and I learned the rules governing the three Blackpool piers. South was posh; Central was common-or-garden; North was the one the Jews used, where people from Leeds could pretend not to notice other people from Leeds.

In my teens I would very occasionally travel venturesomely to Manchester to see a film or a play. Apart from unattainable London, Manchester was the big metropolis where everything went on; it included Belle Vue funfair, which was said to make Blackpool Pleasure Beach look like nothing in particular and had a zoo into the bargain. In those days Manchester was a very big city indeed. My dearest wish was for Leeds to overtake Sheffield – behind which alien place our population always lagged by a maddening handful of thousands – in order to become Britain's sixth biggest city. Even to think of Leeds overtaking Manchester – as it now has – was a phantasmagorical dream.

The Lancashire city with which I first became really well acquainted was Liverpool. When I worked in Harold Wilson's political office at 10 Downing Street, I used to accompany the Prime Minister on his visits to his Merseyside constituency of Huyton. Over a period of more than four years I went there dozens of times. We used to arrive at Lime Street Station, having travelled from Euston in a specially reserved section of the train; Harold, his wife Mary and myself rode in one compartment, with the Garden Girls, often typing busily away under the protection of the Special Branch detectives, located next door. We always caught the train only by the skin of our teeth, Harold and Mary both being nerve-shattering procrastinators. At Lime Street Station, the top-hatted station master would greet us, and we would be whisked away for the drive, lasting only a few seconds, to the magisterial Adelphi Hotel. Mary remembered the Adelphi from her girlhood in New Brighton, as the place above all other places for an elegant afternoon tea in its imposing downstairs lounge.

Unless kept under strict control, Harold would pop across to Lewis's store just over the road. This was part of a chain which included one we had in Leeds and another in Manchester. There, in the men's-wear department, he would try on, and always buy, inexpensive suits, for he had a tremendous eye for a bargain. Then, through semi-derelict streets lined with an extraordinary number of pubs, we would speed to the constituency for whatever engagement he was to carry out.

At that time, the enormous overspill township of Kirkby was in Harold Wilson's constituency, and the newer Cantril Farm estate was being built: huge, menacing tower-blocks stuck, for no particular reason, in the middle of the countryside. Kirkby already had a reputation, of sorts. It housed the biggest teenage population in Europe, and there were tales of children's parties coming into Liverpool by coach to see the Christmas pantomine and looting every pair of the cheap opera-glasses available in the theatre for sixpence in the slot. Kirkby was famous, too, as the home of the tough television series Z-*Cars*.

Eventually, Harold, irritated by the poor room service and annoyed by the high prices at the Adelphi, moved to the Golden Eagle Hotel in Kirkby. It was a humbler (and much less costly) place where he was treated magnificently even though one of his staff once negligently flooded a bathroom.

Harold would hold surgeries in an office at Huyton Labour Club, and afterwards we would go into the big room and have a drink. These sessions introduced me to the special world of Lancashire Labour Clubs, and to the marvellous Scouse humour of Merseyside. There was one comedian, whom we heard several times, whose droll stories made me almost physically sick with laughter.

Then, in 1969, I was adopted as Labour Candidate for the Ardwick constituency of Manchester and became, literally, an adopted Mancunian, an adopted Lancastrian, an adopted North Westerner. In 1970, I was elected to Parliament. Although I was an incomer from across the mountains, I was made very welcome. My welcome, indeed, caused me to notice an important difference between Lancastrians and Yorkshiremen. I recall that this realisation came upon me the very first time I walked down Market Street, then the most popular shopping thoroughfare in Manchester. I was amazed to find that my progress was quite painless. No-one pushed me; nobody poked their elbows into my ribs. It was not at all like that in Market Street's Leeds equivalent, Briggate, where it is every shopper for him- (and especially her-) self. Yorkshiremen, I knew, were tough as the rocks on their moors. Lancashire people, I found, are in their personal relationships as soft as butter. I believe that this contrast is brought about by the difference in climate. Yorkshire people live an existence made harsh by the elements, by the cold winds that sweep in, unobstructed by any barrier, from the Ural Mountains and Siberia. The damper, milder climate of Lancashire is not only gentler for facilitating cotton-processing but for moulding people's characters. This circumstance does not mean that North

Westerners have easier lives. It does help them to be less dour.

*   *   *   *

I became used to the North West. I travelled about it, seeing its extremes from the Scottish border to the boundary with Staffordshire, from the west end of the Wirral peninsula to the Pennine ridges, where Oldham merges uneasily with Huddersfield.

I drove out to Prestbury, in Cheshire, on Manchester's southern commuter belt. Prestbury is indubitably an ancient village, definitely the real thing. Its Parish Church accommodates in its grounds a rough little Norman chapel and even, suitably protected, a genuine Saxon cross. A white cottage, just around the corner and firmly inhabited, was built in 1770. Even older is a former school-house, constructed in 1721. The problem is that Prestbury has been refined almost out of reality. The side of the school-house is adorned with notices announcing that this self-conscious place won the national prize for Best Kept Village in 1977, 1980 and 1982. Best kept it certainly is. There is hardly a fragment of litter to be found, the few odd bits in view no doubt having been spitefully dropped by visitors who were slumming in reverse. The hedges seem manicured. The dry-stone walling looks as though it has been designed by computer. People using Prestbury are instructed to behave themselves. 'No horse riding on footpath or verges', admonishes a notice that clearly means business. Even the birds sing in a specially orderly way.

This is a place of rich people. The cottages, which come in two kinds, old and older, are bijou cottages. The houses, even those fronting the main roads, are often enormous, in capacious grounds. One, called Spinney End, had - when I was there – four cars parked on its drive, with room for many more; perhaps some members of the family were out. The 18th century former school-house shelters a branch of Williams and Glyn's Bank. Next door are Bridgford and Sons, estate agents. I observed that their window displayed details of five properties each costing over £100,000, with three more sneakily demanding £99,500. A few yards further on, John S. Brown's rival establishment scored with one desirable residence obtainable at £182,000.

Prestbury contains numerous establishments to cater for the wants of the occupants of such dwellings. There are little shops with coy names like Artizana, a 'craft gallery' selling extremely expensive nick-nacks that presumably get bought. There is a very up-market confectioner, Ye Chocolate Box. There are several restaurants. One, Prestbury Village Bistro, unnervingly offers such dishes as Courgette and Brie Soup, followed, reassuringly, by Cheshire Turkey with Chestnut and Sausage-meat Stuffing.

Another time, I drove north from Manchester and went steadily on, past the rolling hills of central Lancashire. Here I was in a different, wild world. I turned down a steep hill into the little town of Ramsbottom. Ramsbottom boasted a thoroughfare named Industrial Street and numerous rows of buildings mostly coloured black. I proceeded northwards along roads where chimneys of deserted mills stuck forlornly through the trees. I went through Rawtenstall, with its Newchurch Boot Company, its Co-operation Street, and its advertisements for hot pies; through Dunnockshaw, with sheep on its hillside; through Clowbridge, where the hills began turning into bleak moors. I entered Burnley, with its rows of little houses painted in bright, primary, colours as if they really only existed in a child's painting, and a redolently named pub, The Rifle Volunteer.

From Burnley the hills stretched away to the remote horizon, in successive layers of different shades and different shapes. They loomed over unevenly shaped fields separated by dry-stone walling, rough-and-ready but well constructed, which looked to have been made by entirely different creatures from the artificers of Prestbury's carefully tailored equivalents. Along the road lay places with strange names such as Nappa and Blacko; and then there were no buildings at all, just mile after mile of menacing moorlands. The only route now twisted through a chunk of Yorkshire, and then re-emerged into Lancashire before debouching at Kirkby Lonsdale.

This urban version of a displaced person once lay in Westmorland. When that county was abolished, poor Kirkby Lonsdale, suffering from severe identity problems, became an addendum to the far east of Cumbria. It is a lovely little town, as unaffected as Prestbury is pretentious, crammed with dusty and enticing second-hand bookshops and built haphazardly around a marvellous little Market Square. This has a curious memorial in the middle and, facing each other at either end, the Royal Hotel (on Main Street) and a Trustee Savings Bank housed in an elegant stone building decorated soberly with classical pediments. There are no bistros in Kirkby Lonsdale, the Market Square offering for sustenance only the Vale of Lune Coffee and Eating House, with the day's speciality not Courgette and Brie Soup but home-made scones.

From Kirkby Lonsdale it is possible to get, along narrow, winding, switchback roads, to Carnforth, with its sturdy stone cottages, and from there, via Over Kellet, and a view beyond the hilltops to the grey waters of Morecambe Bay, to the motorway that returns travellers from this remote district back to Manchester in ninety minutes at most.

In Manchester I eventually bought a house, not from Bridgfords or John S. Brown's, and certainly not at their prices. Even so, it was a lovely 1854 coach house. It was in Victoria Park, in my constituency (now redistributed as Gorton), and all of a sudden Manchester had become my home, the place where I most wanted to be. I had really become a North Westerner.

* * * *

What, though, is the North West. When I first came to the region, it consisted geographically and administratively of four counties: Lancashire, Cheshire, Cumberland and Westmorland. Then in the early 1970s Peter Walker, Secretary of State for the Environment, came along and interfered. In his Local Government Act he abolished Westmorland entirely, and gave Cumberland the name Cumbria. He turned the region into a gigantic jigsaw puzzle, plucking, for example, Widnes and Warrington out of Lancashire and dumping them in Cheshire, robbing Lancashire of Barrow-in-Furness and handing it over to Cumbria. He created two completely new counties, Greater Manchester and Merseyside. More than a decade later, his successor, Patrick Jenkin, decided to abolish these two new creations as administrative counties with elected councils.

Political parties, for their organizational purposes, and government departments, for compilation of statistics and wider executive reasons, hive off Cumbria into the Northern region along with Durham and Northumberland. Certainly it's true that, in a softer way, the Cumbrians speak with an accent close to that of the Geordies and their North Eastern neighbours, quite unlike the gallery of related accents in Greater Manchester and Lancashire. However, if speech is the criterion then Liverpool and Merseyside, with their beguilingly muddy vowels and consonants should be all on their own. However, geographically they are indisputably part of the North west, as too, just as certainly, is Cumbria.

The North West is, in population, the most sizeable region of the kingdom outside London. Its seven million inhabitants are more numerous than those of Scotland, Ireland or Denmark, and twice those of Wales. There are great differences between their five counties, as they existed in 1985. Cheshire, apart from that eastern section sharing the Peak district with neighbouring Derbyshire, is mostly flat. It is mainly a farming county, with three-quarters of its area agricultural land, mostly used for dairy-farming. Half of Cheshire's population lives in the Mersey Valley towns of Warrington, Widnes, Runcorn and Ellesmere Port, together with Chester and Crewe. Cumbria, on the other hand, is mountainous, containing the Lake District and part of the Yorkshire Dales National Park. Cumbria covers almost half of the North West's geographical area, but provides only 7 per cent of its population. It is, indeed, the second largest county in England by size, the fortieth by population. Although there are substantial populations in Carlisle, Workington, Whitehaven and Barrow, half of the county's inhabitants live in towns and villages with fewer than ten thousand people.

Lancashire on its eastern side is a land of mountain and forest, but towards the west, much of it is flat and not only agricultural but horticultural. Shorn of its major towns by Peter Walker, it still contains important centres like Lancaster, Preston, Blackburn and Burnley, together with what it refuses to hear of being other than the country's premier seaside resort, Blackpool.

Merseyside, whose dominant centre is Liverpool, also contains St Helens, Bootle, and − incongruously, and unwillingly on both sides − genteel Southport, together with the northern part of the Wirral including Wallasey and Birkenhead. It is the poorest part of Britain, fifth bottom of the 131 European regions, right down there along with Calabria and Sardinia. Greater Manchester has the city of Manchester as its hub, together with that other city of Salford, whose boundaries with Manchester are so difficult to distinguish, plus Wigan, Leigh, Bolton, Stretford, Altrincham, Bury, Rochdale, Oldham, Stockport and Ashton-under-Lyne. Its inner city areas − not only in Manchester but in Bolton, Oldham, Rochdale and Wigan − have seen the greatest exodus of people anywhere in the country. It contains more derelict land than any other English county except Cornwall. 15 per cent of Manchester's sewers are more than a hundred years old and constantly collapsing, causing blockages in the streets.

Even so, Manchester is the regional centre of government for the North of England, containing the offices of most Whitehall departments, as well as the printing works of the northern editions of the national newspapers. In the hideously ugly Arndale Centre it contains − but scarcely boasts − the largest covered shopping centre in Europe. Like Liverpool, Manchester is a commuter centre, drawing vast numbers of workers into its shops and offices every day and complaining that its affluent neighbours use its excellent civic facilities without contributing to them by paying its rates.

*   *   *   *

There are many ways of entering the North West region. The principal place to arrive by air is Ringway International Airport, in the south of Manchester (five million passengers a year), though there are other regional airports at Liverpool, Blackpool, Carlisle, Barrow and Chester. Liverpool is the biggest seaport, although its workforce has been halved in the past ten years. For travellers from London by Inter-City train, the first station of consequence reached is at Crewe. For entrants from Scotland, by road as well as by rail, handsome Carlisle, with its imposing castle, is the main point of entry. Travellers from Yorkshire on the M62 motorway across the Pennines, which is sometimes shrouded in fog in the winter, arrive in the northern suburbs of Manchester.

The North West is, indeed, justifiably vain about its motorways. It has 340 miles of them. The M6, Britain's very first, now runs like a regional spine from Preston to the Scottish border. However, to me the most dramatic way of entering the region is from the south-west, from Wales. Chester is a real border city, only two miles inside England from the Principality, and those who enter Chester coming along the road from Mold have the Welsh mountains looming behind them.

Chester is a Roman city, on to which have been added continual accretions, most notably from Norman, Elizabethan and Victorian times. Just outside the centre of the city itself is the cathedral (promoted from being an abbey in 1536) on St Werburgh Mount with, opposite it, an ostentatiously authentic Elizabethan building housing a computer shop. Turn the corner and you are in the main thoroughfare, Eastgate Street. Here can be seen St Peter's Church, whose original foundation dates from 907 AD. A notice points out that on this site, long before, could be found the headquarters of the Roman governor of Chester.

Further along Eastgate Street may be found Chester's celebrated Rows, the avenue of shops, often refined and expensive, containing elevated pillared arcades, many of them handsomely decorated in wrought iron. Even when the shops are not really old they are made to seem so, branches of Littlewoods and British Home Stores being housed in mock half-timbered buildings. Halfway along Eastgate Street there is a bridge over the road, in the centre of which is a fantastical – more wrought iron – celebratory clock painted brightly in red and green. It is marked: 'This Clock Tower was erected in Commemoration of the 60th year of the Reign of Her Majesty Victoria Queen and Empress'. The date, of course, is 1897, and the inscription points out that the donor was one Edward Lloyd-Evans. Nearby, a further reminder of the proximity of Wales, is an emporium named Taffy's Carpets.

Chester at first appears a thoroughly stately place, in a way an inappropriate introduction to the often scruffy North West. Yet, if you look around the foot of the stairway that leads to Edward Lloyd-Evans' ceremonial clock, you will find yourself ankle-deep in the litter which, too often, becomes almost a regional emblem.

*   *   *   *

Drive north west out of Chester, through rather nasty scrubland, and you will find yourself on the Wirral and heading for the Mersey estuary. The road goes by one of the great industrial monuments of Britain, the Stanlow oil refinery, whose forest of towers and chimneys makes it a modern Bologna. Then the traveller is at the entrance to the Mersey Tunnel (fee a modest 40p), though not about to travel through the original portion, Queensway, which when opened in 1934 was at three miles the longest road tunnel in the kingdom. The road to Liverpool from here lies via the newer Kingsway, opened in 1971 and, at five-and-a-half miles, even longer.

Liverpool possesses some of the sturdiest and most resilient people in our islands and some of the stateliest public buildings. However, too many of these buildings are crumbling. 'Liverpool', a representative of the Victorian Society has said, 'was considered the most exciting Victorian city in the land from the architectural point of view. But it is now full of empty tracts of land where buildings have been demolished and not replaced. It is like a city at war'. Conservationists point almost with tears in their eyes to the fate of St George's Hall, regarded as one of the finest neo-classic buildings in Europe and, according to the Victorian Society, 'far more important as a building than the British Museum'. When the Law Courts were moved from this Hall, the government stopped its grant covering 90 per cent of maintainance costs. The city council could not find the money, and so the Hall was simply boarded up.

Many parts of the centre of Liverpool have certainly become a repulsive mess, with derelict buildings standing like decayed teeth along the roadsides. One of the few bright sights in the inner city is the Albert Dock, refurbished by the controversial Merseyside Development Corporation. Old warehouses have been cleaned up and, although there are too many useless boutiques which clutter up such projects everywhere, there is also a Liverpool F.C. shop, lending a touch of genuine local identity and an Egon Ronay-listed snack bar, What's Cooking, which is as inefficient as the cheerful menu warns in advance that it is going to be. Albert Dock is the site of one of the most important centres for the visual arts to be constructed in Britain for many years, the Tate Gallery of the North.

*   *   *   *

The M62 goes from Liverpool straight across to Manchester and the Pennines. Politically, the journey from Chester to the eastern boundary of the region lies predominantly through Labour-held constituencies. In the 1983 General Election the North West region elected two Liberals (including the redoubtable Cyril Smith), 38 Labour M.P.s and 39 Conservatives. The Conservative lead over Labour in votes was 6 per cent, compared with 19 per cent in England overall; and in every one of the five counties the balance in votes was more favourable to Labour than in the country as a whole.

Indeed, Merseyside and Greater Manchester, each put Labour ahead in both seats and votes. The North West contributed five members to the 1984 Labour Shadow Cabinet, compared with one member of Margaret Thatcher's real Cabinet.

The politics of the North West are explained by the sad fact that it is, despite the affluence of certain parts, a deprived and impoverished region. Its problems are manifested by its population loss, the worst for any part of the United Kingdom, with in addition the steepest predicted rate of further decline. While the populations of Cheshire and Lancashire have risen, the urban areas have shrunk. In half a century, Liverpool's population has fallen from 856,000 to 503,000; Manchester's from 766,000 to 457,000.

Impoverishment displays itself in many ways. The North West contains 36 per cent of the 'grossly polluted' rivers of England, with only 14 per cent of the country's river length. While the level of owner-occupation is very high (71 per cent in Lancashire compared with 59 per cent in the United Kingdom as a whole), the number of new houses built in the region is proportionately the lowest in the country. The age of the existing houses is amongst the oldest, and those houses have a larger than average proportion without an inside W.C. The North West contains the country's lowest percentage of households with central heating or a deep freeze. It has lower than average car-ownership, especially in Merseyside. Its people eat less butter and more margarine than their fellow-countrymen (though they also consume more meat and potatoes, spend more on alcohol than any other Britons, and are the nation's most addicted tea-drinkers).

The North West has the country's highest death-rate, and the highest suicide rate for women. Its men and women are more prone than those in other regions to die of bronchitis, and its men have the highest death rate from heart disease. Although North Westerners (except in Cumbria) have the highest live birth-rate in England, they suffer from greater than average infant and peri-natal mortality and provide the highest rate of illegitimate births. North Western women work full-time more than their sisters in any other part of Great Britain and – coincidentally or not – there are also more children under eighteen in care than in almost any other part of the country. The number of one-parent families is greater than average (again, except in Cumbria). Possibly linked with these phenomena is the morose information that the North West contains the country's largest proportion of divorced men.

Although – with Merseyside outstanding – the North West has the highest percentage of children under five at school, and the highest proportion of day nursery places, it also has one of the worst teacher-pupil ratios. A lower proportion of the region's sixteen-year-olds remain at school than in any other area.

While the region's three shire counties have crime rates well below average, Greater Manchester and Merseyside are afflicted with a disproportionate supply of law-breakers. Violent crime is worst in Merseyside, with robbery and burglary twice the national average. Over the North West as a whole, there exists one of the worst burglary records in England and, intriguingly, by far the worst record of fraud and forgery. Not surprisingly, the region confesses to the highest percentage of guilty people sentenced to prison, both in Crown courts and magistrates' courts.

The inner city areas, in particular, are cursed with crime and vandalism, bad housing, derelict buildings, insufficient open space, too little greenery and recreational provision. There are growing concentrations of disadvantaged people, the elderly, the poor, the ethnic minorities. Public transport gets worse. Redevelopment reduces the availability of local shops. Above all, there is unemployment.

Unemployment, indeed, is the scourge that afflicts the whole of the region, even Cumbria, where it remains below the national average. The North West has, for generations, been a heartland of manufacturing industry, with the country's lowest proportion of workers in agriculture. Many of Britain's – and indeed the world's – industrial processes were born in this part of our islands. As early as 1779, Samuel Crompton invented the spinning mule in Bolton. Textiles became a dominant industry. Manchester led the country in rainwear and hats; Rossendale was a centre of the slipper industry. The region contained, especially in Bury, Radcliffe and Ramsbottom, the greatest concentration of papermaking in the world. There were thriving coal-mines, in Lancashire and Cumbria. There was shipbuilding, in Barrow and on the Mersey. After Henry Royce had built his first car in Manchester in 1904, he went into partnership with C. S. Rolls, and an important Rolls-Royce establishment was developed at Crewe. The vehicle-manufacturing town of Leyland in central Lancashire gave its name to a whole conglomerate based on the internal combustion engine. Ford and Vauxhall were located on Merseyside. Aircraft plants were sited north and south of Manchester.

Then decline set in. Between 1966 and 1983 the region lost 536,000 jobs, more than half of them after 1979. In the six years from 1977 to 1983, the North West, with 11 per cent of national employment, suffered 18 per cent of Britain's redundancies. The region, in fact, had the worst redundancy record in England. The ratio of unemployed to vacancies in mid-1983 was a devastating 27:1. Unemployment became worse than in any English region except the North. The proportion of people out of work in Liverpool became higher than in any other city in Great Britain, and Workington, Widnes and Runcorn, Wigan and St. Helens, Wirral and Chester, Rochdale, Bolton and Bury were almost as bad. What is more, nearly half the unemployed remained out of work for more than a year.

The toll in the once-dominant textile industry (including clothing, footwear and leather goods) was destructive. Employment of 620,000 in 1914 had by 1981 shrunk to 52,700. Other industries were stricken too. In the years between 1965 and 1983, more than half the North West's workforce vanished in mining, metal manufacture and engineering. Trafford Park, in Manchester, once one of the country's most thriving centres of industry, became denuded, almost a ghost town.

County by county, the impact was baneful. Between 1981 and 1983 Cheshire lost 9 per cent of its jobs. At the other end of the region, although tourism provided badly needed employment in the Lake District and surrounding areas, West Cumbria and Furness suffered hard blows. In Greater Manchester, 230,000 manufacturing jobs were lost between 1966 and 1981, a 38 per cent decline. On Merseyside, employment was down between 1971 and 1981 by over 15 per cent. In Lancashire, between 1979 and 1982, 60,000 jobs were lost, most of them in manufacturing. Leyland's workforce alone shrank between 1976 and 1981 from 14,000 to 9,000. This reduction was due partly to a fall in demand, partly − and chillingly − 'as a consequence of a multi-million-pound investment programme'. Not only were textiles hit in north-east Lancashire, Preston and Skelmersdale, but Rossendale's traditional footwear industry was damaged and the Fleetwood fishing industry was hit when its trawlers lost their access to Icelandic waters.

Those remaining in work had to be content with below-average earnings, partly because the region had one of the least qualified workforces in England. Yet, even after having suffered these blows, the North West remains one of the country's most important industrial areas, accounting for one tenth of the United Kingdom's gross domestic product and one eighth of manufacturing output. It is an especially important centre for chemicals and man-made fibres. The home of the computer and of Jodrell Bank radio-telescope, it contains lavish provision for higher education, with five universities and three polytechnics. Manchester is said to have more students per head than any other city in Western Europe.

*   *   *   *

On the cultural and recreational side of things, there are about sixty museums and art galleries throughout the region, many of them reflecting its life and history. The Tonge Moor textile museum in Bolton contains Crompton's Mule, Hargreaves' Jenny and Arkwright's Water Frame. Northwich has a museum devoted to the Cheshire salt industry, beginning in Roman times. Another museum, at Rochdale, houses documents, pictures and other material chronicling the activities of the Rochdale Co-operative Pioneers. Manchester possesses an air and space museum and, in the world's first passenger railway station, a museum of science and industry. Liverpool has a maritime museum; Ellesmere Port a boat museum; Fleetwood a fisheries museum. Salford art gallery possesses a large collection of the works of the Lancashire artist Lowry. At Grasmere, in Cumbria, Wordsworth's home at Dove Cottage can be visited, together with a museum housing many of his manuscripts.

The North West is lavishly supplied with theatres, in profusion in Manchester and Liverpool, and also at Bolton, Chester, Lancaster and Oldham. Local repertory companies compete eagerly with touring productions, although harmony was impaired when Covent Garden opera decided that it could no longer afford to send its performers to the specially adapted Palace Theatre in Manchester. Smug Liverpool audiences continued to enjoy the visits of the Welsh National Opera, even though, at the Empire Theatre, some of the most touching arias were accompanied by the sounds of trains arriving at the adjacent Lime Street station.

The region boasts two major symphony orchestras, the Liverpool Philharmonic and Manchester Halle', this latter being the only major orchestra in the world still named after its founder. There are also eight local radio stations; five run by the BBC, three by commercial companies. Manchester provides premises, brand new, for BBC television's network production centre. Based both in Manchester and Liverpool is Granada Television, which with *Coronation Street* has made England's North West familiar to every truly civilised country in the world. Carlisle has its own television company, Border TV.

In addition to Blackpool, with those three piers, its 518 foot high Tower (now more than ninety years old) and its prideful, almost arrogant Coronation Rock Company ('the undisputed Number One rock and candy specialists'), the North West boasts several other well-known seaside resorts. Of these, New Brighton may be somewhat tatty these days, while Morecambe has always seemed a bit too hilly for some and Southport's beaches are notoriously far from the sea; all the same, they remain stubbornly, even exuberantly, in business.

Tourists seeking a novel outing can also make for the public observation tower at Heysham nuclear power station ('Do we need it. How does it work. Is it really safe?') or Beatle City in Liverpool ('a brilliant multi-media experience' with 'priceless memorabilia', and all for £2 — half-price for swinging pensioners and the unemployed). Leighton Hall, north-east of Morecambe, offers 'flying displays with birds of prey' and, as an extra, an Antique American Doll House. No wonder the proprietors, the Gillow family, won the 1983 Sandford Award for Heritage Education over such strong competitors as Lyme Hall, south-east of Stockport, an Elizabethan house dating from 1560, with its mastiff exhibition; not to mention the Alice in Wonderland Group tours made available at Daresbury, near Runcorn, on the somewhat tenuous pretext that Lewis Carroll was born there. The local hotel at Daresbury does, however, offer 'a memorable three-course meal' — one presumes a tea-party -amid 'new Alice decor'.

The region presents some of the best sport available anywhere on the face of the globe, with football clubs that include the world's most famous team, Manchester United, together with such other crowd-pleasers as Everton, Liverpool, Manchester City, Blackburn Rovers, Oldham Athletic and Carlisle. The North West is — with Yorkshire — the true home of Rugby League football. Its top teams include St. Helens from Merseyside; Wigan, Oldham and Leigh from Greater Manchester; Widnes and Runcorn from Cheshire; and Barrow and Workington from Cumbria. The North West's county cricket team is Lancashire. Test cricket is played at Old Trafford, famous for Jim Laker's nineteen wickets in one match in 1956. Lancashire League cricket is a nursery for many leading players and the home of numerous top world professionals. Nor should we forget Wigan's pride in its pigeon-racing.

The region has given birth to some of the most enticing (and some of the most off-putting) dishes in the international repertoire. They include Blackburn Cracknels, Bolton Hot-Pot, Chorley Cakes, Everton Toffee, Hindle Wakes Fowl, Lancashire Foot, Lancashire Nuts, Lancashire Potato Pie, Lancashire Spiced Loaf, Manchester Collared Pork, Manchester Pudding, Morecambe Bay Shrimps, Oldham Parkin, Preston Parkin, Cheshire Soup, Cheshire Chicken Brawn, Chester Buns, Chester Cake, Chester Fingers, Chester Pudding, Cumberland Raised Pie, Cumberland Shipped Herring, Grasmere Gingerbread, Grasmere Shortcake and Westmorland Cake.

Its characteristic foods cannot claim to be examples of haute cuisine; rather they are the historic evidence of how the poor make the most of what little they can afford. One item is indeed called Poor Man's Cake. Others include sheep's trotters with oatmeal, pig's brain and kidney — and that enigmatic pair, Lobscouse and Wet Nelly. There are, of course, two of the nation's choicest cheeses, Cheshire, the oldest in England and known since the 12th century, and Lancashire (sometimes called Leigh Cheese, after the town where it originated), a crumbly, white delight too little known because it does not travel well. Above all, the region is the nation's benefactor as inventor of that carbohydrate ambrosia, the chip butty.

Other, more exotic foods, are becoming indigenous to the area, thanks to newcomers bringing their own diet or adapting what they have found. Some of the best fish-and-chip shops are owned by Chinese immigrants, who also offer chip butties with curry sauce. Pakistanis, Bangladeshis and Indians have opened restaurants all over the region, but particularly in the districts where they have settled in the largest numbers, especially inner Manchester, Bolton, Rochdale, Blackburn and Preston. They have established their own places of worship, mosques and temples, to add to the plethora of religious establishments available in the North West, ranging from the Spiritual Assembly of the Baha'i of Wigan to the British Mediums' Union of Spiritualists in Salford.

Liverpool is the only city that can claim two cathedrals, the ultra-modern Catholic cathedral, which took a mere seven years to build, and the Anglican cathedral, designed by Sir Giles Gilbert Scott, which required seventy-four years to complete but, when it was ultimately finished in 1978, turned out to be worth the effort as the biggest in Britain. It was a proud day for Liverpool when in 1982 Pope John Paul was a guest speaker at the Anglican cathedral and then went on to say Mass with his fellow-Roman Catholics.

*   *   *   *

In its five counties, from Longtown in the north to Nantwich in the south, the North West offers striking and often dramatic contrasts. The region contains ancient habitations and recently established new towns. Its social range is remarkable. It displays, in places like Prestbury, some of the most affluent and enviable living conditions to be found anywhere in the world, while its inner city areas are often pervaded by misery and squalor. In Stretford, Greater Manchester, 17.2 per cent of the voters are black or of Asian origin; in Copeland, Penrith and Workington, a trifling 0.3 per cent. In the Cheadle parliamentary constituency, 83.1 per cent of households are owner-occupied; in Manchester Central only 19.4 per cent. In Wythenshawe, Manchester, 75.8 per cent of the dwellings are owned by the council; in Southport a mere 6.7 per cent.

Out of 633 constituencies in Great Britain, Knowsley North, on Merseyside (the division now containing Kirkby) is number three of those with the highest proportion of 16-24 year-olds. Morecambe and

Lunesdale, forty miles distant, is number fourteen of those with the highest proportion of people of pensionable age. Of constituencies with the highest proportion of professional and managerial workers, Cheadle, in the southern part of Greater Manchester, comes number two in the whole of the country. Conversely, of those with the highest proportion of semi- and unskilled manual workers, Knowsley North, some twenty-five miles from Cheadle, is number one. Liverpool Riverside is number one in Britain for unemployment, Ribble Valley, thirty miles away in central Lancashire, is number 617.

Although its countryside ranges from the gorgeous mountains and lakes of Cumbria, through the bleak moors of the Pennines, to the lush farmlands of Cheshire, the North West is simply a relatively compact chunk of one of the three countries that make up the not very large island of Great Britain. Yet the prospects of someone from inner city Manchester or poverty-stricken Merseyside achieving the living standards of the most prosperous in suburban Cheadle or semi-rural Ribble Valley are not all that much greater than getting the chance to walk on the moon.

The North West has known many historic and turbulent days, from the Peterloo massacre to the disturbances in Toxteth and Moss Side in 1981. It has nurtured numerous famous folk. The Wirral supplied the House of Commons with an acerbic Speaker, Selwyn Lloyd. The Merseyside constituency of Huyton provided the nation with its longest-serving peace-time Prime Minister, Harold Wilson, who, although born in Yorkshire, had a Lancastrian father. Winston Churchill, later to become Prime Minister in the Second World War, sat for a time as a Conservative for Oldham and as a Liberal for Manchester.

The North West has been the birthplace of one of the world's greatest composers, William Walton, a native of Oldham, and exceptional actors such as Wendy Hiller and Albert Finney. Its history and social vicissitudes, sad and humorous by turns, have been chronicled in plays like *Hobson's Choice* and *Love on the Dole*. The region's most characteristic and admirable sons and daughters, however, are not its offspring with celebrated names, but those whose anonymity has made the North West so remarkable a contributor to the British national mixture: the Cumbrian shepherd, the Lancashire millgirl, the Merseyside boilermaker, the Manchester factory-hand, the Cheshire farm labourer.

They are the seven million North Westerners who have stuck it out and survived – and who always will.

John Watson

John Watson is the Member for Skipton and Ripon. He was educated at Bootham, the Quaker School at York, and then went to the College of Law at Guildford. He is a qualified solicitor as well as a man of business, the Director of a printing and packaging company.

In Parliament he is a member of the Select Committee on Energy and from 1979 to 1982 was Parliamentary Private Secretary to the Secretary of State for Northern Ireland. During the 1970 Election campaign he was Edward Heath's personal assistant.

It was through the Young Conservatives that John Watson rose to prominence in the Conservative Party. He joined them in 1961, held office at all levels and in 1971 was elected National Chairman.

The Duke of Devonshire does not live in Devon, he lives in Derbyshire – but shoots in Yorkshire.

When the miners were on strike his Lordship's beaters included miners. They drove up from South Yorkshire and in the absence of strike pay and Supplementary Benefit it helped to keep the bailiff from the door.

*   *   *   *

The filament of civilisation joining the two subcultures of North and South Yorkshire is to be found in Leeds. A city of 700,000 people with its feet either side of the divisive River Aire, it combines reality with the true finer things of life. Men call a spade a spade. Their wives call two spades 'three no trumps'. With equal pride it claims parentage of the largest fish and chip shop in the world, Harry Ramsden's at Guisley, and 'the world's number one piano competition'.

Actually, Leeds does not receive half the credit it deserves. In the past fifteen years it has witnessed the virtual demise of the tailoring industry, once the city's largest employer. Firms such as Montagu Burton and

Hepworths have laid off thousands of workers as fashions changed and overseas competitors and changing retail habits have played havoc with their previously secure business empires.

Yet at 12.4 per cent by 1985 Leeds' unemployment was now below the national and regional average. The City successfully established itself as the commercial centre of the eastern Pennines. Building Societies, insurance companies and even merchant banks have chosen to make Leeds their regional base. They have brought the jobs to fill the vacuum left by textiles. They have brought a tangible air of prosperity too. The city centre contains many new buildings, yet office rents in Leeds are still the highest in Britain outside London.

Inevitably, it is possible to find older residents who claim that Leeds is not what it was and that the department stores no longer offer the choice or the services of former days. Such people now go to Harrogate. But speak to the national managers of the chain stores and they will tell you that their Leeds branches are among the most profitable.

If credit is deserved, it is hard to know where to award it. The City Council has been subject to a classic case of pendulum politics. Whatever the political complexion at Westminster, the opposite will rule in Leeds Civic Hall (for strangely, Leeds Town Hall is not the seat of the Local Government). The Government Affairs Officer at Leeds City Council must have a very easy job. His task is always to oppose everything being done by the government of the hour.

The Chamber of Commerce is notably more effective than most, but can hardly claim all the praise for the City's economic transition. Possibly the person most responsible is that unknown planner who decided in the 1950s that Leeds should be the source of the M1 motorway.

The rival city, 30 miles to the south, has fared less well. Nursing a desecrated steel industry and an unemployment rate of 15 per cent, Sheffield has the distinction of being possibly the most socialist city in Britain. It is not hard to see why.

Some 32,000 people work for Sheffield City Council. That is 1 in 9 of the working population. A further 5,000 people work for South Yorkshire County Council − popularly known as the 'People's Republic of South Yorkshire' − and 43 per cent of Sheffield families live in houses owned by the city council. Whatever the theoretical attractions of free enterprise, voters are likely to resist them if acceptance means no house or no job.

In 1983, when Margaret Thatcher was sweeping Britain, she did not exactly sweep Sheffield. 54 per cent of all voters remained true to the Labour cause and Michael Foot's party took 5 of the city's 6 seats.

Mind you, the ruling class is not quite dead. Isolated it may be in the leafy enclaves of Dore and Ranmoor, but it does its best to glitter when the occasion arises. One such event is something called the Master Cutlers Feast, held in late spring of each year. It is a splendid affair of white ties, medals, sashes, furs and lots of diamonds. It is an evening dedicated to eating, drinking and complaining about the inadequacy of the government's efforts to control the workers. The Master Cutler pays for the whole thing – personally. Sadly, most cutlery in Britain is now made in Korea and Taiwan.

Local government spending in Sheffield was £1,006 per head of population in 1984/85. Much of it was spent upon a generously subsidised bus service.

It is the industrialists of Sheffield who bear most of the burden – as they are always keen to remind each other. Typically their favourite tale concerns a local manufacturer who decided to extend his premises. He submitted a planning application for his new factory extension. For five weeks nothing happened. Then he was visited by a man in an anorak who asked his views upon lesbianism.

*   *   *   *

If Sheffield and Leeds reflect present day realities in Yorkshire, it is the ancient city of York which holds the key to the county's past.

Julius Caesar visited Britain in 55 BC. He came, he saw but he did not stay to conquer. More pressing business took him back to Rome. It was not until 100 years later that the Romans set about imposing their rule upon the wild Celtic tribes of northern Britain.

In AD 71 the Romans established a powerful fortress at York, which they called Eboracum. Its site had been chosen with characteristic skill. It dominated the two navigable rivers of the Foss and the Ouse. Though most of the land around was swamp, their fortress was built upon a wide and well-drained gravel ridge which stretched for miles on either side. The construction of Eboracum enabled the Brigantes, ultimately, to be subdued and lands further to the north were conquered also.

Around the fortress itself there grew a major Roman city. Emperor Constantius I actually built a splendid palace and was there at the time of his death in the year 306. His son, Constantine the Great, was born in York. Constantine was the first Roman Emperor to become a Christian. In 312 he fought as a Christian and asserted his imperial title at the Battle of Milvian Bridge. No one quite knows where Constantine's Christianity came from. It was certain, however, that there was a Christian presence in York at the time of his childhood there. It was also apparent that the city has been the subject of great Christian attention ever since.

After Constantine's death in 339, the Empire began to collapse in on itself. Roman troops were withdrawn from Eboracum. Then followed the various incursions of the Saxons, Angles and Jutes. By 600 a strong king had emerged. He too established York as his military and economic capital. His southerly province, Deira, covered the same area as present day Yorkshire.

It was, therefore, a couple of Yorkshire lads whose fair hair and blue eyes were so noticeable to Pope Gregory at the slave market in Rome (non Angli sed Angeli). History records they were two Angles from Deira.

Two hundred years later, the Anglo-Saxon armies were no match for the Danes. In 866 a Danish King captured York and gave the city its present name (Jorvik, pronounced Yorwik). Although these Danish Vikings are normally portrayed as sanguineous barbarians, they were, at least so far as York was concerned, a good and civilising influence. A visit to the recently-opened Jorvik Centre in the city reveals a people dedicated to agriculture, crafts and a surprising amount of literature. It is to the Danes as much as its commanding location that York owes its success as a city.

Although William the Conqueror was himself a Norseman of sorts, he did not spare the people of York from the devastation which he delivered upon England after his invasion in 1066. Devastation, however, is a great unifier. It was only after the Norman Conquest and its unruly consequences that the old tribal kingships of Wessex, Deira, Mercia and the others were brought under common rule.

*　　*　　*　　*

Modern York is fuelled by tourism, railways and chocolate. Tourists, particularly from the USA, have provided it in the past couple of years with the busiest hotels in the North of England. The railways, through the vision (and possibly corruption) of 19th century George Hudson have made the city a transport and communications centre. They also provide many jobs.

And chocolates, founded by great Quaker families of the last century, provide the city's manufacturing base. Names like Rowntrees, Terrys and Cravens are given as explanations for the treacly flavour in the air on a still day.

To the eye, however, York is still dominated by its magnificent Minster. Started in 1220 it was not finished until 1470 − a period of almost constant construction which must have made it the mediaeval equivalent of London's Barbican. It is a remarkable building and casts the tone for the whole of central York.

Yet for all its historical pre-eminence and modern success, York has not grown as fast as other Yorkshire cities. There are a number of reasons. Its river is now shallower than before so York is no longer a serious port. Its

Guilds of the 16th and 17th centuries, established to protect their own trades, became so protectionist and restrictive that new businesses simply went elsewhere. Above all, York missed out on the industrial revolution. Nowadays, with a population of just 100,000, York is only a third the size of Bradford. It is also smaller than Huddersfield (130,000) and only slightly larger than Halifax (90,000). Recently Calderdale Borough Council, which incorporates Halifax, held an exhibition at the House of Commons. It was planned as part of a campaign to give the old place a face-lift. 'It's not all dark satanic mills nowadays', proclaimed the opener. He was right. The dark mills have been cleaned and are now light — but they still look pretty satanic.

Bradford, Huddersfield and Halifax are the great Victorian wool towns of West Yorkshire. Their location is logical. Sheep graze in great numbers on the nearby Pennines. The soft water supply has proved ideal for wool processing. Also, it flows rapidly and was originally a good source of power. The towns were sufficiently near to the Yorkshire coal fields to obtain fuel for the steam power their mills quickly demanded.

Working conditions in the early Victorian mills were unspeakable. As farm land outside the towns was enclosed for private use, whole families would find themselves similarly enclosed in factories for survival. There are many records of the noise, dirt and lack of safety within the mills. To people bred in the open countryside, however, it must have been the long hours and numbing monotony of the jobs which caused the greatest distress.

Upon the fruits of such endeavours many fortunes were made. No town or village in the former West Riding of Yorkshire is without its large Victorian mansion. Built, usually, by the textile barons of the last century, these houses are elaborate and ornate. To demonstrate their knowledge of different lands, the mill owners would combine many different styles of architecture into one building. The modern eye tends not to see such buildings as beautiful, but they possess a certain power nonetheless.

The textile towns are struggling now. Wool textiles have endured booms and depressions for nearly two centuries, but the recession of the early 1980s was probably the most severe of all. Comfortable management attitudes were abruptly challenged from overseas; European, East European and Far Eastern manufacturers plunged into the British market. The textile mills were forced to shed jobs dramatically, and in many cases they closed completely.

The managers of those mills which now remain admit quietly that they are 'doing all right', but it has been a bitter experience. Bradford suffered more than most. The decline of its major source of jobs coincided with an increase in its Indian and Pakistani population. Unemployment has not made its consequent social problems any easier to handle. Clearly Bradford has not possessed the size, the location nor the depth of resources to emulate the commercial success of Leeds, just eight miles to the east.

*   *   *   *

To the south and east of the textile towns is the great Yorkshire coalfield. In the hills near Halifax and Huddersfield it is shallow and the seams are not thick. This is where the oldest mines are to be found, now largely exhausted. Further east, the coal is deeper, thicker and richer. The newest pit of all, at Selby, will extract vast quantities of coal actually to the east of the River Ouse. A sixteen feet seam is located beneath York Minster itself. Such a resource was unknown until a few years ago.

The greatest demands upon the coalfield were made in the middle part of the last century. Textile mills needed power. The booming city of Sheffield needed coal for its iron and steel industry. British steamers serving the new Empire needed coal in order to conquer the waves.

Some demands were more esoteric. At Stratford colliery near Penistone an apprentice was always employed to select the brightest pieces of coal from each batch. These were then wrapped in tissue paper for delivery to Buckingham Palace where they would burn — presumably brightly — in their Majesties' grates.

Many of the men (and women, children and ponies too) who went down the mines at that time were from Yorkshire itself. Others came from Scotland or the North East. Together they created attitudes to an industry which still prevail today. Possibly the long miners' strike of 1984 and 1985 will have brought about a change in such attitudes but that seems unlikely. A massive distrust of senior Coal Board management, a disbelief of the press, an unbounded confidence in the power of the National Union of Mineworkers; such self-contained suspicion was generated by the coal owners of the 1800s. It survived both the General Strike of 1928 (which the miners started and lost) and the nationalisation of the industry after the Second World War.

Yorkshire miners also possess a loyalty to their Union which is truly remarkable. In March 1984 they were called out on strike without a ballot — even though it has been argued that their own Union rules made such a strike unconstitutional. To a man they responded. They put absolute faith in their President, Arthur Scargill, when he said that Government coal stocks would have dwindled by the end of the summer. Many television crews seeking to report picket line violence from the miners' own side were often abused and a camera was referred to as 'that lie machine'. A year later they had endured great hardship, and Arthur Scargill's arguments and predictions had been exposed as bankrupt. Yet the vast majority were still on strike. Their loyalty owed far more to the inheritance from previous generations than to any vaunted 'intimidation' by the militants.

The mining and agricultural communities which make up South Yorkshire have never really mixed. Pale stone agricultural villages, frequently very old, survive apparently unscathed in even the densest areas of the mining industry. They are surrounded by the much larger pit communities with their red brick council houses, neon pubs and rugby league clubs. The landscape is now much improved. In a testament to agricultural ingenuity, sheep and cattle are now able to graze the slag heaps and waste tips.

*   *   *   *

The eastern capital of Yorkshire is Hull. Though its Yorkshire status is never seriously in any doubt, it must be reported as a matter of administrative fact that Hull is no longer in the county. Hull now sits uneasily as the capital of something called Humberside.

Until the 1970s Kingston upon Hull was separated from Lincolnshire by the wide Humber estuary. This separation was, of course, a great economic and cultural strength. However, it became fashionable to regard it as a weakness. At a by-election campaign in 1965, Barbara Castle, then a member of a Labour Cabinet, worried about losing the seat to the Tories, promised the voters of Hull that the Humber would be bridged.

Labour won the election by 5,000 votes and sixteen years later the bridge, 'the largest single span suspension construction in the world' was opened to traffic. Not many people use it now. Few people wish to travel from Hull to Lincoln, and even fewer want to travel back. The tolls collected on the bridge are barely sufficient to cover the wages of the maintenance staff.

Still, the bridge has given both sides of the river an economic unity of sorts and this has been enshrined in the new county of Humberside — one of the more cavalier creations of the 1973 Local Government Reorganisation.

Though it is now a base for such modern companies as Reckitt & Colman, Northern Foods and (hopefully) Nissan, Hull owes its past prosperity to its position as a port and as a centre of the fishing industry. Its role as a port is still substantial in spite of union problems. Its fishing fleet, however, has all but gone.

Surprisingly, fishing did not become a major industry in Hull until the end of the last century. By 1990 it accounted for a quarter of the city's jobs, but the first fishing smacks did not arrive until 1835. They came because ladies from London society would migrate annually to Scarborough bringing with them a desire for the same fresh fish as that caught near Ramsgate. Finally, when Britain emerged in 1973 as the loser in a long series of 'cod wars' with Iceland, the fate of the fishermen was sealed.

Now, with a population of 290,000 and an unemployment rate of 17 per cent, Hull is trying hard, but the gap left by fishing has not yet been filled.

*   *   *   *

The Yorkshire coast is not the warmest in England. It must have relied upon attractions other than meteorological to make it a favourite Victorian playground. But its wide sandy bays would have made a change from the toe-crunching shingle of Brighton or Eastbourne; its cliffs and caves would have contrasted with the foggy flatness of Lincolnshire or Norfolk.

In the smaller resorts of Bridlington and Filey, most of the bigger hotels have now been converted into holiday flats. They are filled in the summer months by young couples and thousands of children.

Scarborough, however, still reflects the atmosphere of fresh air and fun which first attracted the Victorian damsels for a naughty frolic. The grand hotels remain, though The Grand itself has just embarked upon that rapid succession of ownership and purpose which reveals too big a building in too wrong a place. A giant sandcastle of a structure, cascading dangerously down the cliff face, the hotel has probably witnessed more secret affairs, more sales seminars and more Liberal conferences than any other in Britain. It was here that the Young Liberals created their memorable slogan 'Make love not war'. It was here, years earlier, that Lloyd George made both.

*   *   *   *

The great expanse of North Yorkshire which stretches for more than 90 miles from Scarborough to Bentham is the breathing space of the county. In West and South Yorkshire there are more than ten people per acre; in the North there is less than one. Between Upper Wharfdale and Nidderdale, it is possible to walk for twenty miles over the open moorland without seeing any sign of humanity or organised agriculture.

Unemployment at 9 per cent is well below national average. Outside the relative industrialisation of York itself, North Yorkshire is maintained by farming, quarrying, tourism and a wide variety of small industries. At the last General Election the Conservatives won all seven of North Yorkshire's Parliamentary seats. The local council is the most northerly in Britain to be controlled by the Conservative Party.

The villages around Harrogate, and York have expanded rapidly in recent years as young executives from Bradford and Leeds have moved in to take advantage of rural living — and lower rates. As they have done so the social structures of the communities have become strangely reversed. In the local pub on a Sunday lunchtime you will find the saloon bar filled with jeans-clad 35 year olds drinking lager. The public bar will be full of locals drinking mild. It being Sunday, they will be wearing dark suits and will have been to church.

Yet the more remote villages of North Yorkshire are facing a new kind of problem, fashionably called rural deprivation. Most such villages have their complement of elderly people who have retired there from the big cities. When they moved in they had cars. Successive petrol price increases have now caused the cars to be sold. At the same time the village shop has closed through lack of custom (distant hypermarkets are cheaper) and the school has closed through lack of children. Most disastrously of all, the local bus service has come to an end as soaring subsidies could not match dwindling passengers. So the elderly remain, isolated and unserved. The village communities do respond well to such problems; real hardship is very rare. Nonetheless, in its impact upon many rural residents, the recent phenomenon of rural deprivation is at least as great as the inner city deprivation about which so much has been written.

It is the farmers who provide the backbone of North Yorkshire. In the east and west they are the dairy farmers whose land will not grow grain. Either side of the River Ouse in the centre they are arable farmers whose recent crops have filled European storage capacity to bursting point. The arable men are doing very well but recognise it probably cannot last for ever. Many of the dairy farmers are suffering. Having enormously increased production in the decade to 1984, but not having seen their standard of living rise as a result, they were suddenly clobbered by quota limits on their output.

Change is not welcome in North Yorkshire. In their attitudes to it, the people display one of the most fundamental characteristics of the county as a whole. The battle to save the Settle to Carlisle railway is a case in point.

Whoever wrote that it is better to travel in hope than to arrive was probably travelling from Settle to Carlisle. The line was built as a result of a combination of railway disagreements and parliamentary bloody-mindedness. Until 1875, the only railway line from the West of England to Scotland was operated by the London and North West Railway. The rival Midland Railway tried unsuccessfully to negotiate terms for its own traffic to be carried on the line. Having failed, it then laid down plans for the Settle to Carlisle route, running roughly parallel with the LNWR line. When such plans were approved by Parliament in 1866 the LNWR backed down and agreed to allow Midland traffic over their line. The Midland then introduced another Bill to Parliament asking to be released from their commitment – and Parliament refused.

The line was, therefore, superfluous even before it was constructed. Its construction was also bitterly opposed at the time by most local opinion.

However, it *is* the highest and most scenic in England. The building of it represented Victorian engineering at its finest. It has many fans nationally, but it also loses money. Recent plans to close it on economic grounds are thus opposed by local people as strongly as they once opposed its construction.

*   *   *   *

It is deeply difficult to describe the Yorkshire character. Attempts to do so usually carry frequent inclusions of the word 'stubborn'. It is not hard to see why. What else is Scargillism if not the stubborn refusal to accept what others regard as the inevitable. A Yorkshireman will greet every proposal with a raised eyebrow. It is notable that many of our largest companies in Britain have Yorkshiremen as Finance Directors.

But 'stubborn' is neither sufficient nor fair. It neglects entirely the enthusiasm which can be generated within a Yorkshire soul. It neglects the unconscious humour which can arise without intention, but which, once pointed out, can be the basis for self-mockery.

A more typical attribute is common sense; a flat, no nonsense approach in which questions are asked directly and answers reviewed for their accuracy. It is no coincidence that two of the best British interviewers, Alan Whicker and Michael Parkinson, are both from Yorkshire.

Overall, the Yorkshire character is better described by example than analysis.

A Magistrate in Leeds once sentenced a car thief with the words: 'Now then, I don't know whether you're guilty or not. There's an element of doubt in your case – but you're not getting the benefit of it. I'm sending you to prison for six months. If you're guilty, you've got off lightly. If you're innocent, let it be a lesson to you'.

The modern Yorkshire character arises most clearly from the county's sporting activities. Yorkshiremen like to see their sporting heroes as social outcasts with massive talent. Harvey Smith is seen as the greatest showjumper of all time. He was, of course, justified in giving a V sign to those toffee-nosed judges from the South East. Leeds United in the early 1970s beat just about anyone in sight but didn't get half the credit they deserved. Don Revie, their manager, could have done wonders for the

England football team but was not allowed to do his job properly. Who could blame him for going off to train the Saudis instead?

It is in cricket, however, that all Yorkshire characteristics are suddenly rolled into one. Readers should understand that Yorkshire plays cricket in a different way from all other counties. Elsewhere in England, the cricket season is played from April to September. In Yorkshire those are regarded as the closed months reserved only for the formalities of hitting balls on pitches. The real action comes between September and April.

That is when there are committee meetings, special general meetings, motions of no confidence in the committee and no end of secret deals which overflow into the columns of the *Yorkshire Post*. It is all terrific sport. The essential question of the moment is simple; is Geoffrey Boycott a good cricketer. It is difficult to find a single member of the Yorkshire County Cricket Club who will answer that question using fewer words than the Chancellor employs in introducing his budget.

*   *   *   *

Yorkshire has an accent all of its own. It is clearly distinguishable from the dialects of Lancashire, Nottinghamshire or the North East. People in London cannot usually tell the difference, perceiving merely that the voice is that of 'a northerner'. But to a person from Leeds the Lancashire accent is as different as cockney.

The accent has led to much amusement. Edwin Wainwright was a coal miner until he was elected as Labour M.P. for Dearne Valley in 1959. On an overseas fact-finding mission he was seated, characteristically, in the hotel bar. A Conservative M.P. with the same delegation entered the bar with a pocketful of toffee wrappers. He was anxious to dispose of them: 'Where's the bin?,' he asked. 'Nowhere lad, I've bin here all the time,' replied Mr Wainwright.

On one occasion that same dialect has also led to tragedy. It happened at Riccall level crossing on the line between Selby and York. When the old gates were replaced by an automatic lifting barrier, a sign was erected saying 'Wait while lights flash'. The use of the word 'while' was misunderstood. In London it means 'during', in Yorkshire it means 'until'. An elderly couple approached the crossing and duly waited until the lights started flashing — whereupon they ventured across and were instantly hit by a goods train.

*   *   *   *

Yorkshire has produced slightly more than its share of the great and famous. They tend to be remarkable for their relatively humble backgrounds. The two Yorkshire Prime Ministers of the 20th century,

Herbert Asquith and Harold Wilson, were born in Morley and Huddersfield, respectively. Neither had a privileged background. Both succeeded initially through academic excellence.

There have also been two 20th century Chancellors of the Exchequer, Philip Snowden and Ian Macleod. Both were born to middle class parents near Skipton.

Happily, the one Yorkshireman of noble birth who tried to change the course of parliamentary history had little success. His name was Guy Fawkes.

Yorkshire inventors have tended to concentrate upon the practical. Many of the great automation devices of the industrial revolution came from the Yorkshire mills. Joseph Bramah is not famous, yet he deserves to be. He was the creator of a machine which has arguably had a greater impact upon our everyday lives than the motorcar or the television. Mr Bramah invented the flushing lavatory.

It is a fact that Yorkshire has been the birthplace of more great explorers than any other county. The most famous were William Scoresby, Martin Frobisher and Captain Cook. Their success, however, seems more closely related to their practical skills of navigation than to their natural valour.

Yet even the practical common sense aspect of Yorkshire people can be exaggerated. There is a clear creative and artistic heritage in the county, frequently in surprising places. The composer Delius was born in Bradford; so was J.B. Priestley. Sculptor Henry Moore came from Castleford and Barbara Hepworth was born nearby in Wakefield.

The true essence of Yorkshire has been captured by just four authors; Emily Bronte', Charlotte Bronte', Winifred Holtby and James Herriot.

The Bronte' sisters possessed a genius gift for words which enabled them to project both the wild countryside of the Yorkshire Pennines and also the intense human feelings which they contained. Readers of their books frequently develop a close curiosity about the authors, their lives and the land in which they lived. Their books were written, mostly by candlelight, in the parsonage at Haworth, near Keighley. It stands today and visitors to it do not trail round in glum observation, as is usually the case with museums. They ask questions by the thousand. Then they set off to tramp over the heather moors to catch the spirit of Heathcliff, Mr Rochester and Jane Eyre.

A book of equivalent atmosphere is *South Riding* by Winifred Holtby. There is, of course, no South Riding and there never was — but there cannot be a better description of life between the Wars around Hull and Bridlington.

James Herriot is actually a Scot but he has written exclusively about his experiences as a country vet in North Yorkshire. Contemporary literary opinion tends to dismiss the works of Mr Herriot — largely because they are so popular. Their acclaim will come, however. Their economy of language, their wit and the accuracy of his characters will make his books required reading for the 'A' level students of the next century.

*   *   *   *

All people develop a pride in their own county. What is surprising about Yorkshire is that other people develop a pride in it as well. Large companies experience little difficulty in moving executives to Yorkshire but often face domestic opposition when they seek to move them away again. The British Diplomatic Service is littered with Yorkshiremen in different parts of the world. Almost to a man they will return to Yorkshire.

The welcome we give there is more cautious than genuine. The countryside we have is less tidy yet more natural. The communities we have created are sometimes not beautiful, are frequently not rich but yet are communities in every sense.

Lord Cledwyn of Penrhos

Baron Cledwyn of Penrhos is the Leader of the Labour party in the House of Lords. As Cledwyn Hughes he was the M.P. for Anglesey from 1951 to 1979 and a former chairman of the Labour party and Minister of Agriculture under Harold Wilson.

Lord Cledwyn is from North Wales, with a passion for that region's topography and people. A Welsh speaker, he is in the long tradition of distinguished Welshmen whose passion and Nonconformity have made such a happy contribution to the national life.

U nless the weather happens to be unusually bad, the average visitor to North Wales enjoys his stay here. The seaside resorts are very pleasant; there is a variety of beautiful scenery within a comparatively small area and walkers, ramblers and climbers are well provided for.

Another advantage of the region is that the main lines of communication run east to west. Liverpool has been called the capital of North Wales and it is easier — as I well know — to travel to London than to Wales' capital city of Cardiff. Geography has been kinder to the invader than it has to the native.

The old North Wales is still there for those who keep their eyes and ears open; and you hear more Welsh spoken in Marks and Spencers at Llandudno than you would imagine. Its charm is its great variety in so small a compass. Wrexham has its woodlands and farms as well as its pit machinery. The Vale of Clwyd has been called 'The fairest Valley within this Isle' and the Clwydian Range is gentle compared with the sterner moorlands of the Berwyn Mountains: westward again the Conwy River divides moorland and mountain as the Carneddau leads the way to the last fastness of Eryri, Snowdonia, with its pointed peaks. To the west again is the peninsula of Lleyn with its lesser range Yr Eifl, anglicised as The Rivals, and finally Anglesey, or Mona, the Mother of Wales.

Cardigan Bay sweeps past Harlech and Barmouth to the estuaries of the Mawddach and the Dyfi, where North Wales merges into Ceredigion and the South. The great castle of Harlech held out during a merciless siege in the Wars of the Roses. It was also the last stronghold in England and Wales to fly the flag of Charles I in the Civil War. North Wales comprises the six counties created by the Tudor Acts of Union of 1536 and 1543 on the pattern of the English shires and they are: Anglesey, Caernarfon, Meirionnydd, Denbigh, Flint and Montgomery. The Local Government Act of 1973 amalgamated the first three to form the new county of Gwynedd. The second two became the County of Clwyd, and Montgomery was detached to form the new County of Powys.

* * * *

The accession of Henry Tudor to the English throne as Henry VII after his victory at Bosworth in 1485 appeared to many Welshmen to fulfil the bardic prophesies that a Welshman would once again rule over the land of Britain. North Wales had for centuries been the scene of invasion — Roman, Saxon, Norman and English — and almost unceasing conflict. Little is known of the post-Roman period, but a Romano-British society emerged from the chaos. Missionaries appeared in North Wales, bringing Roman influence as well as the Christian message, and gave the Welsh language a large vocabulary of Latin words. By the middle of the 6th century, Welsh was emerging out of the parent British tongue. The Welsh called themselves Cymry, the Saxon invaders called them Walles, meaning 'strangers or unknown people'. The Cymry had become a distinct people by the mid 19th century. The great dyke built by King Offa of Mercia established for the first time a frontier with England, and, for all the raids and incursions, Wales was a relatively independent country from the end of the Roman occupation until the Norman Conquest of 1066. Gwynedd, which comprised almost the whole of modern North Wales, resisted the Norman invader under courageous princes like Llewelyn the Great (1173-1240), while Norman lordships were carved out of the Marches and the South. He created a strong native state and married off his son and four of his daughters to great Norman houses. He even succeeded in inserting three clauses, promising the righting of Welsh wrongs, into Magna Carta.

Civil War followed the great man's death, but eventually his grandson Llewelyn ap Griffith emerged as Master of Gwynedd and was recognised by Henry III as Prince of Wales (Princeps Walie). Edward I, however, was too much for him. He was killed in 1282. The victorious Edward imposed a harsh regime, which was much resented, though most of the gentry settled down to it and so became eligible for public office and built his ring of formidable castles. After Llewelyn, Wales had no frontier or unifying principle save the language and culture. As the 14th century developed, discontent against the repression grew in North Wales and erupted in Owain Glyndwr's uprising; he inspired Wales with a national consciousness which persists to this day. Owain held the four corners of Wales in his hands, called several parliaments, planned two universities and an archbishopric in St Davids and signed treaties with foreign powers. But by 1408 Gwynedd alone stood loyal to him and when Anglesey, his granary, fell to the forces of the Crown, his days were numbered though he was never defeated in the field. His son accepted a free pardon, as did many of his followers, and went to serve in the English Court with his Anglesey cousin, Owain Tudor who married Henry V's widow. Hence came the Tudor dynasty, for Henry VII, the victor of Bosworth, was his grandson.

It is doubtful whether Henry or his successors deserved this encomium, for they seemed to act on the principle that the best solution to the Welsh problem was to erase that country's separate identity and merge Wales with England on the Cornish model. Whether this was fully comprehended at the time is not clear, but a profound revolution occurred in Wales. At the end of the Tudor period, the ruling class was anglicised and the language still spoken by the country people was in danger of losing its standards. The Act of Union set out to abolish it once and for all. It is hardly too much to say that the translation of the Bible by Bishop Morgan saved the language from denegration and eventual extinction. The most important effect of the Act of Union was to bring Wales under the English Common Law, although Welsh law and custom continued to influence social practice. Gavelkind went out for ever and primogeniture came in to stay. The new shires and boroughs also sent Welsh members to Parliament. Thus was created the link between North Wales and the two Houses of Parliament.

The Acts of Union brought a thousand years of history to an end. Their objective was to create a uniform state comprising England and Wales. The 'daily use of a Speech nothing like or consonant to the natural Mother Tongue used within this Realm' was a profound disadvantage. It made 'Distinction and Diversity' between the English and the Welsh 'whereby great Discord, Variance, Debate, Division, Murmur and Sedition hath grown between his said Subjects'. The Act of 1536 decreed that English was to be the sole official language of all legal and government business and Welshmen who were not conversant with English were disqualified from holding public office. A Tudor King advised by a most capable civil servant, Thomas Cromwell, believed he was doing the Welsh a favour by converting them into Englishmen and incorporating Wales into his realm of England. Of course, there were military as well as political implications, as in the case of Ireland. An English speaking Wales adhering to the established religion was far more likely to show a hostile front to a foreign aggressor. The great majority of Welsh gentry warmly embraced the new order; they became anglicised absentee landlords and forgot the obligations which they had always hitherto honoured, as well as forgetting the old traditions.

This break between the upper landowning class and the common people was a major factor in Wales' subsequent history. Things were never the same again. The native Welsh toiled to sustain a propertied class which divorced itself from the old Welsh society and it took over three centuries for them to reassert themselves.

This explains the tendency of the Welsh people to radicalism in politics whenever the opportunity came to express themselves, especially after the Reform Act of 1868 and the subsequent activities of the 'Cymru Fydd' Movement. It was the reaction of the people against a ruling class and a Church which was out of sympathy with their way of life and their aspirations.

But the radicalism was never revolutionary. Even Robert Owen, the father of British socialism, born in Newtown and therefore a North Walian, believed reforms should be achieved by consent of the people.

As it developed in the consciousness of the people of North Wales, political radicalism was genuine and deepfelt, but it was tempered by the more meaningful religious observance which grew slowly during the 16th century and culminated explosively in the great Methodist Revival of 1735. This and the Industrial Revolution are the two most impactive events to shape modern Wales. North Wales was full of churches; the numerous 'Llans' bear witness to that. The old dissenters exercised an influence out of all proportion to their numbers.

Yet the Church generally had lost its influence, despite the efforts of a few conscientious priests like Griffith Jones, whose circulating schools had taught 158,000 to read by the time of his death in 1761. Howell Harris, Daniel Rowlands and William Williams, the three remarkable men, whose religious experiences set off the Great Revival, were in fact Churchmen whose aim was to work within the Anglican Church in Wales and to remove its inadequacies. This proved impossible, as their preaching and their methods provoked hostility and because Bishops refused to ordain Methodist supporters and all because hostile clergy refused to give communion to Methodists, the latter were compelled in 1811 to ordain ministers of their own. Thus they became a nonconformist denomination and the only section of the Church founded in Wales itself. Their enthusiasm gradually infected the old dissenters, who greatly increased their membership, especially in South Wales. The Revival which swept South Wales like wildfire came slowly to the North, but it was here that it took root and made its more permanent gains. It used to be said that if you put a roof over Anglesey, it would make a good Methodist chapel. Howell Harris and his colleagues had no thought of saving the Welsh language and culture; their objective was to save souls and Sion Williams writing about the state of Anglesey on the eve of the Revival, made the case for this:

> '... the common people (except one in a thousand) had no more knowledge than the wild creatures of the Mountains. They delighted in nothing except empty sport and carnal pleasures............
> They used the Sunday like a market day to gratify every wicked whim and passion............
> Within the last sixty years there has been many an entire parish in Anglesey where not one single inhabitant could read one letter in a book, and not one in a thousand who saw the least necessity for such an accomplishment.'

There is no doubt in the evidence that nonconformity transformed life in Anglesey and North Wales. The Sunday School Movement awoke a desire for education and there was a surge of activity which led to primary schools, training colleges and eventually to the University of Wales. Newspapers and periodicals, many of them denominational, mushroomed. The chapels were organised and run on democratic lines; they taught people to debate and prepared them for participation in public affairs as the franchise was widened and local government developed. Many of the ministers were leaders and orators of the highest quality, and several hymn writers were gifted poets. The reawakening generated a creativity and a vitality which Michael Polyani has described as 'the spilling over of Christian aspirations into man's secular thoughts.'

During this period, a small group of Anglesey men were active in London which, in the absence of a capital city, became the focus of several Welsh movements. Goronwy Owen, an Anglican priest, brilliantly revived Welsh strict metre poetry and the Morris brothers, versatile explorers of Welsh antiquities who came from small Anglesey farms, in 1751 formed the Honourable Society of Cymmrodorion. This was the second oldest learned society in Britain, formed 'for the encouragement of literature, science and art as connected with Wales'. Its members met convivially in London taverns and were therefore not entirely at one with the growing band of Methodists as they began to build their Welsh chapels in London as in Wales itself. If one has to make a choice out of so distinguished a generation, I would say that three from North Wales made an outstanding contribution to Welsh education. Dr Thomas Charles of Bala, who organised the structure of Sunday Schools; Sir Hugh Owen, the Anglesey boy who walked with the drovers to London and who became the prime mover in the establishment of the University of Wales, the only national university and today the second largest in Britain; and Sir Owen Edwards, writer and educationist of immense influence.

*   *   *   *

Looking from Westminster, what have the occupations and invasions, the hardships and the revivals, the Acts of repression and of Union made of us politically?

As the eighteenth century wore on another powerful influence began to play its part in the shaping of modern North Wales. Agriculture did not march with the times, partly due to poor soil and communications, but mainly owing to lack of leadership. There were a few enterprising farmers in Anglesey and Clwyd and shortages caused by the Napoleonic Wars stimulated a modest agrarian revolution. This was short lived, however, and enclosure, whilst it brought some general benefit, bore hard on the smallholder and the farm labourer. They emigrated, mainly to America, or sought work in the new industries of North East and South East Wales.

In Flintshire and Denbighshire, coal and lead were mined and iron was smelted with coke (then an exciting new process) at Bersham near Wrexham, later better known for its coalmine. From 1761, when rich and easily mined copper ore was at last discovered in Parys mountain in Amlwch, Anglesey became for half a century the centre of the world's copper trade. At the same time, the woollen trade in Montgomery began to prosper. Both industries declined and virtually died out by the middle of the 19th century. However, the slate industry of Gwynedd was larger, more significant and lasted longer. In the Ogwen Valley, Llanberis, Nantlle and Ffestiniog formed the greatest centre of slate production in the world. Ports at Bangor, Portdinorwic and Portmadoc thrived as they small sailing ships carried the slates to Northern Europe where they shipped other cargoes to distant parts of the world. Towards the end of the last century this industry employed over 14,000 workers. They were Welsh-speaking and they formed a powerful and articulate community with strong religious and political views.

The improvement of communications and the start of the railway age had significantly different effects in North and South Wales. In the south, the railways were built to serve the industrial areas, whilst the line from Chester to Holyhead was constructed primarily to deal with the Irish traffic.

George Stephenson took his railway along the invader's route, the narrow strip between the mountains and the sea, and across the Menai Straits, over or through his great Britannia Tubular Bridge, a wonder of the age and a worthy match for Telford's elegant suspension built in 1826.

The extensive damage caused to the Britannia Bridge by fire in 1970 gave rise to some acute problems, not least the economic effect on Anglesey and Holyhead and its port in particular. Regular meetings were held, which I attended, and a decision was taken to dismantle Stephenson's tubes and reconstruct the bridge as an open one with supporting arches. When Anglesey's County Surveyor, an able engineer, suggested that with stronger arches, a road span could be constructed above the railway line, thus giving Anglesey a second road bridge and enabling Bangor to be by-passed, the Fine Arts Commission, whose approval was required, feared the new design would detract from the elegance of the great bridge, but finally agreed the new plan, so that out of the fiery tragedy emerged a second road bridge into Anglesey. This has eased the traffic problem for the tourist and the traveller to Ireland and the completion of the new road through Colwyn Bay and the tunnel under the River Conway will substantially reduce the journey time from Chester to Holyhead. Before the new road span was opened by the Prince of Wales, a wag placed a large board at the entrance to the bridge with the words 'Anglesey Full' painted upon it, turning away many visitors.

Improved communications always change the character of a community and if it is small and vulnerable the change can be traumatic. Up to a certain point the old can absorb the newcomer and benefit from fresh blood but the new intake, if it is too numerous, can also hybridise and, in due course, swamp the old culture. That is the problem of North Wales.

But good communications are also essential if new industry is to be attracted and, as quarrying and mining declined and the heavy industries of Deeside faltered, unemployment, which has always afflicted North Wales especially Gwynedd, is today a major problem. Industrial estates have been established in the larger towns and if these have been affected by recurrent recessions, there are also bright spots like Newtown and Caersws, which the late Laura Ashley's enterprise has revived. New industry also involves an influx of construction workers and, later, managerial staff who are not Welsh.

*　　*　　*　　*

North Wales was a province or a state according to whether Gwynedd shrank or expanded with the fortunes of the princes. It is richly endowed with fascinating remains and the enquiring visitor can examine the milestones of its history from Chester to Machynlleth or Aberdaron or Holyhead. He can still wonder at the ruins of great tombs or temples of the Iberian neolithic immigrant (about 3 to 4,000 BC); Bryn Celli Du near Llanddaniel in Anglesey is a splendid example and Barclodiad y Gawres near Aberffraw is another. I cannot say what religious rituals or ceremonies were conducted at these shrines, but our ancestors certainly knew how to choose their sites. From Bryn there is a magnificent view of the Snowdon range and from Barclodiad a vista from the mountains in the southwest to Holyhead Mountain in the north.

The experts say that the short, dark and tough Welshman is a descendant of this important wave of settlers who also brought with them a knowledge of crop husbandry and the makings of a more stable society. In the 7th century the warlike Celts brought conflict and the iron age. The hillforts date from this period and the walled settlement of Tre'r Ceiri sixteen hundred feet above Llanaelhaearn in Lleyn is a striking example, again with a breathtaking view. The Roman occupation has not left many traces in North Wales. Segontium, whose name is still celebrated in the River Seiont, was one of the outposts of the great empire and its remains, as well as a small museum, may be seen outside Caernarfon on the Beddgelert road. The remains of Canovium may be seen at Caerhun near Conwy on the river of that name and the herringbone walls which now surround St Cybi's Church at Holyhead, once a Roman fortification, are further examples.

Nor, sadly, is there a great deal to remind us of our native princes. The glory of Aberffraw on the west coast of Anglesey, once the capital and seat of the princes of North Wales and, for short periods, of all Wales has vanished for ever although I am always conscious of an unique atmosphere when I stand on the little stone bridge over the Ffraw. The royal residence and other buildings were timbered and this is said to have been used to build the Conqueror's castle of Caernarfon. But Llywelyn the last native prince built Criccieth Castle of stone and that remains. From 1282 onwards however until the Industrial Revolution, it was the Norman castles which dominated the North Wales landscape: Edward I's castles at Caernarfon is the grandest (1283); Conwy, the most elegant; Harlech the most forbidding; and Beaumaris the most modest, yet it is said to be the finest example of mediaeval military architecture. All today are great tourist attractions. Pandit Nehru must have been thinking of these when he asked his architects, who were explaining their plans for rebuilding part of Delhi, if they would make good ruins. But things were different in 1295 when the King started building at Beaumaris the last of his eight castles. Reporting on progress, the Master of Edward's works in Wales wrote to the Exchequer:

'As to how things are in the land of Wales, we still cannot be any too sure. But, as you well know, Welshmen are Welshmen, and you need to understand them properly. . .'

The Master Builder was a perceptive coloniser and England produced not a few of these in the following seven hundred years.

If the King's great castles stand supreme, the border castles built by the Lords Marcher are also impressive and Chirk (1310), close to Offa's Dyke, with its splendid wrought iron gates (made by the famous Davies Brothers of Bersham in the early 18th century) also command admiration. Additions to Chirk Castle have improved rather than spoilt it and the great Augustus Pugin, whom we associate with the Houses of Parliament, had a hand in these.

Poverty and the departure of so many leading Welsh families to London after 1485 account for the comparative paucity of domestic architecture in North Wales up to the 19th century. Plas Mawr, an Elizabethan town house in the shadow of the great castle is outstanding and Nerquis Hall and Plas Teg in Flintshire have great charm.

However, it is the influence of the Church which, from the earliest times, still permeates North Wales. Everyone becomes aware of the Llans (Llannau) of Wales, the enclosure within which the Celtic saint (I always think of him as a forceful Welsh preacher) planted his cross and built his little cell.

The remote Celtic churches of Anglesey and Lleyn, Lady Margaret Beaufort's shrine to St Winifred at Holywell (she was the mother of Henry VII), the great perpendicular church at Wrexham, Clynnog Fawr's remarkable Parish Church as well as the Gothic creations of Victorian architects like Benjamin Ferrey (Christchurch, Bala, is an attractive example), mark the North Walian's search for spiritual sustenance.

The cathedral churches of Bangor and St Asaph are well worth a visit, perhaps more for the atmosphere than the architecture. Although the old 1385 tower remains, St Asaph was restored by Sir Gilbert Scott, we do not forget that the old church was burnt by Edward I, Owain Glyndwr and Cromwell. Bangor, the oldest diocese in Britain, nearly a century older than Canterbury, was also destroyed in the 11th and 15th centuries and redesigned by Scott and his son.

Bala on the shores of Llyn Tegid, the largest natural lake in Wales is of historical importance for two reasons. It was in 1784, that Thomas Charles, who has already been referred to as a religious organiser of genius, settled there and made the town the focus of North Wales Methodism. It has been called the Welsh Geneva because the Methodism was and remains Calvinistic, although the denomination is now officially the Presbyterian Church of Wales. The High Street is also dignified by a statue of T. E. (Tom) Ellis, the first of the outstanding young Welsh radicals to enter Parliament; Lloyd George, five years later in 1880, was the second. They gave a sharp political edge to the Cymru Fydd (Wales To Be) Movement which was formed in 1886 and, in Parliament itself, formed a party within a party.

The importance of Lloyd George to the people of North Wales cannot be overestimated. One is tempted to make comparison with Henry Tudor. After years of struggle for education, for political recognition, for respect for the language and tradition, and against privilege and church domination which was then equated with English dominance, here was a nonconformist, Welsh-speaking Welshman who stormed the very bastions of imperial power at its zenith. Like Henry, but for different reasons, he was charged with neglecting Wales during the ascent, but on the whole he was forgiven for it. Welshmen walked with a little more confidence because of Lloyd George, and his memorial by Clough William Ellis above the rushing River Dwyfor deserves obeisance.

Dr Kenneth Morgan has said that if there is one constant theme in Welsh politics during the last century it is the devotion of the Welsh to the political left. This has been progressively less apparent in the north than the south. Every Welsh seat returned a Liberal in 1905 for historical and religious reasons, rural Welsh people declined to vote Conservative. The highpoint of the Labour Party in North Wales came in 1966 when six Labour Members of Parliament were returned out of nine, one of which was a Liberal. It is not without significance that five of the Labour Members were Welsh speaking nonconformists and the sixth, Eirene White, was in this tradition. Political and, to some extent, population change has weakened both Labour and Liberal appeal with the result that the 1983 General Election produced five Conservative Members, with two each for Labour and Plaid Cymru and one Liberal in Montgomery after a brief Tory interlude. It is a significant change in political fortunes in what has always been a radical area, and one must await further elections to discover whether the new pattern has permanence.

*   *   *   *

To understand North Wales, one must pause again to consider the Welsh language, 'yr hen iaith' (the ancient tongue), the oldest spoken language in Europe. It arouses high passion. It is loved and cherished, in many cases regarded with indifference and sometimes denigrated as being an obstacle to progress. Sixty percent of the people of Wales spoke Welsh at the turn of the century, and the ratio was much higher in the North, but today only one fifth speak Welsh; the percentage in Gwynedd is sixty-one and in Clwyd nineteen. The tide ebbs to the west as the east becomes anglicised. Rhyl and Prestatyn are not greatly distinguishable from Blackpool and Southport.

There are some Welshmen who regard their compatriot's defence of their language as odd or 'nationalistic' and Englishmen can be more tolerant and understanding. A report from Whitehall's Board of Education in 1927 reflected this sympathetic attitude:

'We shall never be able to take a wide and reasonable view of the Welsh language and its literature until we realise that from the very first beginnings of its history Welsh has been one of the great literary languages of the world, and that its use as an instrument of culture and enlightenment must not be measured by the subordinate or insignificant political position of the country in which it was, and is, spoken. Welsh social history can neither be learnt nor taught unless it is clearly understood that the history of Wales is the history of the language'

It was also a perceptive statement which recognised the gravity of the decline of the language in the inter-war years, although it appeared to most people to be secure in Gwynedd, Powys, Dyfed and even in part of West Glamorgan. A realisation that its demise might be at hand rallied varied elements to fight for its survival. The Government, especially after the creation of the Welsh Office with a Secretary of State in the Cabinet, gave practical support. This was both administrative in the shape of the Welsh Language Act of 1967, and financial through grants to Welsh language schools, the National Eisteddfod and to other Welsh language agencies. The high passion has found expression, mainly among young people, through the Welsh Language Society (Cymdeithas yr Iaith) whose activities have included breaches of the law such as the burning of holiday homes. It is a poignant story whose end cannot be predicted.

What kind of people are we today who live in Gwynedd and Clwyd and north Powys. Gerald the Welshman was able to define us and, some would say, flatter us:

'This people is live and active, hardy rather than strong and entirely bred up to the use of arms......
No one of this nation ever begs, for the houses of all are common to all; and they consider liberality and hospitality amongst the first virtues......
..... in each family the art of playing the harp is held preferable to any other learning.
Both sexes exceed any other nation in attention to their teeth, which

they render like ivory, by constantly rubbing them with green hazel and wiping them with a woollen cloth. These people being of a sharp and acute intellect and gifted with a rich and powerful understanding, excel in whatever studies they pursue and are more quick and cunning than the inhabitants of a western clime. In their musical concerts they do not sing in unison like the inhabitants of other countries but in many different parts......'

But this was written in the 12th century and if most of these and the other characteristics described by Gerald have vanished, the survival of choral singing throughout the centuries is remarkable.

Llywellyn Powys tried to compare the English and the Welsh in this way:

'The English have shown all the world how valuable are the qualities of good sense, and good nature and a steadfast character. The spirited contribution of the Welsh is of a different sort − a civility in social contacts, and extreme sensibility to the whole of their conscious existence, but especially with what has to do with the physical world from star to leaf. It is this nervous awareness of existence and nervous consideration of the feelings of others that cause them so often to be misunderstood. It is their very skin to try to please.....'

I must confess that I have a sense of this characteristic in myself and at times thought it to be a weakness. A stark declaration which may hurt or offend, although it may be the truth, does not come naturally; the way must be paved with some emollient sentences or an explanatory paragraph or two. The slings and arrows of a long political life has, no doubt, blunted this instinct, but I am conscious from time to time that it still lurks in the background.

Just before the war, John Cowper Powys wrote about the 'spirit of the Welsh character'. It is not so easy to find or to identify today. There is no omnibus North Wales character. There is still the Welsh-speaking community of the upland area, shyer and more introverted than its southern counterpart, and here one senses a stubborn determination to preserve what is called 'the Welsh way of life'. The new Welsh language television channel, S4C, reflects a good deal of this activity and, whilst it is concentrated in the small towns and villages of the west, the chapels and schools of centres like Mold, Rhyl and Wrexham produce their quota of gifted competitors in Eisteddodau.

Today the population of Clwyd is 392,000 and that of Gwynedd

224,000; the projection for the year 2001 is 485,000 and 232,000 respectively. The more anglicised area will become more and more dominant and this will inevitably reflect itself in the character and customs of the people. Notwithstanding economic difficulties, the population growth of the North East, which includes the Deeside coastal strip and the Wrexham area, is the second fastest in Britain. It is significant, however, that industrialists throughout the region pay a warm tribute to Welsh workers for their adaptability and hard work. A good example is the Anglesey aluminium smelter at Holyhead which was built on a green field site and manned by mainly inexperienced workforce; today it has a record of production and productivity which compares more than favourably with any smelter in the world.

The tradition of hard work and thrift, as well as the quickness of mind which Gerald detected, are still to be found in the people of east and west, Welsh-speaking and non-Welsh-speaking. Recent times have not been easy for them and unemployment is nearly the highest in Britain. I must again emphasise that the need for jobs is pre-eminent and must be tackled if any other problems are to be dealt with. Updated plans for the Welsh economy as a whole are urgently required and the Welsh Office should set its hand to the task.

Thus far, the North Walian, for all his success in other walks of life, has not distinguished himself on the managerial side of industry. Native Welshmen are not numerous amongst higher or even middle rank executives in the region's industries. There is a growing awareness of this especially in some schools and colleges of higher education. If Welsh men and women can become consultants and judges and top academics they can also run plants and factories and become civil engineers. There are some poets of one degree or another, a few of rare merit, in the small towns and villages of Gwynedd and Clwyd and if you go to a small local eisteddfod, you may hear singers who will surprise you. But you will not find many Welsh industrialists. Up to now it is not greatly in our tradition, but it must become so and we must change if we are to survive.

O. M. Edwards, the educationist and former Member of Parliament for Merioneth, wrote this in his *History of Wales*:

> 'Wales is not the home of one ancient race; it is not the home of one ancient language. Many races have reached its glens and hills; some have died away; some remain. Many languages have died on its mountains; many may be spoken again again and pass away. But while races and language go, the mountains remain. And they give a unity of character to the people who live among them. And here it is that we are to look for continuity in Welsh history....'

There must be truth in this, but the enormous changes of the last seventy years, including the two great wars, have created problems which Edwards could not have foreseen. Agriculture, coalmining and quarrying have declined as leading occupations of the people as indeed has seafaring. It is recorded that more Anglesey men *pro rata* served at sea in the two wars than from any other part of Britain and there are those living today who remember the small ports and harbours of North Wales throbbing with activity. The unity and character of which Edwards wrote may prove impossible to preserve in village and small town communities which are perceptibly losing their old character because the industries which sustained them are no longer there. The growth industry which benefits the region throughout is tourism. The work of the Wales Tourist Board is admirable, but it must remain doubtful whether sufficient jobs can be created in the service sector, including tourism, in order to compensate for all the losses in the old traditional industries.

I attended a preaching meeting the other day in the small Anglesey village of Bryn Du and listened to an excellent sermon delivered well and with great sincerity. Afterwards, I chatted to old friends amongst ministers and elders about the state of the Church and politics and old times. But the congregation was sparse and elderly; thirty years ago the chapel would have been full, and fifty years ago overflowing. The theological debate and the discussion about last Sunday's sermons in sunday school and chapel meetings are things of the past.

As a child, staying with my grandparents in Pontrhyddallt, I remember the quarrymen marching four abreast from their work. That quarry at Dinorwig which employed over three thousand men and was the largest open slate quarry in the world, with a proud tradition of self education, is closed.

In the 1950s, as a young M.P., I addressed a packed meeting at the Miner's Institute in Rhosllannerchrugog, reputedly the largest village in Wales. The Institute was the centre of cultural and political activity in an area dependent on coalmining. The industry has declined sharply and the old enthusiasm for extra-mural education and debate has waned.

The story is told of the Ministry expert visiting the hill farms of Gwynedd and, after a day of wind and driving rain, seeking refuge and a cup of tea in one of the small farmhouses and, asking in exasperation: 'What can you produce here?'. The old farmer took his pipe from his mouth and said, 'Men'.

And so one could go on, but perhaps it is not profitable to dwell on the past. The old order has changed and is still changing, and we must hope that the new will be worthwhile. The best of the young generation has spirit and drive and there are still more poets to the square mile in the region than in any other part of Britain.

Ceiriog was not one of our greatest poets but he is much loved for his lyrics. Sir Idris Bell translated his long poem about the shepherd, Alun Mabon, and the last verse conveys a nostalgia most of us feel:

'Ebbing with the passing years
Ancient customs change and flow;
Fraught with doom of joy or tears,
Generations come and go.
Out of tears and tempest's reach
Alun Mabon sleeps secure;
Still lives on the ancient speech,
Still the ancient songs endure'.

THE WEST MIDLANDS
Nicholas Budgen

Nicholas Budgen reveals, in his essay on the West Midlands, his knowledge of the complexities of Birmingham and the practical problems of farming in these counties. As one can see from the orderly presentation of his subject matter, he is a barrister as well as a farmer

His schooling was at St Edward's School at Oxford, from which he went to Corpus Christi College, Cambridge. He has been a Conservative Member of the House since 1974 and was a Government Whip in 1981-82. Before that he had been a Secretary of the Conservative Finance Committee, and a Member of the Public Accounts Committee of the House in 1980-81. He was Chairman of the Birmingham Bow Group for two years.

In short, Nicholas Budgen is a steady representative of the parliamentary establishment, but his interests are far from being confined to Party politics, and in 1984 he was 'the backbencher of the year'.

Where to begin. With the vulgarity of Lady Docker, the wisdom of Doctor Johnson, or with the moralizing chicanery of Joe Chamberlain. The West Midlands, where hammer once rung on iron, covers all these things and more.

The West Midlands can be seen as a fan. The outer arc is Warwickshire, Worcestershire, Shropshire and Staffordshire. The hinge is the conurbation of Birmingham and the Black Country.

Thus, the creation of the West Midlands County Council in 1974 may have been a political mistake with many economic disadvantages. But its creation did draw attention to the importance that the conurbation has long had to the shire counties surrounding it. For at least two hundred years, the industrial towns have fertilised the country areas with money and, in recent years, development. Since 1974, Herefordshire has formed one county with Worcestershire. Herefordshire still sits uneasily in the West Midlands. The wealth and influence of Bristol spread out to

Gloucestershire and Herefordshire. Herefordshire still has stronger links with Bristol, the West Country and Wales than Birmingham. Its people still tend more to the sleepy than the brassy. However much they may resent it Warwickshire, Worcestershire, Shropshire and Staffordshire belong to the West Midlands. There may be an important exception as far as the Potteries are concerned. Somewhere between Stone and Stoke on Trent a line may be drawn. Above that the towns become like the mill towns of the north. The people look more to Manchester than to Birmingham. The people tend to be slower and less assertive in their attitudes. They are Northerners and not West Midlanders.

Let me declare my interest. I am a West Midlander. Almost all the experiences, prejudices and responsibilities that are important to me are rooted in the West Midlands. Like many West Midlanders, I cannot claim that my family has been continuously resident in the same place for many years. We have moved as the necessity of earning a living obliged us; but within the West Midlands. My paternal grandfather fled from the South East and his vulgar background in the grocery trade to what he thought was the respectability of a Shropshire vicarage. My maternal grandfather left the genteel poverty of another Shropshire vicarage to find the vulgarity of the Black Country where he bought and expanded a foundry business. Apart from my time at University, I have spent all my adult life in the West Midlands. Since 1962, when not a politician, I have been a travelling salesman in the law – going out from Birmingham to the Courts of Birmingham, the Black Country and the shire counties. My prejudices have been influenced by reflecting upon the communities that solicitors serve and represent. The nature of the counties was often reflected by the people who did business at the local Government offices near to the Courts or who sat on juries or as magistrates. To this was added another obsession. As soon as I started to earn a reasonable living at the Bar, I began to keep horses and to race and hunt them. Thus I judged the countryside by its suitability for my licensed vandalism. How much was it developed by suburbia. How much was it ploughed up. Where were the racecourses and point-to-point meetings. These were trivial enough questions as I motored around the towns of the West Midlands, but they made me think about the changes in agriculture and the countryside that occurred in twenty or so years.

*   *   *   *

Let us start at the south and work around the arc of the shire counties. Warwickshire has always had a most important position in the Midlands. In the Civil Wars it was the area in which the armies from the North met the armies from the South. The rich have long been attracted by the beauty and fertility of this county. Thus Warwickshire has many fine country houses. Leamington Spa has much elegant 19th century architecture. In Victorian times, Indian Army officers retired to Cheltenham. It now has a large Asian population who appear to have settled in with less tension than was experienced in other parts of the country.

Today Warwickshire remains the smartest place for 'Brummies' to live. It is near Oxford; it is convenient for London and Birmingham; wealth can be enjoyed; investments can be easily managed from a modernised farm house; cultural interests can be enjoyed in Stratford-upon-Avon. But most of all, Warwickshire still has all the marks of money and success. The 'Brummy' who has made it moves from Solihull to Kineton. Once at Kineton, his wife stops complaining about the inefficiency of the local hairdresser and worries about the effects of ploughland on hunting. Warwickshire has become not unlike Buckinghamshire.

The middle class are in control. Like a sergeant major in a Guards battalion, they believe that, if it is stationary, you should paint it every year. The rich farm land is increasingly arable. The antique dealers and the actors at Stratford are more concerned about the dollar pound exchange rate than the Chancellor of the Exchequer. The politics are Conservative − though not so assertive as urban Conservatives. The style of Margaret Thatcher has not yet entirely driven out the memory of Anthony Eden.

They − the Planners and Politicians − have done their best to ruin Worcester. But it remains an attractive city. The recession in the Black Country has its effects in Worcester. The man with a carpet factory in Kidderminster, who lives in Worcester, may not have painted his house since 1979. But Worcestershire has benefitted from the great surge in farming incomes over the last decade. When Peter Walker was Minister of Agriculture his message of 'Produce, Produce' was well received in his home county. I wonder if his words will be remembered with much gratitude if the EEC ever gets round to reducing agricultural prices.

Herefordshire is different. The people and the politics are different. Their links and attitudes are more those of the West Country and Wales. The sharpness and volatility of the Black Country and Birmingham is replaced by a softer and more concilliatory attitude. Thus, in both Hereford and Leominster, the real threat to the Tories comes from the Liberals and the Alliance. The Alliance of the Liberals and the Social Democratic Party forged in the late 1970s may not have a clear position on a number of important issues. But they proclaim their moderation and attack the alleged extremism of both Labour and the Conservatives. This is a suitable area for the Alliance, since in one section of these communities we find the desire to trim and the tradition of non-conformity. It will be interesting to see how areas which are rural but not necessarily dominated by farmers react to the end of the bonanza after going into the EEC. Will restrictions on the production of milk make Liberals?

*　　*　　*　　*

As we travel on to Shropshire we find ourselves in a rich varied county. South Shropshire has the hills and grassland of Church Stretton. To the north we find large flat farms producing much corn and milk for farmers who, in two generations since the 1930s, have moved from being frightened tenant farmers into proud millionaires. In the early 1930s, around three-quarters of the land was still owned by the great landowning families. They had endured about fifty years of agricultural depression interrupted only briefly by the Great War. In spite of some inflation after the Great War, land values from 1880 to 1930 fell from about £80 an acre to about £25 an acre. In the 1930s the tenant farmers started to buy the land they farmed. The process continues and the land now changes hands at around £2,000 an acre.

The ownership of the land reflects also the changes in industrial fortune. To the north we find Liverpool money from slaves and soap. The east of Shropshire reflects the Black Country's good years in the motor boom of the 1930s and the advantages to businessmen of cost plus 10 per cent in the War years.

The outer Parliamentary constituencies of Shropshire, Shrewsbury and Atcham, Shropshire North and Ludlow, demonstrate the pull of Wales. Also the combination of learning and leisure does not always make for full appreciation of either Mrs Thatcher or Mr Kinnock. The farmers and shopkeepers of Shrewsbury admire Mrs Thatcher but many of the masters at Shrewsbury School prefer to be civilised and vote for a plague on both their houses. Ludlow and Church Stretton attract people in retirement. They are often more concerned to preserve their environment rather than their immediate economic interests. In each of these seats at the last General Election, the Liberal or SDP candidate came second with over 30 per cent of the vote. In the West Midlands the attraction of the third party becomes stronger the further you are away from the conurbation. The Wrekin, which includes Telford New Town, reasserts the battle between the two larger parties. Telford is mainly populated by people from the conurbation, where the political traditions are more assertive and decisive.

Staffordshire is remarkable for its variety. Around the conurbation, the county is much affected by the spread of Black Country attitudes and by the housing and industrial development which looks to the Black Country. Thus, it has constituencies like Cannock and Burntwood, Mid-Staffordshire, and Staffordshire South East which reflect many of the attitudes seen in the marginal seats of the Birmingham areas in the 1950s and 1960s. For the history of Birmingham and the Black Country did exert some common pressures on its people. For over two hundred years, men left the suffocating conformity and paternalism of the country areas and went for better wages to the industrial areas. They became critical, direct, humorous, self reliant and sometimes acquisitive. Their decisiveness makes them poor trimmers and reluctant compromisers. They have neither the culture nor the inclination for the Alliance — or at any rate the Alliance of David Steel and Roy Jenkins. And so, in these critical and recently changed Staffordshire seats, we see an area which reflects the volatility of the West Midlands and which makes it a crucial area in deciding the outcome of a General Election.

Further away from the conurbation, the political and economic character of the county becomes more static. Burton shows the reduced floor space and reduced labour force required for the modern production of beer. The town has become more middle class. The prosperous farmers vote, at least for the present, like Tory squires of the 1840s.

Stafford is not a town of the charm of Worcester, or the distinction of Warwick or even the beauty of Shrewsbury. But it is a substantial industrial and county town and it has in the last recession been hit a good deal less badly than the Black Country. Unlike the Black Country, it did not have a heavy dependence on the manufacture of the motor car. Also its most important employer, GEC, was much reorganised by Lord Weinstock when he first shook up the amalgamated concern. Thus, the town was in quite good shape to face the recession of the 1980s.

Mining has long been important to the economy of Staffordshire. The availability of coal was important to the growth of metal bashing in south Staffordshire and to the Potteries in north Staffordshire. The big mine at Lea Hall in central Staffordshire supplies the power station at Rugeley on the Trent. Rugeley expanded greatly in the 1950s and 1960s. Miners from Scotland were brought down to Rugeley to work the mine there. In the coal strike of 1984-85 the miners of Staffordshire were remarkable for the way in which the vast majority worked through the strike. No doubt the reasons for this varied from miner to miner. But it is a feature of the Staffordshire coalfield that the miners tend to live scattered among a wider community.

Staffordshire Moorland is different. So are Stoke and Newcastle-under-Lyme. Both are more part of the North than of the West Midlands. Staffordshire Moorland has some well established textile businesses. But the character of the constituency is dominated by the high grasslands of the moors. It is wet, cold land mainly devoted to livestock farming though with some quarries to be found there as well. It has little in common with the metal bashers of south Staffordshire or even the rich arable farmers of central Staffordshire.

Stoke and Newcastle depend upon the Potteries and upon coal mining. Warwickshire is home for the merchant bankers, the antique dealers and the actors who live in Warwickshire so as to be near to London, Birmingham and Stratford. It is a county of solid wealth from the land and some elements of pretension and fashion. By comparison, Stoke is still a place of small squat men and women working hard for men like Tellwright − Victorians working for Victorians. They once had the protected markets of the Empire. They are now much affected by the sterling dollar exchange rate. A low pound is good for Wedgwood, Spode and Minton − even when the Prime Minister says it is undervalued. In Stoke, there has been since the 1930s no great influx of people − save perhaps for the Poles who settled there as miners after the War. But the Poles were and are more Victorian in their values than the Victorians.

The politicians of north Staffordshire are old fashioned: a paternalist Tory in Staffordshire Moorland wanting a better deal for his farmers and more reflation. While Labour in Stoke has a recent history of selecting men who revere Mr Atlee. In Stoke Central, Bob Cant was a monetarist and had Gladstonian views about public expenditure long before Dennis Healey learned the error of his ways in 1976. He was followed in 1983 by Mark Fisher, who is the grandson of an Earl; and the son of a Tory M.P. and educated at Eton and Cambridge and − what is even more surprising − not particularly ashamed of it. While, from Stoke South, Jack Ashley concentrates more on the disabled than upon Marx or Trotsky.

*   *   *   *

I have described the outer arc of the fan of the West Midlands. In the 1950s and the 1960s the politicians and the planners decreed that there should be an inner arc of satellite towns. It was held that the prosperity and growth of the conurbation would continue unabated and that, therefore, it was both necessary and just to spread the growth of the West Midlands around the inner arc of settlements. Fashion has now turned against these ideas.

The inner arc below Birmingham starts with Chelmsley Wood between Birmingham and Coleshill. I remember Chelmsley Wood well from the late 1960s. From 1967 to 1970 I was the Conservative candidate at Birmingham Small Heath. It was a time when the Borough Engineer was King, the Borough Planner was the Archbishop of Canterbury and the

Bulldozer was to the Town Hall army what the arrow had been to our forces at Agincourt. The roads like Kimberley and Salisbury and Churchill may have had many rat-infested houses, but I never knocked on a door and found anyone who wanted to go out to Chelmsley Wood.

Then we move on to Redditch New Town and around the inner arc to Telford New Town. The vast housing estates were used to house problem families from the conurbation. Telford in particular attracted industry by most vigorous marketing and state incentives (I must be careful not to call them bribes). I shall never forget defending a lady from Birmingham who lived in Telford and who knifed her husband to death. She had gone to Telford in the belief that there would be new life there. There was plenty of new housing but there were no relatives, no friends and not much in the way of corner shops or even fish and chip shops. She was desperate. She was not typical in her action but I am sure she was typical in her misery.

The business that went to Telford tended to be of the larger sort. The great firms, able to raise plenty of capital, but most of all with respectable and responsible directors who knew and respected politicians and civil servants; men who knew how to take a bit of trouble in filling out a complicated application form for discretionary grants; men who had almost no shareholding in the firm for which they worked but who would be sound men; were they to be appointed to a quango upon retirement. Many of these firms closed in the recession of 1980 to 1982. The men on the shop floor were sacked and the managers moved back to head office.

The West Midlands County of 1974 is an extraordinary formation. From the south it starts with Coventry and then widens to take in Birmingham and the Black Country. Coventry in the past had important ancient buildings. Many of these buildings were knocked down by bombing in the last war. Since the Second World War, Coventry has been a town which has concentrated upon the manufacture of the motor car. Politically it has been dominated by the Labour Party. Two of its recent M.P.s, Mrs Audrey Wise (no longer in the House) and Dave Nellist, take their lead from Tony Benn. The middle class managers and professionals who work there have tended to live in the surrounding countryside or at Kenilworth, Warwick or Stratford-upon-Avon. John Butcher achieved a significant victory when he won Coventry South West in 1979 to make him the only Tory M.P. from Coventry.

Birmingham remains the Victorian creation of the non-conformist families who assisted Joe Chamberlain in his plans for municipal reform. It has splendid public buildings, some of which have, in recent years, been cleaned. The 1960s in Birmingham were times of progress and the property developer. A large inner ring road was built. It is easy to drive into the City of Birmingham but some of its dignity has been lost as a result.

It was a feature of the 1983 General Election that the Labour vote held better in the Birmingham seats than in, for instance, Inner London or, to a greater extent, Outer London. In Birmingham, the swing to the Conservatives was 2 per cent, in Outer London it was 4.6 per cent. The Labour Party in Birmingham has traditionally been more moderate than in London. Also the depth of the recession in Birmingham brought its own political reaction.

West Bromwich, Warley and Walsall have grown and sprawled out of their small town beginnings. None of these towns would lay claim to great architectural distinction, but all would claim that their earlier periods of prosperity had left them with many skills and much available factory space for any businessman with capital and ideas.

Dudley is an ancient town, with a castle on an important site commanding the town and much of the surrounding area. It reminds us, most of all, how rich the great families were up to 1945. The Earls of Dudley owned many of the local steel mills and mines. They were not mere landowners. They were active industrialists and, on occasions, politicians.

Wolverhampton is an ancient town. It is prosperous and important in the manufacture of cloth. It moved from wool into metal. It retains some distinguished buildings in the centre. Wolverhampton now includes the, still prosperous, residential areas in and around Tettenhall.

*   *   *   *

The passing visitor to the West Midlands will most of all be amazed at the very good communications and transport system. The old methods of communication remain in partial use. The canal system has been tidied and cleaned and, in some instances, repaired by groups of young people employed on the various schemes funded by the taxpayer. It is possible to get a train almost every half-hour from Birmingham to London. It takes a little over one-and-a-half hours. But most of all the West Midlands is memorable for its convenience to the motorways. It takes no longer to go from central Birmingham to Stafford than it takes to go from Kennington to Chelsea during the middle of a working day in London. Communications are not good to the East Coast. But in all other directions the West Midlands has the most direct and convenient communications.

The most dramatic view in the West Midlands is the view from the train between Birmingham New Street Station and Wolverhampton. It passes through Handsworth, West Bromwich, Sandwell and Bilston. Those places were the home of the great metal bashing boom that started in the early 1930s and continued without very obvious interruption until the end of the 1970s. On both sides of the line we can see great works empty. At Bilston, the once vast steelworks produces no more. The journey makes vivid the description that many businessmen give of the squeeze which they and their companies felt between 1979 and 1982. I suppose that the most graphic image of the 1960s and early 1970s is that of the Marxist shop steward, Red Robbo, organising a strike at Longbridge in a car park with many new cars owned by the workers.

Why did this happen and what happened. Birmingham was known as the City of a Thousand Trades. In the same way Coventry, Wolverhampton and Walsall were all known for their amazing diversity. Then came the motor car and the Second World War. Certainly, the manufacture of motor cars provided some opportunities for economies of scale. The War gave great opportunities for the West Midlands. It certainly encouraged extra production. My mother's family made quite a lot of money making hand grenades. They were paid at the cost of production plus 10 per cent. I would expect it was some time after that before they worried much about production costs or worried about finding new markets. Then the West Midlands supplied a shattered Europe with its bashed metal.

But the 1960s saw the start of two of the main trends which made the 1980s so difficult. From Coventry to Wolverhampton the conurbation became increasingly dependent upon car manufacturing. Moreover, the conventional wisdom, as expressed by exhortation and the tax system, was towards larger professionally managed units of production which were also more heavily unionised than the old, often privately owned, factories.

When the gathering inflation of the 1960s and early 1970s was checked in 1976 and further slowed in 1979 to 1982, the West Midlands suffered perhaps more than any other area of the country. I assert this because I believe that their years of prosperity and good fortune had rendered them less able to anticipate and accommodate recession than areas where the dole had long been a feature of everyday life. But it was not just a social or psychological difficulty. Cars are and were internationally traded. The West Midlands was caught with too much capacity for the production of cars. With the pound worth 2.40 dollars, the cars could not be sold abroad. The great manufacturers of motor cars hoped that the recession was a mere minor kink in a rising curve of production. It was not and they were as ill equipped to look for new markets as their heavily unionised workforces were prepared to accept new conditions of work.

*   *   *   *

So what are the main features of the West Midlands County today. YES – the unemployment is the most important feature. It stands at nearly 17 per cent of the working population. But why did the Tories win seats in and near the conurbation. Why have not the Tories been branded with high unemployment as they were in the 1930s. This is not the place for partisan political explanations. However, there is a strong rumour and impression that the Black Economy is widespread in the West Midlands and that it provides an important supplement to the state benefits which the unemployed and their families receive.

An argument used by West Midland industrialists to explain some of the difficulties of their region is lack of capital. 'Oh', say they, 'But no one from the City wishes to come North of Watford', or, 'The present Government is uninterested in manufacturing business'. This may be special pleading. Tarmac, in Wolverhampton, is regarded as one of the most successful businesses based in the U.K. Birmingham is the financial capital of the West Midlands. More and more merchant banks from London have their Birmingham branches. The Bank of England and the clearing banks set up an organisation which provides capital upon commercial terms.

I believe the difficulties of Midlands industries have been more that of declining markets and inability for one reason or another to compete with technical changes and foreign competition than lack of capital. However, there is a widespread view in the Midlands that the financial men are too important and that 'they' (undefined) in the City do not like or understand manufacturing industry. To the extent that markets have become dominated by institutional money and the pension funds, there may be less opportunity for the Birmingham businessman to meet and assess lenders of capital than is available to the London businessman. As an M.P. with an interest in economic problems, I notice the difference between the varied and vigorous social life of the City of London with its livery companies and its banks and its stockbrokers ever anxious for a whiff of information and the tendency in the Black Country to work harder and concentrate upon production and not marketing or dealing. I suspect that this may be good for getting work done but less good for raising capital.

A persistent complaint of the businessmen in the West Midlands is the level of rates. The most obvious feature of Local Government in the West Midlands is its size and recent growth. In Wolverhampton the Council directly employs about 10 per cent of the persons in employment. Other people employed in the public sector amount to at least another 10 per cent of the persons in employment. These two groups, if mobilised to vote, can be very significant in local elections where only about one third of the electorate vote. The Council supports activities ranging from the Grand Theatre to the Afro-Caribbean Cultural Centre and the Black Country Development Agency. The role of the Council is constantly expanding. To the traditional roles of education, highways, markets, social services and planning the Council has added committees dealing with training and temporary employment, the inner areas, Race Relations and Equal Opportunities and Economic Development. There is much duplication with the work of the West Midlands Council. But, most of all, the Council draws into its net people who have an interest in more Council activity. The councillors attend more and more committee meetings. The Tories fight a gallant rearguard action but the role of the councillor becomes more and more time consuming and people with careers in business or the professions are less and less able to play an active part in local politics. Each section of the community affected by the Council's activity becomes anxious to reduce expenditure in other activities. Few are prepared to ask what is the proper role of the Council. As the private sector gets smaller, so it becomes more difficult to persuade the electorate to reduce services which help or employ them or their relatives.

The system of rent and rate support also tends to make financial restraint less attractive to the electorate. When 18 per cent of the employable population is unemployed, then more and more people become indifferent to rates they do not pay. The business vote is no more. Businessmen often live outside the borough in which they work. The connection between enjoying services and paying for them has been much eroded.

*   *   *   *

Finally, the West Midlands is known for its population of West Indians and Asians. In the 1981 Census, 10 per cent of the population of the West Midlands County were of non-British origin. 2 per cent of the population were of African or Caribbean origin and 3 per cent of Asian origin. The post-war immigration was different from earlier immigrations in that the colour and culture of the immigrants marked them out. But there is a long history of immigration into the Black Country. The Irish helped build the canals and the railways. Immediately after the Second World War many Poles settled in Wolverhampton.

Enoch Powell, who fell out with Ted Heath over his views on race, did not make immigration an important issue. Its importance was demonstrated for all to see in the General Election of 1964 when Peter Griffiths defeated Patrick Gordon-Walker at Smethwick and when this issue helped a Tory win at Perry Barr. It has continued to be an important issue throughout the West Midlands.

I notice, most of all, the differences between the development of the Afro-Caribbean races here and that of the Asians. The West Indians often believe themselves to be different and distinct. A 1983 Harris Poll suggested that only a small proportion of the West Indian community voted. My dealings with them make me think that they are unlikely to become politically significant for some time. Many West Indians feel apathetic, alienated and disenchanted with their experience of Britain. They resent the success of the Asians and this resentment prevents them from successful organisation for any political purpose.

The behaviour of the West Indian young people causes much concern. They suffer very high levels of unemployment. Few are to be found in skilled jobs or the professions. Many are found in the criminal courts facing charges involving violence. Neither their culture nor their family life has adapted easily to traditional British life. Their young men feel, in general, a deeper sense of alienation from the remainder of the population than any other section of it.

In 1975, the Community Relations Commission carried out a survey into the voting habits of West Indians and Asians. The CRE confirmed its findings in the General Election of 1979. It found that the Asian turnout was about the national average. In my experience in Wolverhampton it is not now possible to make wide generalisations about the Asian community. There are, of course, some Asians who have remained in the heavy manual jobs which they first took up. But, for the rest, the common characteristic which they exhibit is drive and industry. In the inner areas a high proportion of the corner shops are now run by Asians. In all the professions Asians, usually younger Asians, are to be found.

The most dramatic example of Asian enterprise is to be found in the clothing trade. The West Midland Low Pay Unit (an activity of the County Council, as you would rightly expect) estimates that in 1984 there were around 400 small clothing factories employing about 20,000 people. At least 62 per cent of these firms are owned by Asians. And it is said that 80 per cent of the new firms are Asian. Also, since the late 1970s, a wholesale clothing market serving small manufacturers has grown up. This too is in Asian ownership. This new, and mainly Asian industry has become one of the major employers in the West Midlands. The reasons for its success are various. Asians tend to employ the family on low wages. The attack made by the Low Pay Unit does teach us something when it says that the wages paid are, on average, about 50 per cent below the wages ordered by the Industry's Wages Council.

The tradition of the West Midlands and its surrounding counties has long been self reliant. When prosperity has come few have ascribed it principally to the genius of Government, whether central or local. When disaster has come some have helped the wounded, but others have been more concerned to reclaim the scrap metal. Let us grieve for the Black Country. But also notice that the men most admired in the Black Country have always made money and not shed tears.

THE EAST MIDLANDS
Matthew Parris

Matthew Parris was M.P. for Derbyshire West from 1979 to 1986. He was educated in Swaziland at Waterford School, from which he went to Clare College, Cambridge and thence to Yale. He then served for two years in the Foreign and Commonwealth Office and was next from 1976 to 1979 in the Conservative Research Department.

He was a member of Mrs Thatcher's private office when she was leader of the Opposition and in Parliament he was the Secretary of two Conservative backbench committees, on transport and on sports. He is an occasional contributor to The Times *and other journals and from September 1986 is to be presenter of television's* Weekend World.

> 'When I am living in the Midlands
> Which are sodden and unkind'
>
> Hilaire Belloc

Somewhere in the centre of the East Midlands, overshadowed by the great power stations of the foggy Trent basin, lies the little town of Kegworth. During the last election campaign Mrs Thatcher's car stopped in Kegworth. The Prime Minister got out. 'Where am I?' she said, and got back in. She could not have put it better.

The East Midlands has no sharp features. Our boundaries blend slowly into neighbouring areas, and the core region itself has no single focus, but instead a series of centres – Northampton, Leicester, Nottingham and Derby which dominate their immediate region but not the whole area (though Nottingham occasionally tries!).

If the East Midlands is a region at all then the only county which could claim to be utterly within it is tiny Rutland!. Unfortunately, the Government has abolished Rutland: or perhaps it would be kinder to say that Rutland has been asked to take Leicestershire under its wing!

Derbyshire, with its moors and dales is already a land of transition. Lincolnshire starts, self-confidently enough with Lincoln (one of the less twee cathedral cities), but subsides drearily into the East Anglian Fens. Its northern region has been removed completely and is now in the rather doubtful entity of 'Humberside' (another planners' invention, cordially despised by its inhabitants). Leicestershire and Northamptonshire are substantially East Midlands counties, but the West Midlands breathes down the necks of both.

*   *   *   *

Approach the region from the South − from the Home Counties via Luton where they make hats and cars and will soon be a suburb of London, and by Luton, you are nearly in the East Midlands. Then you come to Northampton. An enormous town, about twice as big as anyone realises: described to me by its maverick M.P. Tony Marlow as 'moderate, low-profile'. A boring and business-like town with a fine church, a huge and impressive market square, a town-hall in sub-St Pancras style and little else to distinguish it.

As everybody knows, they make ball-bearings and shoes in Northampton: and its museum's display includes Dame Margot Fonteyn's ballet pumps, a boot in which an elephant crossed the Alps in 1959, and Queen Victoria's wedding slippers. That at least is more in Tony's style.

So were two worthy predecessors-in-office; one was Henry Labouchere, the radical journalist and M.P.; another the atheist Charles Bradlaugh of Northampton, prosecuted in 1877 for distributing impertinent pamphlets. Unseated by the House in 1880, the electors of Northampton sent him back in 1881. He was forcibly ejected by ten policemen. Twice re-elected, twice again (in 1883 and 1885) excluded − the House finally admitted defeat and accepted him. His statue still stands, gesticulating at Radio Northampton.

Or approach the region from the North West. Take the little train from Stockport, Manchester. Climb through some of the highest altitude slums in England until you reach Buxton in Derbyshire − where Mary Queen of Scots used to take the waters for her rheumatism. Buxton is the only town in the northern hemisphere where a cricket match has been snowed-off in June. Gaze through the inevitable drizzle across this faded spa-resort (a sort of minature, down-market Bath), its grey roofs and urban sprawl relieved only by the distant prospect of my own constituency, West Derbyshire. You are on the edge of the East Midlands. The scary and desolate moorlands of the Dark Peak lie over your left shoulder. The wretched little towns of Staffordshire lie over your right. But ahead −

paradise! The White Peak: West Derbyshire: play-ground of the East Midlands: jewel of the Pennines!

Hyperbole apart, it is gentle and pretty country. Nottinghamshire's D. H. Lawrence wrote much about it. Bakewell, your next stop, was as far as Bonny Prince Charlie ever got — and as far as I ever hope to get too! Jane Austen stayed and wrote a good deal at the Rutland Arms Hotel. So did my mother, who has seen her ghost there.

Chatsworth House, the seat of the Dukes of Devonshire, is nearby. It is magnificent: for my taste, too magnificent. Besides, I shall never forgive the present Duke (Andrew), the previous president of the West Derbyshire Conservative Association. It is not for joining the SDP that I condemn him — we all have our moments of folly — but for doing so after I had just had five years' supply of our notepaper, with his name at the head of it, printed. My agent spent three days crossing it all out. I remember the time he told me he was planning to defect. He and I had just unveiled a plaque commemorating the Centenary of the Matlock Conservative Club, of which he was President, and I was seeing him into his Bentley. It came as rather a shock. Fortunately the Duchess remains a Conservative and sends more pheasant than ever for our fund-raising raffles.

The Duke of Rutland, however, has never quit, even though we are honeycombing the whole of his cherished Vale of Belvoir for the extraction of coal. He bitterly opposed it — one Conservative Councillor even lay down in front of the bulldozers — but never wavered in his support for the party. He owns (apart from Belvoir Castle) Haddon Hall, not far from Bakewell, an altogether more intimate and romantic place, sweeping down to the banks of the Derbyshire Wye.

Driving on, you reach Matlock, along with Belper the largest town in my constituency. Belper produces 90 per cent of Britain's petroleum jelly. Matlock, the headquarters of the Derbyshire County Council, produces 100 per cent of Derbyshire's red tape.

From Matlock you could go over the hills to Ashbourne (where the sparkling water comes from), an attractive and civilised little market town, 'gateway to Dovedale', its centre not greatly altered from the days when Boswell and Johnson used to visit. I shall secure a by-pass here if it's the last thing I do! The church, St Oswald's, has a delicate sculpture of a little girl who died aged five. Penelope Boothby was an only child and her death in 1791 broke her parents' marriage. The inscription reads:

'She was in form and intellect most exquisite.
The unfortunate parents ventured their frail barque,
and the wreck was total.'

Or you could drive down the gentle valley of the Derbyshire Derwent, the little communities of Holloway, Lea (where Florence Nightingale lived as a girl) and Whatstandwell in the hills to your left. Soon you would reach Crich 'The straggling grey village of Crich ...where the hills of Derbyshire fall into the monotony of the Midlands' (D. H. Lawrence).

Or try an approach to the East Midlands from the east – from Gothenburg, for instance – as I once did on a Swedish ship. A pamphlet was circulated amongst passengers as we neared the oil flares of Immingham Docks. It appeared to have been drafted by the East Midlands Tourist Board in Swedish. Translated back into English (as my version was) the result was curious. It read:

'Skegness

Behind the sea wall at Skegness are pleasures scarcely to be found elsewhere in the United Kingdom'.

Sadly, they have eluded me.

Actually, Skegness is rather better than its reputation. Certainly its landladies (for of whom else would the Skegness Conservative branch be composed ?) can give a guest speaker a jollier evening than most – as I can testify. And it is only fair to allow that the alligator park no longer exists. It was Skegness's answer to Disneyworld. And to think that Walt Disney's ancestors came from Norton Disney, in the East Midlands!

From Skegness you might drive down the coast for a donkey ride in Cleethorpes whose youthful Member of Parliament, Michael Brown, is the only Tory in the House who failed his 11-plus examination and went to a Secondary Modern School. His father was furious when he threw over a steady career as a bank clerk to try his hand as a Conservative candidate for the seemingly impossible seat of Scunthorpe. He won. But still his courage knew no bounds. Within weeks he was calling for the closure of steel-making capacity in that one-industry town. We gasped in admiration. When, though, he drove down to the docks in his Japanese car to join a protest against the import of foreign steel, some of us thought that even Michael had gone too far. And when (in 1980) he told the newspapers that rebellious Tory colleagues were 'like rats leaving a sinking ship' there was a general view that he had humoured neither the rats nor the captain. A plucky lad, nevertheless, and my best friend in Parliament.

Or you might like to drive across the flat Lincolnshire countryside – lit by the flares of industry (and, perhaps, be reminded of Flixborough, site of the incident which came as close to a major industrial disaster as we have ever come). For industry – with or without accident – has scarred most of the East Midlands irreparably. Open, featureless, countryside is so easily spoilt.

The constituency of Gainsborough is an example. Its last Member of Parliament, Sir Marcus Kimball, represented 'the countryside' with an ardent and old-fashioned integrity. No debate on fur or feather, hunting, shooting or fishing was complete without him and I can still remember my astonishment when, in an obscure Standing Committee, at an unsocial house, speaking upon some agricultural Bill, Sir Marcus revealed himself to be an expert not just upon the broad outline but upon the minutest veterinary detail, of Whirling Disease in Trout.

Marcus was immensely respected. Yet Gainsborough is not the Gainsborough of George Eliot's novels. The East Midlands is not like that anymore. Not to say, of course, that in the field sports, we are not still supreme. Whyte Melville's great hunting novel *Market Harborough* was set in the region. Isaac Walton, who wrote *The Compleat Angler* is particularly linked with Ashbourne and the River Dove. The Quorn, Belvoir, Cottesmore, Pytchley and Meynell Hunts are famous. And that other traditional country sport, hunt the hunt saboteurs, can still be enjoyed by all! Very much on the side of the huntsmen is my co-contributor, Nick Budgen, who regularly invades my patch for just such a purpose, and has been seen in ditches all over South Derbyshire.

No, neither the traditional pursuits, nor the ancient beauties of the region have disappeared. Some areas are drab in scenery and architecture, like the featureless country between the cities of Nottingham and Derby, and the coal-mining areas of East Derbyshire. But among them remain areas of character: what is left of Sherwood Forest and Dukeries, the strange little crag of Charnwood Forest, the cliff, heath, wold, fen and marsh of Lincolnshire, and the huge skies and marshland as you approach the North Sea ...all these things retain their beauty.

It is the industry itself which has left some of the most striking landscapes. The huge quarries around Buxton, the bird-watchers' paradise created by the gravel lagoons of the Trent Valley, the vast cooling towers of the Central Electricity Generating Board power station near Castle Donnington, magical in certain lights and weather, and the extraordinary array of chimneys rising out of a pastoral landscape, created by the brick industry of Bedfordshire — these are what strike the traveller. It must be said of the East Midlands that the iron has entered its soul. We must learn to love it if we are to be East Midlanders.

*   *   *   *

'They paid their two halfpennies at the turnstile and crossed the bridge. The Trent was very full. It swept silently and insidious under the bridge, travelling in a soft body. On the

river levels were flat gleams of flood water. The sky was grey,
with glisten of silver ...'.

D. H. Lawrence.

Our region is not a region of great cities. Apart from Leicester and
Nottingham which have almost half-a-million inhabitants apiece, the
other large towns in the area, some claiming to be cities are only towns:
Derby, Northampton, Lincoln, Bedford.

Of our cities, the liveliest is Nottingham, 'Queen of the Midlands'. Her
site is a fine one, spread over hills just above the River Trent. But she has
treated her past poorly, and the old and mediocre are jumbled
unsatisfactorily together with the new. Yet, somehow, Nottingham
retains the vitality for which it has long been known as a cultural centre,
with university, concert hall, playhouse and old Theatre; as a shopping,
sports and media centre; and as the site for Goose Fair, which lives on!

Lace-making, once a dominant industry, has given way to bicycles,
drugs, and cigarettes – a trio of Boots, Raleigh and Players – and the city
and surrounding country are not without a quiet prosperity.

'Leicestershire is not a county of extremes'.

Sir N. Pevsner.

Leicester and its county are richer but the mix is less successful. Once
the wealthiest city (per capita) in the Commonwealth, Leicester has a
proud historic and archeological heritage, and (today) the university, the
great institutions, and the financial and administrative power that make it
the dominant city in its region. But there is a terrible evenness about both
town and country. There are no dominant employers. The city lacks civic
grandeur. Its prosperity is reflected more in its suburbs. The results are
pleasant, leafy outskirts and a hollow centre. Leicester was an early
experiment by a Polish architect (Smigiellski) in city planning. It has not
succeeded. The city is an incoherent mish-mash of warehouses,
ringroads, Roman ruins and public lavatories. Its siting is dull and flat
and its river bedraggled. Its ruins are puny and a huge highway cuts off
its most historic area from the rest of the centre. Its two fine churches of St
Mary de Castro and St Nicholas are separated by the Holiday Inn. For all
that, though, the city has a bustling and competent feel to it; and Leicester
is changing. For it has one distinctive character. Nowadays, it is one of
the most Asian of all British cities. A high proportion of Ugandan Asians
have made their way here. In two out of three of Leicester's Westminster
constituencies Asians make up a quarter of the electorate. Labour's
Australian born candidate, Patricia Hewitt, could be seen in a sari in her
narrowly unsuccessful campaign in the 1983 General Election. Nor,
perhaps, is the business energy or family-centred culture of the Asian
community alien to the spirit of Leicester. The National Front are said to

be dismayed by their failure to appeal to the white citizens of Leicester.

Derby is the poor relation of the trio. It is really just a glorified railway town – and the glory has worn a bit thin. Its other great employer, Rolls Royce, the battered flagship of the British aero-engine industry, staggers on hopefully. A meanly-proportioned town, its townspeople solid and civil, Derby too has a high proportion of Asian inhabitants. Unemployment is rather high, and commerce and industry are hard-pressed: but Derby is not yet on the ropes and will probably pull through – principally, I believe, on the soundness of its citizens.

Derbyshire's second town, Chesterfield, is harder hit by unemployment. A surprisingly hard-bitten place, it boasts two great curiosities: its buckled church spire, and its Member of Parliament, the Rt. Hon. Tony Benn, M.P. Both met, initially, with widespread public dismay. With time, though, both in an eccentric way, have found a place in the hearts of the public – and it is hard to imagine (now) how we could do without either of them.

Bedford has, proportionate to its size, the largest colony of Italians. Italian political posters go up in the streets, and Italian political parties send over representatives. The new BBC local radio station includes Italian. The Italians originally came over to work in the brickworks and many have stayed. They even have ice-cream wars!

And then there are the Clydesiders of Corby, who moved here from Scotland when Corby was a boom town, steelworks following on iron deposits. Corby was one of Britain's most incongruous industrial towns with the steelworks rising out of unspoilt farmland. But it was also vulnerable, like other single industry communities, and the loss of the steelworks threatened its existence. Today, despite hopeful signs of regeneration, the town has a sad and hollow feeling: not so much a town at all – more a developmental node. It is now the only development area, eligible for national and EEC regional aid, in the whole of the East Midlands. Being a Tory marginal seat has worked wonders!

The East Midlands' urban scene is not one of unmixed decline. There are some areas of considerable growth; and new towns have been grafted on to old. Peterborough, for instance, has a fine cathedral, is on the frontier of the Fens, is bleak, and is growing fast. Too fast. I know, because my secretary used to work for its M.P., Brian Mawhinney – and resigned in the face of his mountainous constituency correspondence and perpetual telephone calls.

And there are some quieter and pleasant market towns: Melton Mowbray (where they make pork pies), Market Harborough (where they make liberty bodices), and Loughborough (where they cast the biggest bell in England and – equally unlikely – have their own University and

College of Physical Education. (No one is quite sure why).

There is Southwell with its Minster on whose mediaeval carvings of plants and flowers an entire book 'Leaves of Southwell', has been written; and Louth, with its Georgian houses. Oakham and Uppingham in the *soi-disant* county of Rutland are pleasant towns; and perhaps above all, there is Stamford – a town with no special or monumental building, but somehow a marvellous whole.

Grantham, once voted the most boring town in England, has entirely redeemed itself by producing first Isaac Newton and then Margaret Thatcher. Newton only saw the light when the apple fell at Woolsthorpe in Lincolnshire. To Mrs Thatcher, however, it was probably all quite obvious from the start.

*　　*　　*　　*

It may well be legitimate to take famous people from, say, Wales or Cornwall and examine them in terms of their Welshness, or Cornishness. But in the East Midlands it is hardly the 'East Midlandishness' of an individual that adds to his fascination. Do our people, in fact, have anything in common. We do seem to specialise in rebels and pioneers – perhaps because of a certain rootlessness which is almost the theme of this essay.

Will Lee revolutionised Nottinghamshire's economy in Elizabethan times by inventing a machine for knitting stockings. The first machine for the spinning of cotton was built by James Watt at Linby in Nottingham. The first silkmill in the United Kingdom was in Derby. The first time water power was used to drive a cottonmill in 1771 was by Arkwright at Cromford, 'the cradle of the industrial revolution'.

The very first package tour was organised in the East Midlands: a railway excursion by Thos. Cook & Sons from Leicester to Loughborough and back!

The same spirit, perhaps, inspires the rebels – of all types. Robin Hood's reputation still gives an undeserved interest to the relics of Sherwood Forest. (Personally, I always had more sympathy with King John and the Sheriff of Nottingham – the true underdogs!).

If Robin deserves a prize for getting the best press from the most unpromising material, then other East Midlands rebels have received more mixed publicity. Titus Oates, of Popish Plot fame, has gone down as 'terrorist' rather than 'freedom fighter'; and those other fine rebels, the Luddites of Nottingham, deserve (but rarely get) respect for romanticism if not realism. Byron, at least, (another East Midlands figure) would have approved.

We can also claim many religious rebels: John Wycliffe of

Leicestershire, the Mayflower pilgrims (who, contrary to most schoolboys' belief did not actually *come* from Plymouth); Charles Doddridge of Northampton, who founded the Congregationalists; General Booth, of the Salvation Army; and, of course, John Wesley. William Bagshaw, 'the apostle of the Peak', was ejected as rector of Glossop because of his refusal to accept the prayerbook.

Like D. H. Lawrence, John Bunyan was as much a rebel as an author, and wrote *Pilgrim's Progess'* in Bedford Jail. I often wonder whether some prophetic vision of the clay pits and gravel ponds that industry was to leave in the county, lay behind the inspiration for the landscape of pits and sloughs through which Pilgrim journeyed. 'Despond' is certainly the word for the view of parts of Bedfordshire, from the railway line!

Bunyan has been forgiven. Simon de Montfort, said to be the founder of our most ancient of Parliaments, has certainly been forgiven by his home town of Leicester. Sir Edward Digby of Rutland, who financed Guy Fawkes and the Gunpowder Plotters (they met, among other places, in Northamptonshire and Bedfordshire) has certainly not. Nor, I imagine, has the Headmasters' Conference forgiven F. W. Sanderson, Head of Oundle in the 1890s, who turned against beating: 'Punishment I declare, from years of experience in this experiment, is a crime. Not only a crime but a blunder!'

So many of the names that I have mentioned have been nobles. In mediaeval England, the East Midlands were one of the feudal heartlands and this is still visible in the landscape and in the villages. The fields of Laxton, in Nottinghamshire, are the best place to see what a mediaeval open-field farming pattern looks like. But our great nobles are not only figures of the past. Besides the Dukes of Rutland and of Devonshire, we can offer the packaged' Duke of Bedford, with whom rich American tourists can dine for a fee.

Scattered throughout the East Midlands are the sites where the great killed each other, with evocative names like Naseby, and Bosworth Field, where Richard III was unable to exchange his kingdom for a horse. Ironic that its M.P., Adam Butler, should be quite the least swashbuckling or cavalier sort of man one could imagine!

The East Midlands of the famous is easier to describe than the East Midlands of the 'people'. Are any generalisations possible about this zone of transition from southern to northern characteristics. Already the people of Derbyshire are more open, direct and blunt than southerners, as anyone who has taken part in a political campaign can testify!

*　　*　　*　　*

Only in the Derbyshire hill farms does 'horn' predominate. Elsewhere, 'corn' is the crop, especially in Lincolnshire, which has more agricultural constituencies than any other county. At the head of this list comes Holland with Boston. The heroism of their Member of Parliament, Richard Body, is remarkable; an East Midlands rebel, if ever there was one. He will never be forgiven for his opinions about agricultural subsidy, which are so obviously true as to be deeply offensive. He believes that the Common Agricultural Policy of the EEC is illogical and wasteful. He thinks it crazy that Europe gets its sugar from beet instead of buying more sugar-cane from the third world. He has been saying so for years. He is evidently right — so it is not surprising that no-one takes any notice of his views; and the Government pretends that he simply doesn't exist.

The East Midlands is a great region for mining: based of course upon coal and iron which were twin pillars for the region's economy. Much of the Roman Empire's lead came from the hills of Derbyshire and the last mine was only closed after the Second World War. In Wirksworth, in my constituency, the Barmote Court, which deals with all claims relating to lead mining, is still in existence. Quarrying is an enormously important part of the local economy.

Nowhere is the evidence of mining, past and present, more visible than in Derbyshire. It is the first thing you notice on Ordnance Survey maps of the Peak District. The great lime quarries outside Buxton are perhaps the most visually striking in Britain, huge craters on the bleak moor. Some of the mines are tourist attractions, like the Blue John Mine at Castleton. Even Derbyshire's political preferences have been affected in places which are no longer mining areas, but where there is still a residual Labour vote from mining days. My constituency is dotted with hundreds of abandoned lead mines, down which unsuspecting ramblers still occasionally disappear (and, I suspect, to the delight of local farmers).

Iron mining, like lead, is over; coal mining, however, is still expanding. Coal has been mined in the East Midlands since Roman times. The great Elizabethan mansion, Wollaton Hall, in Nottingham, was built in 1588 on the profits of coal. There are fields in Leicestershire, Nottinghamshire and north and south Derbyshire. Bolsover in Derbyshire has more people employed in the coal industry than in any other constituency. It was bitter news for Dennis Skinner, the left-wing M.P. for Bolsover, when his constituents began to break the recent miners' strike. Nottinghamshire has some of the largest, most modern mines in Britain, and is second only to adjacent South Yorkshire as a mining region. Here, and in Leicestershire, new fields are still being opened up.

The East Midlands have been the stronghold of the strike-breaking miners, not only in the 1984/85 strike but in the last one earlier in this century. Last time, they even set up a separate union. The political effects

MATTHEW PARRIS · 145

of all this are clear. Some of the most implausible Tory wins in the 1983 General Election, such as Sherwood, are clearly attributable to the moderate traditions of the East Midlands coalfield. Behind the politics, ideology and personality, the strike of 1984/85 was about the shift in investment from the coalfields of Yorkshire, Scotland, Wales and Kent into the East Midlands. Whether or not it is true that working miners waved £5 notes from the windows of buses ferrying them through the angry picket lines, it has become a legend in the region: because, like all legends, it touches upon something central if imperfectly articulated.

Farming and mining stock mark the region distinctively. But it would be a mistake to suppose that most East Midlanders are engaged in either. It is the variousness of the industry, old as well as new, rather than its reliance upon any one sector, which characterises the East Midlands economy. A list of what is provided, manufactured, or sold in the East Midlands would read like the Yellow Pages of the telephone directory. There is everything from jet engines to barrels of beer — indeed, it was the innovative Ruddles of Rutland which sold all its pubs minus one in order to concentrate on supermarkets and the free trade.

*   *   *   *

Nottinghamshire has a splendid cricketing history. Trent Bridge is still a name to conjure with; and it was Nottinghamshire fast-bowlers Larwood and Voce who were responsible for the body-line bowling in the 1932/33 tour which helped to provoke the only major crisis to date in relations between the United Kingdom and Australia. In football, too, Nottingham Forest is a famous team while Notts County is the oldest football league club in England.

Royal Shrovetide Football, played in Ashbourne each Shrove Tuesday, is very different. The whole town (and anyone else besides) can play. The goalposts are three miles apart. Those born to one side of the river (the 'Uppards') try to capture the ball and bring it to their own goalpost. The 'Downards' do the same. By the time the final whistle is blown on Wednesday, the ball has been all over the town and (usually) down and through and out the other side of a man-sized drain which carries the river under the centre of the town! The scrums are extraordinary: TV scenes of picket-line violence leave Ashbourne Shrovetiders unmoved by comparison! I started the game — once. A dull successor (I imagine) to Princes of Wales and Dukes of Devonshire, I was hustled to the dais, with the crowds lunging and baying at me for action. I understood what it must feel like to be carried through the mob for a public execution! Eat your hearts out Torville and Dean! (Nottingham's ice-skating world beaters).

Yet there are gentler recreations. The Peak District National Park (much of it in my constituency) preserves countryside of great natural beauty: hills and dales, rivers and caves, climbing, walking, riding and camping. In one of those night-photographs taken from satellite, it would appear as a patch of warm and illuminating darkness, encircled by the sightless glare of industry and habitation. It is discomforting to reflect that at the time when the National Parks were created, I would almost certainly have been against the idea. I would have made a predictable speech about individual liberty, attacking planners. Fortunately, other views prevailed.

In the Peak Park, and our great houses, churches and cathedrals, the 'Olde Englande' which foreign tourists seek, survives more in the tangible relics, in the 'furniture' of the region, than in its spirit or customs.

If there ever was an East Midlands cuisine certainly it does not exist today, but the cheese Stilton from Leicestershire and Derbyshire and, of course, Sage Derby is excellent.

*   *   *   *

Perhaps because of this heterogeneity, loyalty to community, class, or Party is uncommonly weak. This, I suggest, is why Labour's decline came earlier and is proceeding faster than elsewhere.

Before 1979, Northamptonshire had one seat, Kettering, that had been Labour since the War. Now there are two separate seats, Kettering and Corby, and both are in Conservative hands. In Leicestershire, the reversal is even more striking. Now there is only one Labour M.P. in the whole county, Greville Janner. (And Greville is only technically in the Labour Party, these days!).

Lincolnshire has always had more Tory strength, but even here the Scunthorpe and Lincoln seats have been captured from Labour. Most striking has been the collapse of the Labour-leaning farmworker vote around the Wash. In 1966, Labour were only 316 votes behind the Conservatives in the seat of Holland and Boston. Now it is a rock-solid Tory seat.

The trend in Nottinghamshire can partly be explained by the 'new race of miners' (D. H. Lawrence) in the coalfields. Here too, Labour have lost ground, not even winning the apparently tailor-made seat in Sherwood. Ashfield saw one of the biggest ever swings from Labour to Tory in the 1977 by-election.

In Derbyshire, the Conservative Party channelled all their forces, in the 1983 election, into what we thought were the marginals of South Derbyshire, Amber Valley, and Derby North. We won all of them comfortably. We hardly bothered with North East Derbyshire and Derby

South: they did not look like marginals. They were, and we kicked ourselves for ignoring them.

As for Bedfordshire, it is now entirely Conservative in its representation in Parliament and it is hard to believe that Labour was once so strong there.

Is there any regional explanation for Labour's decline. I have mentioned a heterogeneity and a certain rootlessness, and implied a sort of 'new Britain' materialism: an 'upwardly socially mobile region' a region of 'strivers', as the jargon would have it. The moderate tradition in the coalfields (partly because miners there are doing so well), the lack of any great concentrations of heavy industry, the high percentage of women in many sectors, all draw the voter away from ideological dogma, and stubborn Party loyalty.

Certainly, one cannot blame any supposed extremism in the local Labour Party. Apart from the Tony Benn−Dennis Skinner enclave in North east Derbyshire, the Labour Party in the East Midlands has lagged embarassingly behind the leftward movement of the Party as a whole. There have been a striking number of right-wing or maverick Labour politicians from the region: the fox-hunting, pro-hanging M.P., Sir Reginald Pagett of Northampton, Philip Whitehead from Derby North, George Brown from Belper, Don Concannon from Mansfield, and Woodrow Wyatt, as well as a considerable number of local Labour politicians who have become active in the SDP: David Marquand, Dick Taverne and Ken Bradley. But the fashionable and intellectual appeal of the SDP has not so far proved a great attraction to East Midlanders. We are not, on the whole, fashionable or intellectual people!

*   *   *   *

What we are, as the East Midlands, is an area of comparative personal mobility. Does a fixed address lead more easily to a fixated political standpoint. I think it can. For that very reason the Conservative Party would be unwise to rely upon its new supporters in the East Midlands, any more than the Labour Party could rely upon its old. The population of Northamptonshire is burgeoning (up by 13 per cent from 1971 to 1981). Nottingham's population has sunk fast (down by 19 per cent in the 1970s). All is flux: and in these circumstances political parties are unwise to count their chickens.

Especially is this true because the regional economy is wavering uncertainly. We have not suffered a wholesale collapse and we are not going to. Unemployment is still slightly lower than the national average and far below (for instance) that of the West Midlands. But the picture is a doubtful and patchy one. Cheese-and-wine parties are perhaps no reliable guide to the economic fortunes of the people, but I find that no more than a bowl of peanuts and a cocktail-dip may separate the businessman who tells me that business has never been better from the businessman who tells me that it couldn't be worse. I hear many success stories and see many bankruptcies. There is no clear trend.

EAST ANGLIA
Richard Ryder

Richard Ryder O.B.E., director of a family farming business in Ely and a journalist, describes in his essay the economy and growing prosperity of a part of England normally regarded as sleepy. Though it can never recover the pre-eminence it held in the Middle Ages when the wool-trade made it the most populous and the richest part, it is remarkable for the growth of smaller businesses and the freedom of its ports from industrial disputes.

Richard Ryder is 37. He was educated at Radley and Magdalene College, Cambridge. He was the Conservative candidate for Gateshead East in both the 1974 elections and won the Mid-Norfolk seat in 1983. He was political secretary to Margaret Thatcher from 1975 to 1981. He was also Vice Chairman of the Eastern Regional Council for Sport and Recreation.

East Anglian folk are often stereotyped as living many years behind the times in feudally-run villages. According to this absurd view, East Anglian men are hearty, ruddy-cheeked simpletons, who spend days tilling the land, evenings quaffing pints of real Adnams ale and nights resisting eviction by wicked landlords. East Anglian women are portrayed too as jolly and overweight, forced to top up subsistence family incomes by picking and riddling potatoes and hoeing sugar beet in sub-zero temperatures caused by the piercing east winds.

East Anglian scenery also matches the eyes of outside beholders, some of whom regard it as dull and featureless, the more so now that the prairie farming has taken its toll on hedgerows and trees. 'Very flat, Norfolk', remarked Noel Coward, a stylised townee. To sportsmen, the region is either a marshland crawling with wildfowl; or deciduous trees, conifer belts and fields bulging with pheasants and partridges. To holidaymakers on the Broads it brims with lagoons, meres and lakes; seemingly natural but which were dug out by men searching for peat a thousand years ago.

What would conservationists have said then, I wonder?

Disentangling facts from fiction, realities from romance, in East Anglia is almost as tricky as securing a natural vantage point on the open spaces of the Fens, or finding the sea at low tide on a vast Norfolk beach, say at Brancaster or at Wells. It is tricky, partly because a little of the mythical East Anglia survives in a few concealed villages. Whereas, in fact, most of it faded when the region's population began to multiply faster than other areas of Britain twenty years ago, due to the creation of hundreds of light industrial firms, huge insurance offices in Norwich and Ipswich, London 'overspill' and an influx of retired people buying post-war, picture-window bungalows and unused farm cottages at competitive prices. All of this happened in villages expanded for the first time since the emigration caused by the agricultural and industrial revolutions. It is this massive increase in population which has irretrievably changed the face of East Anglia, for better or for worse, certainly for richer rather than poorer. It means that perhaps nearly half the residents were not born in the region. Indeed, you are now likelier to hear Cockney spoken in Thetford and Haverhill than the unmistakable East Anglian dialect — which, like all other regional sounds, is gradually disappearing in any event. So references to East Anglian characteristics are misleading to the extent that great labour and social mobility have transformed the region, with the squire and the vicar no longer the only cornerstones of the community. Yet, it is still easy to observe amongst natives of East Anglia many of the sinews of independence which have given them marked distinctions for centuries.

East Anglians do not resemble garrulous caricatures, as Colonel Trevor West found on retiring from the army to farm pigs in Akenfield, Ronald Blyth's Suffolk village, in the 1950s. West harshly described original Akenfield inhabitants as 'cold and hidden'. East Anglians tend to avoid direct statements, answers are non-commital, meanings hinted at, attitudes cautious, and malapropisms common. They are reserved and guarded in their approach to life, perhaps because their livelihoods depended for generations on the vagaries of the changing seasons over which they had no mortal influence. The only East Anglians who will talk their heads off are the fishermen. Thus, events are accepted without apparent surprise or emotion, seldom are they made to happen. It makes them hard workers and excellent soldiers. Alas, the Territorial Division of East Anglian Territorial Army Regiments were sent out to Singapore in 1941, fought with distinction against the Japanese and more than 10,000 of them were captured and endured a fearful captivity.

The East Anglian disposition would also make them outstanding Whitehall press officers and splendid spies, never submitting under interrogation, or at least never in danger of being understood if they did, because their dialect is a language apart.

The word 'it' is redundant in the dialect; the word 'that' is employed instead. The words 'do' and 'don't' mean 'if you do' and 'if you don't'. So a farmworker quizzed about the whereabouts of a radio-set would reply. 'That lay agin the shed, don't that did do, don't I shall be surprised, and that'll be a rum un'.

'Ber' or 'bor' means mate, and is still in frequent usage, as is their plural which is 'together'. So 'let's go mate(s)' is 'rightaway ber' and 'rightaway together'.

The 's' at the end of the third person singular of any verb does not exist, and so when poet Robert Bloomfield wrote the *Farmer's Boy*, his publishers Cafel Loftt had to edit in the 's's.

Among older, native East Anglians, conversations are often marked by their insularity and Irish irrelevance, as in the case of a Tunstall lady chatting to a friend:

'Did you here my boy Bill a-bin called up?'
'Noo. Where they be a sendin him?'
'Ong Kong, he say'.
'Wheriver's that?'
'Well, I don't rightly know but he tell me he have ter change at Wickham Market'.

Or of two men walking to a neighbouring village:
'What are they doing over there, ber, I shouldn't wonder'.
'I don't know, so they tell me'.
'We ain't far off here now, are we ber?'
'No, we might as well be here, as where we are'.

*　　*　　*　　*

Despite their insularity and the irrelevance of some of their conversation, East Anglians have a varied ancestry resulting from waves of European immigration after the region cast off the continent in about 6000 BC.

Now, three-quarters of East Anglia is surrounded by the sea, or land below sea-level in the case of the Fens, where the dwellers in this rich black soil are called 'Tigers', a name acquired during their resistance to the 17th century drainage schemes, which they thought to be depriving Fenmen of their ancient occupations of fishing and wild fowling.

Many Englishmen, who have never set foot in East Anglia, depict the bleak Fenland landscape as typical of the region. But it is not, as the writer, Robert Reyce, testified:

> 'East Anglia is void of any great hills, high mountains
>   or steep rocks; notwithstanding the which it is not always
>   so low, or flat, but that in every place it is serene and divided with little hills easy for ascent and pleasant rivers watering the low valleys'.

Reyce was right. East Anglia possesses a variety of landscape without the dramatic scenery for at only a few points in south west Suffolk does the land rise to 400 feet. Yet, within this parameter, delicate folds soften a landscape not widely savoured or even known – despite its proximity to London.

There are, at least, two common 'inland' physiographical features. A wide tract of rich boulder clay, which bisects the hearts of Norfolk and Suffolk; and a ridge of chalkland, about six miles wide, which forms a belt on the west of boulder clay and stretches from Hunstanton, on the Norfolk coast, through south-west Suffolk and the Gog Magog hills in Cambridgeshire eventually joining East Anglia to Southern England.

But the variety of the landscape is the unappreciated essence of East Anglia, be it the wooded river valleys such as Constable's Stour or Parson Woodforde's Wensum; the Broads; the Sandlings, a coastal strip of former heathland running from Lowestoft to Felixstowe; or Breckland, an area around Thetford and Brandon which is the driest and most arid part of the British Isles and now dominated by the Forestry Commission, airforce bases, army training grounds and housing developments.

Few deny that modern housing developments are as necessary to East Anglia as they are the inevitable results of its new prosperity. Yet, many assert that agricultural changes have wrought havoc to the landscape by destroying hedges and trees. Since 1945, the region has lost many of these features in order to make way for extra arable acreages and huge new machines like the Claas and Clayson Combine and giant tractors, the new dinosaurs of rural England. The doubling of England's barley acreage in the 1950s represented a governmental bid to enable Britain to be self-sufficient in food. Inevitably, the landscape suffered – between 1945 and 1970 Norfolk lost 45 per cent of its hedges and in 1977 alone 8,000 hedgerow trees – because hedges became almost valueless to arable farmers. Once, they alone checked soil erosion by forming windbreaks, but now the same aim can be achieved by using mulches and oils in the soil. With more and more farmers switching from livestock to arable produce stock proof barriers, like hedges, are no longer wanted. Besides, they require more sympathetic and professional maintenance than that provided by flail cutters, which frequently scythe hedges down to knee high, at which point they lose their wildlife and aesthetic functions.

Up to now, Ministry of Agriculture, Fisheries and Food (MAFF) officials have claimed that the state of the environment is a matter for subjective taste. Indeed, on a recent visit to Norfolk, an Environment Minister asked a farmer, who wants to drain and plough up the Halvergate Marshes — 2,000 acres of rough grazing ground — what aspect of the county he found most aesthetically pleasing. The farmer took the Minister aback for a second by replying 'skies'. A perfectly legitimate answer. After all, the reputations of painters John Cotman and John Crome and that of the Norwich School partly rested on their appreciation of skyscapes — and no-one grasped that quicker than the discerning Minister, a Fellow of All Souls.

Be that as it may, farmers have faced criticism in recent years for, at worst, ravaging the environment or, at best, taking it for granted. Lately, the National Farmers Union (NFU) and the Country Landowners Association (CLA) in particular, have begun to make efforts to alter the attitudes of their members, a task made harder by a contradictory system of farm subsidies. In 1979, the NFU and CLA proposed unsuccessfully the creation of a Ministry of Rural Affairs out of the present MAFF and the conservation section of the Department of the Environment. Despite this suggestion, and subsequent policy documents, a suspicion still lurks in conservation quarters, that the MAFF and the NFU enjoy an incestuous relationship, at the expense of environmentalists. This is a feeling confirmed by the continued removal of landscape features and a refusal to overhaul the system of subsidies. In a poem, Philip Larkin (who ought to have succeeded Sir John Betjeman as Poet Laureate) underlined the importance of trees to the landscape 'Where has the tree gone, that locked earth to sky?'.

*   *   *   *

On a slightly different but associated point, Betjeman went a step further by observing that East Anglian earth was also locked to sky by the spires and towers of its churches whose profusion and beauty are unrivalled in Britain. To be more precise, in his gem of a book *Norfolk Country Churches and the Future*, he declared: 'When a church has been pulled down, the country seems empty or is like a necklace with a jewel missing'.

At the time of the Norman Conquest, high Suffolk (the broad middle belt) and central Norfolk were populated more densely than other parts of England, the result of earlier Anglo-Saxon river valley colonisations. The

Domesday Book recorded no less than 300 churches each in Suffolk and Norfolk. Later, when East Anglia became England's manufacturing heartland, thanks to the acumen of Flemish weaver immigrants, between the 12th and 15th centuries, sumptuous churches such as Blythburgh, Lavenham and Sall were built from the profits of the wool and weaving trades. Worstead in Norfolk, and Kersey and Lindsey in Suffolk gave their names to well known fabrics originating from this period.

The new churches were constructed chiefly in the perpendicular style with flint. Even existing churches were re-shaped in this fashion, leaving only key features like Norman porches and round, 10th century towers, of which over 100 still survive. (Contrary to some beliefs, the style did not dawn in East Anglia but in the West Country, where Gloucester Cathedral remains a classic model.)

Significant damage has been committed at different times, to these 'monuments to the golden fleece'. During the civil war destruction was widespread and neglect triumphed over preservation in the 18th century. Though, in many cases, this indifference was preferable to the later 19th century embellishments, like the craze for pictured glass, to which numerous churches were subjected without apparent resistance. The craze inflicted on light what Dutch Elm Disease has done to slices of the countryside, notably the two-and-a-half mile long avenue at Wimpole Hall in Cambridgeshire, once the finest in England but now just another blot on the landscape.

Visitors to East Anglia are sometimes struck by the isolated churches whose locations are invariably ascribed to the Black Death. Yet, this is half the story, other reasons for their isolation endure too. The location of a church may have been determined because it lay between two communities, as at Cockfield; because of its proximity to a hall or moated site, as at Biddleston; or even because of its relationship to an existing pagan site.

Churches can get no remoter after disappearing into the sea. Yet Dunwich, with sub-marine churches, still boasts a terrestrial Suffragan Bishop. A small museum with the seals and maces of its former Corporation and the remains of a priory, is about all that stands fast of an important town, the last of whose nine churches tumbled over the cliffs in 1919. Near Dunwich is the tiny village of Erwarton, on the Shotley peninsula, between the Orwell and Stour estuaries, where Arthur Ransome set many of his splendid children's adventure stories and the churchyard is alleged to contain the heart of Ann Boleyn, one of Henry VIII's beheaded wives who used to stay with her aunt at the hall next door. Rumour contends that on certain nights of the year, she can be glimpsed sitting in a coach, drawn by four headless horses, with her severed head in her hands. This tale, though, does not apply to Erwarton, but to the village of Blickling, the vicinity of Norfolk from which the Boleyn family came and which still possesses one of England's outstanding Jacobean-style, red brick houses now cared for by the National Trust.

Norfolk is blessed with several other fine houses of which Holkham, Raynham and Houghton are best known.

The Palladian Holkham on the sandy edge of the marshy north Norfolk coast testifies to man's gradual success over nature. It was the brainchild of Thomas Coke, whose great-nephew and heir, Thomas William Coke, was a pioneer of agricultural revolution with Charles 'Turnip' Townshend of Raynham. Theirs was land which had to be worked, not rich ground as in Herefordshire whose grass grew whether you wanted it or not.

Townshend retired to Raynham from national politics after a dispute with his Norfolk neighbour, the Prime Minister, Sir Robert Walpole. He evolved a farming sequence of his own called the Norfolk four-course rotation consisting of roots (turnips and swedes) and seeds (red clover). Forty years after his death, Thomas William Coke inherited Holkham where he introduced bone manure and cattle cake, as well as paying special attention to breeding and selecting grass seeds.

Although Sir Robert Walpole's achievements are beyond dispute – he was Prime Minister for 20 years – he took an entrepreneurial approach to politics that would have provided colourful reading in an 18th century register of Members of Parliament's interests. Walpole began building the magnificently proportioned Holkham Hall the year before becoming Prime Minister. He put the affairs of State into context by opening letters from his gamekeeper and huntsman before those from his sovereign. After his death the house and grounds deteriorated rapidly, prior to eventual rehabilitation, much to the dismay of his youngest son, the writer Horace Walpole. He wrote that 'art and life ought to be hurriedly remarried and brought to live together'. This is exactly what has happened at Heveningham Hall – interior designed by James Wyatt, grounds by Capability Brown – which has been bought by Arabs.

By far the best known country house is Sandringham, one of the Royal Family's homes. The Prince of Wales, later King Edward VII, bought the estate in 1862 largely for sporting potential. He built a new house, resembling a well appointed Victorian seaside hotel, and entertained on a grand scale. Shooting was the main outdoor pursuit and up to 3,000 pheasants would be despatched on a single day.

Yet no sport has enjoyed wider Royal patronage, for the past 300 years, than horse racing. Few towns in Britain have sustained closer links with Royalty than Newmarket, the headquarters of racing and the cradle and playground of sporting art, a school unique to this country, some of whose best graduates, Adam Wyck, Tillermans, Sartorius, Alken and Herring were of immigrant stock.

James I originally favoured Newmarket by constructing a hunting lodge in the town. Charles II followed suit. In fact, his mistress Nell Gwyn's house still stands there. The pleasure seeker was nicknamed 'Old Rowley' by his Newmarket admirers after an energetic stallion of that name.

Today, Newmarket boasts a thriving bloodstock industry, a National Stud, a racing museum, Tattersall's sale paddocks, where millions of pounds change hands each year, and two racecourses, the Rowley Mile and the July. Yet for all the excitement of witnessing the pageantry at these forays and betting on horses from instinct or expertise, no spectacle in Newmarket can compare with the dawn sight and sound of a string of moody thoroughbred racehorses twitching and dancing their way to the gallops for exercise.

Apart from racing and sailing East Anglia is not renowned for sport. Its counties play minor county cricket with major mediocrity. Although the University ground in Cambridge, Fenners, possesses a true batting wicket, rare in this seamer's age and on which dozens of cricketers such as Peter May, Ted Dexter and Majid Khan learned to display their elegant skills. Alas, none of these strokemakers have been East Anglian by birth, upbringing, or adoption. That privilege belongs to Bill Edrich and Peter Parfitt, both born in Norfolk. The Edrich family still fields a team of its own near the Hoveton home of the journalist, Henry Blofeld, whose enthusiastic radio commentaries have made him a cult figure in Australia where appreciation for the English language exists, but it is not always apparent in its spoken form.

Whereas few claims can be entered for the quality of East Anglian cricket, they can be lodged for football. The friendly Norwich City, under the astute chairmanship of fur trader, Sir Arthur South, former Labour Leader of the City Council, and Chairman of the Regional Health Authority, have reached the final of the Milk Cup thrice during the past 12 years, winning it on the last occasion. Next to Liverpool, Norwich's local rivals, Ipswich Town, have been the most consistent club in English football over the past 15 years, carrying off the FA Cup in 1978 and EUFA Cup in 1981 with one of the most attractive sides assembled in British football since the War. It was overwhelmingly a home-grown team, managed by Bobby Robson, containing two Dutch mid-field craftsmen, Arnold Muhren and Frans Thijssen, and all too seldom the injury-prone defender, Kevin Beattie, a genius whose career ended in his early twenties.

Stories abound in the football world about the antics and hospitality of the Cobbolds, a brewing family, who have controlled the club since its election to the League nearly 50 years ago.

*　　*　　*　　*

Even Mr John Cobbold's personality was not enough to secure him election to Parliament in the 1950s when he twice contested Ipswich for the Conservatives against Sir Dingle Foot, Michael's brother. Ipswich reflects many of East Anglia's political characteristics, non-conformity and 'doing different', chief among them. Today, Ipswich is one of the two constituencies in the region without a Conservative representative. Its M.P., Ken Weetch, is a Labour man of the old school who held the seat in 1983 by bravely rejecting the Marxist influence in his Party's manifesto, thereby preventing the Alliance from splitting the centre-left vote which would have allowed the Conservative candidate to stroll through the middle.

Ipswich also 'did different' in February 1974 when the Conservative M.P., Ernie Money, increased his majority despite sweeping Labour advances across the country.

The other non-Conservative in East Anglia is Clement Freud, cook and journalist, who represents North-east Cambridgeshire, in truth the Fens. Freud, a Liberal, attracts Conservative and Labour votes on the back of his celebrity status. Were he to retire, the Conservatives would fancy their chances of regaining the constituency, which they lost to him in a notorious by-election.

Norfolk has a longer reputation for 'doing different' than other parts of the region. Constituencies in the county have often gone against the national trend, though less so lately now that Conservatives have established their grip in county areas, outside Norwich, where radical agricultural and non-conformists used to tilt the balance in favour of the Liberals and then Labour. Today, the decline in numbers of agricultural workers and of non-conformist political solidarity, together with the growth of home ownership and general prosperity have contributed to the emergence of East Anglia as a Conservative citadel — at least for the moment.

Campaigning methods have altered too. A denizen of the 'old politics' was the widely respected Conservative M.P. for Eye from 1951-79, Colonel Sir Harwood Harrison. A tale is told that during an election campaign a senior U.S. Senator was sent to Eye by Conservative Central Office to learn about British politics. Back home, the Senator's own campaigns were, of course, meticulously arranged by scores of 'advance' men with a view to producing the sort of razamatazz and flesh pressing adored by television news editors. Soon after reaching the Harrison headquarters in Eye, the Senator was bundled into the back of a battered car. The candidate, Colonel Sir Harwood, sat erect and purposeful in front beside the driver. Off they went, conversation limited, concentration absolute. Having negotiated Suffolk lanes for half-an-hour, passing only a handful of voters, the car drew to a dignified halt on a small village green. Colonel Sir Harwood climbed out and proceeded to address an empty green for 15 minutes on the subject of the Polaris missile. During the morning three such village greens received the same speech. As lunchtime approached, Colonel Sir Harwood seemed to relax:

'Going well. Yes, in fact, going very well, don't you agree, Senator'.

'I'm sure', replied the Senator, mustering courtesy. 'But I didn't see the voters'.

'I did', growled Colonel Sir Harwood, 'behind the trees and net curtains. Very shy people, East Anglians. Can't stand the sight of strangers'.

*   *   *   *

The exception to almost every East Anglian political rule, in so far as there are any, has often been Cambridge with its potent mixture of town and gown. Its present M.P. is a distinguished historian, Robert Rhodes James, who also happens to be a Fellow of All Souls, Oxford, and so keeps a foot in both camps.

Cambridge has avoided Oxford's tragedy by not becoming an impersonal city; it is still a county town beside a river on the edge of the Fens, mirroring East Anglia's insularity, caution and privacy and containing some of Europe's finest architecture – King's Chapel and Trinity's Wren Library – so much of which can be glimpsed by merely walking for five minutes down King's Parade or the Backs.

Cambridge's self-confident calm has provided the perfect setting for scientists to pursue their skills, and no city in the world can lay claim to a weightier catalogue of talents – Isaac Newton, J. J. Thompson and Ernest Rutherford, J. D. Cockcroft, the discoverer of the neutron, J. A. Ratcliffe, the radar pioneer and more recently, Alan Turning, the computer scientist.

Yet too often, the research and discoveries of Cambridge scientists have been developed for commercial purposes elsewhere in Britain or more typically overseas. At last, entrepreneurship has come to Cambridge with companies that specialise in computer software, laser scanning and genetic engineering. By the end of 1984 more than 300 'high tech' firms were prospering around Cambridge compared with only 40 some five years earlier. Co-operation between academic researchers and free enterprise, long regarded with patronising disdain, has finally emerged, due in part to the Governmental spur in curbing grants to University-based researchers, and the liberalisation of reactionary planning guidelines. Silicon Fen is small compared with California's Silicon Valley, but its presence symbolises not only an appreciation that Britain's people should profit from its brains, but also a reason why East Anglia is Britain's most go-ahead area in terms of productivity with the lowest incidence of strikes.

*　　*　　*　　*

Cambridge does not preside as East Anglia's regional city, that honour falls rightly to Norwich. Most people, who have never set foot in Norwich, picture it as flat and worthy. Yet it is one of the least flat of all Britain's regional cities. Less flat than York, less flat than Newcastle and less flat than Gloucester. A brisk walk from the railway station to the Trollopian Close at the heart of the city or Mousehold Heath on the inner outskirts suffices to emphasise a point to doubters and the uninformed.

Mediaeval Norwich, with many of its winding streets, alleys and parish churches still intact, was the second or third city of England and only Bristol and perhaps York, competed with it. A lack of coal and fast flowing rivers prevented Norwich from participating fully in the Industrial Revolution, although at the height of the 19th century some 9,000 people were employed in the shoe industry, which exists in leaner shape today, in a city where prosperity has never been far away.

Norwich is a great English city, with one of the finest parish churches in the country, St Peter Mancroft, a provincial museum and art gallery housed in the commanding castle with a Norman keep on its artificial mound.

John Ivory's Octagonal chapel praised by John Wesley as 'the most elegant meeting house in Europe', and the Norwich Union Building designed by the prolific local architect, G. J. Skipper, with its unmatchable marble entrance hall symbolise the city's remarkable self-confidence which, like Cambridge's, is quiet and understated. In fact, the Norwich equivalent of tea at the Ritz ought to be the collection of a clutch of life insurance forms from the marble hall.

Ipswich does not approach the beauty, or status, of Cambridge or Norwich. To some extent, it is overshadowed historically, even within Suffolk, by Bury St Edmunds which was once a centre of greater importance than Ipswich ever reached or aspires to today. The barons met at Bury St Edmunds before facing King John at Runnymede.

To be fair, Ipswich possessed a busy mediaeval port and still contains more parish churches of that period than other English towns of equivalent size. But for two centuries following the death of its favourite son, Cardinal Wolsey, Ipswich failed to expand as quickly as Norwich and so lacks the variety, abundance or quality of its rival's architecture.

A tourist in Tuscany may consider that after a day or two ambling through Florence and Sienna he knows it well. How wrong he would be. It is only by taking in the places in between that Tuscany's diversity can be measured. It is no different with East Anglia, where the uncluttered market towns reveal ingredients of the regional menu such as Diss, Betjeman's favourite, Hingham, a nursery of puritanism, Sudbury, Gainsborough's quarters, Wisbech with its two brinks, one on either side of the river Nene amongst the most perfect Georgian streets in England and Ely, Hereward the Wake's haunt, with a cathedral to rank alongside the finest.

*   *   *   *

When William Cobbett visited the places in between, 150 years ago, he abominated 'progress' and regarded change as an assault on the old order of rural society. Subsequent writers on East Anglia – and none of national renown exist today – have usually agreed. Local people are not earning their crusts from the land worked in 'lethargic disrelation to their surroundings' according to Adrian Bell, a fine anthologist of country life who conquered his own lethergy by compiling *The Times* crossword puzzle for many years. To the Cobbett school, 'growth' and 'gross national product' are inadequate measures of prosperity. They may have a point.

But most led comfortable existences and could offer lofty, romantic observations about the poverty and backwardness of their fellow citizens. Goodness knows what Adrian Bell would have made of East Anglia today?

Their housing is the most modern and housing amenities are the most up to date in Britain. More homes possess central heating, tumble dryers and freezers than anywhere else. East Anglians are the lowest consumers of alcohol and cigarettes and East Anglia enjoys, unsurprisingly, Britain's smallest crime rate. No wonder the region boasts the country's lowest death rate from heart disease, cancer, bronchitis and infant mortality. Yet the utopian life-style must produce its draw-backs, for a few, otherwise East Anglia would not suffer from the highest suicide level. This cannot be attributed to population density – still the scantest in England – but perhaps from torment caused by a reserve and introspection which cannot, it seems, be relieved even by sniffing fresh air or acquiring consumer durables. Alas, a cottage in the heart of the Suffolk countryside did not turn Arthur Koestler into a happier man in his later years, although its land and seascape inspired Benjamin Britten and Imogen Holst and did nothing to impair George Crabbe's dour talent.

*　　*　　*　　*

No town better illustrates change in East Anglia than Felixstowe, once solely a holiday resort, but now a major container terminal, providing thousands of jobs directly and in ancillary industries. Rotterdam and Zeebrugge claim to handle almost as much UK traffic as Felixstowe and yet quaint British Luddites oppose its expansion.

Whereas Felixstowe's success has been furthered by the quality of its road communications with the Midlands and the South, Norfolk's commercial expansion has been hampered by the worst trunk roads in England. Politicians and civil servants in Westminster and Whitehall have long neglected the county, assuming it to be content with insularity and a mere dozen of dual carriageways. Proper road networks are not only a matter of personal convenience but, in Norfolk's case, economic necessity also. British Rail have just lavished more than £100 million in East Anglia, the money would have been better spent on roads.

East Anglia is lucky. It combines the peace and wisdom of rural life with the benefits of material progress. As Bernard Matthews, the region's famous indigenous entrepreneur, proclaims in the vernacular tongue – it is 'bootiful', not on a grand Cotswoldian scale but in a private discreet sense, which only those who know it properly, understand. As to getting to know the people, the act of doing so may take years and years, but the achievement more than repays the toil.

Neil Kinnock

The Rt. Hon. Neil Kinnock was elected Leader of the Labour Party, in succession to Michael Foot, in October 1983. It was not long before his manner of speech and agreeable appearance on television had made him a popular figure in the country. He has represented Bedwelty in South Wales from 1970, two years after being elected to the National Executive Committee of the Party, till 1983, and is now the Member for Islwyn. There is no doubt that he knows very well the people of the mining valleys and of the mountainous countryside of South Wales as well as those of Cardiff and the ports, a part of the country in which less Welsh is spoken and there is less nationalist sentiment than in North Wales, though bi-lingualism is the rule.

Neil Kinnock has been a member of the General Advisory Council of the BBC since 1977 and was the former Chairman of the Welsh Group of the Parliamentary Labour Party. He has long been a member of the Tribune Group. He has been closely associated with two movements of protest, the Anti-Apartheid Movement and the 'Get Britain out of the EEC Campaign' sponsored by the Transport and General Workers Union. He was born in 1942 and educated at Lewis School, Glamorgan and University College, Cardiff.

'Who loves not the land of his birth
Should hide himself in the earth
Who loves not these derelict vales
Is no true son of eternal Wales
Who curses not the vandal's crime
Is the simple pawn of lust and time.
Who learns no lesson from history
Sleeps in the slough of slavery'.

Idris Davies
The Angry Summer; A poem of 1926

There is no real agreement about where South Wales starts and where it stops − Henry VIII was only precise about some things. But most would settle for the Rugby bible belt from Newport, where England really peters out, and along the coast to Llanelli and from Pontypool across the Heads of the Valleys roads to Ammanford where West Wales more or less begins.

South Wales is a lovely rich mixture. Nothing is really as simple and straightforward as it seems. In the valleys, landscaping and tree planting are healing the flesh wounds of earlier generations. But the communities still suffer the internal injuries of closure and redundancy. The Vales of Glamorgan and Neath are sylvan and still a bit snooty in the parts that housing estates and purpose-built factories haven't reached. The coast is a contrast between the surf and gorse of Gower, and the mucky banks of the Severn. The accents vary from the singsong of the valleys to the flat vowels of the port cities, from the round resonance of the Welsh West to the rural burr of the English East.

There is no border of South Wales, no simple emblem. But a mixture of cheeky daffodil, pungent leek and roaring red dragon would do nicely to represent an area that is more of a feeling than a neat region.

*   *   *   *

The essential character of South Wales is a product of nearly 250 years of industrial development and change. Before the 1750s, Wales had a significant cloth industry and even boasted a copper and tinplate industry which accounted for most of the total British production. It was, nevertheless, the Industrial Revolution which shattered the dominant rural character of Wales in the most emphatic way and, in so doing, created modern Wales.

The first phase of the Industrial Revolution was the expansion of the iron industry. Entrepreneurs − mainly English − located and ruthlessly exploited the raw materials which they found in abundance at the 'heads' of the South Wales valleys. The availability of capital coincided with rural crises and thousands upon thousands of Welsh men and women uprooted themselves and their families from north and west Wales to find employment and a higher standard of living in Merthyr Tydfil, the unofficial capital of the new Wales.

From then on, there was no looking back. No sooner had the iron industry transformed South Wales, than its pre-eminence was supplanted by the coal industry. In the middle of the 19th century, the Admiralty recognised and demonstrated the quality of Welsh steam coal, and the navies of other countries soon followed this lead. Now it was the turn of Welsh entrepreneurs to seize the initiative. With speed and aggression, men like David Davies of Llandinam ripped into the heart of South Wales. With no regard for the natural beauty of the valleys and with scant attention to the working conditions of the miners, the coal owners extracted the valleys' wealth. They left behind a legacy of ill-health, bitterness, and slag heaps, many of which continue to stand as monuments to their rapaciousness. It is not by accident that the initials of the coal owners, Powell and Duffryn, came to stand for 'Poverty and Death'.

Throughout the latter half of the 19th century and the first decade of the 20th, the population of Wales grew at a phenomenal rate. From 1871 to 1911, the population of the country leaped from under 1.5 million to just under 2.5 million. And nearly all that growth occurred in the industrial South. Around that time Archie Kinnock of Dundee *via* Bristol was courting Margaret Herbert of Tredegar and William Howells and Sarah Griffiths were arriving in Aberdare from Carmarthenshire. My grandparents, who between them begat 11 live children out of 16 confinements, were only four of the many thousands who poured in.

At first it was the Welsh themselves who moved into the region, then the immigrants increasingly came from England and even more exotic ends of the Earth.

The result was the creation of a bustling cosmopolitan society. Alongside the rural Welsh came thousands of Irish, often establishing large communities in towns like Merthyr and Maesteg, hundreds of Spaniards who came to Dowlais, as well as Portuguese, French, Belgians and Italians who scattered themselves all over the coalfield. In the ports of the region, the racial mix was even more pronounced. Edwardian Cardiff was especially cosmopolitan. London, with the beginnings of the African and Arabic communities alongside the Latin peoples who came to search for fortune, was the only other city of the time with a larger proportion of its population that had been born outside Britain.

The most significant feature (which eventually determined the overall character of South Wales) was the way in which the number of non-Welsh arrivals in the coalfield gradually outstripped the Welsh migrants. Initially, by concentrating so many Welsh speakers in the South, industrialisation went some way towards preserving the Welsh language and until the turn of the 20th century the rate of non-Welsh migration was at a level which allowed the Welsh language to maintain its linguistic dominance. But at the end of the 19th century the balance began to slip in the other direction.

Bert Coombes, an Englishman who came to South Wales to work in the coal mines, described vividly in his autobiography *The Poor Hands* (1939), just how diverse was the speech of the people of South Wales:

'What a mixture of languages and dialects were there sometimes!. Yorkshire and Durham men, Londoners, men from the Forest of Dean, North Welshmen — whose language is much deeper and more pure than the others from South Wales — two Australians, four Frenchmen, and several coloured gentlemen'.

In such a situation it was sadly inevitable that English would emerge as the dominant tongue. English, as Bert Coombes explained, had to be used in miner's lodge meetings:

'because most of the Welshmen could express themselves to some extent in English, while the majority of the English maintained a frightened silence whenever Welsh was spoken'.

The bi-lingual generosity built solidarity. It did the opposite for the Welsh language. And that eventually inflicted as much damage on the language as did the attacks of bureaucratic ignoramuses and prissy anglophile pedagogues.

The working-class communities which sprang up in the South Wales valleys dictated the atmosphere and tone of the entire region. To this day, despite all the mid-Atlantic influences and the exodus of 3 or 4 young generations, their resilience is remarkable. The catalysts for their formation were industrialisation and demographic upheaval, both of which continued of course, to exert a large influence over their subsequent development. But other factors too have helped to shape the unique working-class culture of the region.

One of the most important of these elements is the tradition of Religious non-conformity. South Wales was never as pious as the chapel and choir image suggests. But undoubtedly non-conformity, and its associated social values, were at the heart of Welsh society during the latter half of the 19th century. Chapels, whether Calvinistic, Baptist or Independent, were the fulcrums of community life in both rural and industrial Wales. And therein lay their importance; the Chapels were institutions which gave Wales — all Wales — a measure of cultural and political unity and provided rehearsal and performing facilities for music and poetry, philosophy and politics. The cement for that unity was the Welsh language and Liberalism.

However, in the first decade or so of this century, when the language was going into decline, the Liberalism of Lloyd George began to give way to the Socialism of Keir Hardie. Men and women increasingly became disillusioned with the 'other-worldly' approach of some of the denominations and sought their answers instead in the Labour

Movement. In the valleys of South Wales, that Movement was virtually synonymous with the mighty 'Fed' — the South Wales Miners' Federation.

But the divide between the old and the new was never clear cut. Many of the values and traditions of non-conformity continued to influence the Labour Movement and the whole of South Walian society, even though congregations diminished in size as the years went by.

* * * *

The South Wales choral tradition is a case in point of that less than obvious break. In the valleys, choral music was nurtured by, and developed alongside religious non-conformity. The best known Welsh composer of the 19th century was Joseph Parry of Merthyr Tydfil, who went on to become the first Professor of Music at the College of Aberystwyth. He achieved fame, if not fortune, through hymns such as *Aberystwyth* and *Duw A'n Gwnaeth* which became two of the staples for *Cymanfau Ganu* (singing festivals). From the middle of the 19th century these festivals became important musical occasions, and even today they are still a regular feature of chapel life in South Wales. To attend one, or better still, to participate in a Cymanfa is a heady experience. Some would say that the Temperance crusades that swept across South Wales owed much of their success to the superior intoxication of the Cymanfau.

To know your part. To whisper and roar, to drone and soar with others of your kind and *against* others in different parts conflicting in a sweet chord. To feel resonance coming from the collision of voices. To follow the raised eyebrow or the clenched fist or the pursed lips of the conductor as if he were breathing for you. That is to be in a choir in a Cymanfa Ganu.

The Welsh choral tradition is not confined to the composition and singing of hymns. The large choral societies have few qualms about tackling some of the most demanding works in the choral repertoire: Verdi's *Requiem*, Dvorak's *Stabat Mater*, Walton's *Belshazzar's Feast*, Handel's Oratorios — particularly *Messiah* and *Judas Maccabaeus* — are Christmas and Easter conquests.

And contests too — an oratoria audience composed largely of the members of another choir is a terrifying prospect, especially when their lips move with the words and their eyes flash messages of patronising promise or acid criticism or — even worst of all — supercilious toleration. And if that weren't enough there is — in chapel performances — the eerie anticlimax of smashing out a wall-bending 'Amen' following ceiling cracking 'Alleluliahs' and then being greeted by ....silence.

Crinkling sweet papers, coughing and shushing children are allowed in chapel. Smiling and weeping — *quiet* weeping, not sobbing or wailing — are allowed in chapel. Clapping isn't — not for anything other than very special occasions anyway, and that's newfangled.

Applause is allowed for male voice choirs, of course. And there is plenty to applaud. For me the *Cor Meibion*, the Orpheus — even groups of twenty or so who call themselves songsters or Glee Parties and fit nicely on small club and Institute stages for the beer and bus hire — are a delight. There is a pecking order through the National Eisteddford winners and Investiture performers, to the album recorders and the foreign tour makers, to the scrubbed and blazered boy's night outers. The repertoire does not have such variation.

Everyone will have *Tannhauser* (the Pilgrims Chorus), *Nabucco* (the Slaves Chorus), *Il Trovatore* (the Anvil Chorus), a list of immemorial Welsh hymns that have been heard more times than *White Christmas*, and a few Lehar and Offenbach frothies to finish off the first half of any concert. To all of that the big battalion choirs will add complicated and demanding new arrangements and composers whose names all sound — in the words of a near and dear chorister — 'like bloody lagers'. And the medium sized and mini bus choirs will have John Denver, Neil Diamond, Lennon-McCartney and Rice-Lloyd Webber. They all sing when they come off stage too. Where else would Buddy Holly follow the *Pearl Fishers* or the *Gendarmes Duet* come after Police — with wives adding voices — in the bar or the bus. Or the aeroplane too. After a bumpy ride to Berlin a Rhondda choir was heard in full Pratt-and-Witney-drowning four-part harmony to sing 'For he's a Jolly Good Pilot' and a version of 'We'll Take Good Care of You — Fly The Flag' that would have graced La Scala, Milan.

The biggest male voice choir meets, of course, at the National Stadium in Cardiff on International Day. Gwyn Thomas, the Rabelais of the Rhondda and Baudelaire of Barry, recommended anyone with that 'over forty' feeling to stand in a capacity crowd when one of the great hymns was being sung:

> 'The sadder the hymns the better, because that allows the boys to dig deep for their harmonies. It is typical of us that if the hospitality is lavish, we are often married and buried to the rhythm of the same superb graveside chants. At the Arms Park it is like being caught up in some mightily natural force; it gives you a taste of what it must have been like to be caught up in the fierce, hypnotic frenzies of tribalism'.

It is no coincidence that on occasions hymn singing and rugby football should so easily come together; both have their roots deep in the same society. One of the most remarkable features of modern Welsh history is the way a public school amateur game came from Oxbridge curates to South Wales and was commandeered by the South Walian working class. From a game which was controlled, administered and played by the middle-class, rugby was transformed into a peoples' game by the people themselves.

Rugby — never 'rugger' in South Wales — has a life-style and a life-force all of its own. It is the focus of passion and politics in the hundreds of clubs and communities. The playing ground can be the stylish Stadium of Cardiff RFC or the neat mid-valley municipal pitches now spreading to replace the corrugated-iron, cold-dribble-shower, flat-slab-cut-out-of-the-side-of-the-mountain platforms where the half-backs perfect their game side-stepping sheep. None of that matters much. The game has the same thrills and anger, the same ponderous committee cabbalas, the same sages and stars, local heroes and galactic giants of the game.

*   *   *   *

If South Wales experienced a heyday, it was in the Edwardian Age, before the First World War. This was when the coal industry was booming, the ports were expanding and people were flooding into the valleys. It was when the coalowners and union militants shared a confidence and optimism; the former because of the size of their profits, and the latter because of their faith in 'syndicalism' as the means of emancipation. After the First World War, however, it all turned sour. With the onset of the post-war depression, the brittle, coal-dependent South Wales economy collapsed. The heady days of expansion gave way to catastrophic decline. Colliery after colliery was closed, sending unemployment in Wales up to 23.3 Percent in 1927, 27.2 Percent in 1930, and even touching 32 Percent before levelling off in the mid 1930s. In some mining communities unemployment was as high as 70 Percent or more.

Inevitably, long-term unemployment on such a scale led to widespread misery and hardship. For South Wales this was not exceptional. In response to their plight, the people of the valleys reacted in a variety of ways. Some simply left for the Midlands or the South East of England in search of jobs. Others stayed and fought, and participated in the famous Hunger Marches and committed themselves to the National Unemployed Workers' Movement which vigorously opposed the hated 'Means Test', the low level of Relief and the government 'training camps' which my father was made to attend on pain of losing his dole. He learned furniture stuffing — and then got back to the pits as soon as the prospect of war brought the hiring days again.

The severity of the depression meant that the very fabric of South Walian society was seriously eroded. Nevertheless, the vitality of South Wales was apparent not only in the scale of extra-Parliamentary opposition to governmental oppression or indifference, it was also visible in the culture of the valleys. Choral societies and brass bands continued to perform, literary and debating societies continued to discuss the issues of the day, the working -class educational tradition continued through the contrasting approaches of the NCLC and the WEA, and the Miners' Institutes, despite constant financial pressures, maintained their role as the focal points for valley communities. Indeed, it was during the periods of the most acute adversity that the vitality of the culture was most apparent. During the six month lock-out of 1926 we have one of the clearest examples of this. Throughout the long, hot summer of that year a proliferation of jazz and comic bands complemented the mass participation in the more traditional cultural activities, thereby reinforcing the communities' solidarity.

*   *   *   *

Importantly too, the 1930s saw the emergence of a number of South Walian working-class writers who expressed themselves through the English language. Frequently labelled as 'Anglo-Welsh' these writers were, in fact, as 'Welsh' as anyone in Wales. As they wrote in the majority tongue, it could even be argued that they were more Welsh, certainly more representative of Welsh working people than those Welsh speakers who formed the cultural establishment.

Two of these writers who stand out are Gwyn Thomas and the poet Idris Davies. Their brilliance lay in their understanding of the ins and outs of South Wales, and their ability to describe, explain and sometimes criticise the nuances of coalfield society. Gwyn Thomas, through his novels, short stories, plays, radio broadcasts and television appearances presented a running social commentary on South Wales until his death in 1981. Although his lacerating humour, perceptiveness, and satire aggravated many an exposed Welsh nerve, his colourful prose and effulgent speech were, in many ways, typically Welsh.

Idris Davies was equally in tune with his native South Wales. Born in Rhymney, he worked as a miner, then qualified as a teacher in England before returning to South Wales in later life. One of Davies' most powerful works is a collection of 36 short poems dealing with developments in the valleys between the two World Wars. In one of these short poems, he sums up, with his characteristic verse, the defiance and passion of 1926:

'Do you remember 1926? That summer of soups and
speeches
The sunlight on the idle wheels and the deserted
crossings,
And the laughter and the cursing in the moonlit
streets?
Do you remember 1926? The slogans and the penny
concerts,
The jazz bands and the moorland picnics,
And the slanderous tongues of famous cities?
Do you remember 1926? the great dream and the
swift disaster,
The fanatic and the traitor, and more than all,
The bravery of the simple, faithful folk?
'Ay, ay, we remember 1926' said Dai and Shimkin,
As they stood on the kerb in Charing Cross Road,
'And we shall remember 1926 until our blood is
dry".

*   *   *   *

If the poetry and writing of Idris Davies and Gwyn Thomas reflected the idealism and protest of South Wales in the 1930s, it was Aneurin Bevan, more than anyone else, who succeeded in giving political expression, coherence and direction to the people's aspirations. Born into a Welsh family in Tredegar in 1897, Bevan emerged as the most outstanding representative of a generation of working-class leaders who made South Wales pulsate with political fervour and optimism in the face of economic decline and poverty. As a young man, Bevan gained his knowledge from reading the classic socialist texts in the Tredegar Workingmen's Library and Central Labour College; but he also learnt through the struggles of his own people. Whether it was opposition to the Means Test, fascism, unemployment or company unionism, Bevan was to the fore. Not for him the posturing sectarianism of the far left or polite parliamentary politics.

Bevan's message was clear and powerful; the objective of political activity is individual liberty — political industrial and international collective action is the means of securing that and it could only be satisfactorily achieved through Parliament and with popular consent. Equally, it could not be simply handed down by Members of Parliament; it had to be promoted, argued and struggled for by the working people themselves. This was, and is still the essence of Democratic Socialism.

Aneurin Bevan's strength lay in the fact that his creed was rooted in, and drawn from, the collective experience of the people with whom he lived and later represented. Bevan understood that Democratic Socialism would achieve little unless there existed an intimate relationship between leaders and led. In his book *In Place of Fear* published in 1952, Bevan explained what the precise nature of this relationship should be:

> 'The first function of a political leader is advocacy. It is he who must make articulate the wants, the frustration, and the aspiration of the masses. Their hearts must be moved by his words, and so his words must be attuned to their realities ....a representative person is one who will act in a given situation in much the same way as those he represents would act in that same situation. In short, he must be of their kind ....he need not share their vernacular but he should share their values; that is, be in touch with their realities'.

Bevan himself was eloquent testimony to the effectiveness of such an organic unity. There has been no other politician who has been so in touch with the realities of working-class life. Most of Bevan's formative years were spent in Tredegar, and throughout his life he always maintained a close identification with South Wales. It was because of his background that Aneurin Bevan rejected so firmly the Welsh Nationalism of some of his contemporaries in favour of an outlook which was the very antithesis of parochialism. At no time did Nye feel restricted by imposed horizons; his vision was always extended beyond Offa's Dyke into the rest of Britain and the wider world.

For Bevan there was no contradiction in being a Welshman and an Internationalist; in being intensely proud of a local community and adhering to a cosmopolitan perspective. This was why he was able to utilise his experiences at a local level when he was thrust onto the national, British stage. As Minister of Health in 1945, much of the inspiration and many of the ideas for his blue-print for the future National Health Service came from the Medical Aid schemes in South Wales, which the miners had organised and financed for themselves.

Above Tredegar, on the wind-swept mountain known as Waunpound, there stands a memorial to Bevan. The words on that memorial accurately declare that Aneurin Bevan 'spoke to the world' from that point in South Wales.

* * * *

Today, the message and example of Aneurin Bevan is more relevant to

South Wales than ever before. What is happening to Wales in the 1980s is a replay of what happened in the 1930s. As a direct consequence of the combination of government policies and careless economic system, South Wales is bleeding to death. The optimism of the late 1940s and 1950s, and the sense of hope which continued into the 1970s is being bludgeoned by economic collapse and social deprivation. The 'psychoses of poverty and dread' which mutilated Gwyn Thomas' Rhondda in the 1930s have returned with a vengeance.

After 1945, South Wales benefitted enormously from the interventionist industrial policies which were pioneered by Clem Attlee's Labour government. Industrial estates were opened, the ports prospered, and new nationalised industries brought stability, and the giant steel works at Port Talbot and later Llanwern served as the flag ships of sustained prosperity.

However, by the mid-1960s, it was clear that the confidence had been misplaced. The coal industry in particular, fell foul to the new conventional wisdom that coal had had its day as a major energy source and was destined to be replaced by oil.

The acceptance of this view had devastating consequences for South Wales. In the twenty years after 1958, some 104 collieries were closed and manpower was reduced by over 64,000. By 1984, there were barely 20,000 miners in South Wales.

During the 1960s and 1970s, many miners found employment outside the coal industry; for example in the steel and motor industries, or in the new light industries which were locating in the region because of government incentives. Others were transferred to different collieries and some took redundancy payments. For individual miners and their families, the dislocation of these years was traumatic. But the wholesale closure of collieries also had a profound impact on entire mining communities throughout the valleys. In so many villages when the local pit was closed, it was as if the heart of the community had been removed. Dozen upon dozen of local Miners' Institutes either closed completely or were converted into bingo halls. As miners, like most other people, became drawn by the magnet of television, the magnificent collections of books in the Library Institutes were sold for a pittance to profiteering, second-hand book merchants.

Nor were the Institutes the only valley institutions which suffered in these years. Literally hundreds of non-conformist chapels closed their doors for the last time, some to later re-open in the form of mammon's minor temples as warehouses or tyre markets.

Over the past six years the crisis with which South Wales has been grappling for two decades has become crushing. There has been a reduction in the labour force in virtually every sector of the region's economy. In many valley communities, unemployment is well over 20 per cent, and in Wales as a whole over 40 per cent of the 185,000 plus who are unemployed have been without a job for a year or more.

Should the NCB and the government decide to close all but a few of the coalfield's remaining collieries, as has been suggested, it is probable that South Wales will lose a total of 40,000 jobs in coal and its related industries and services. This would mean a male unemployment rate of over 50 per cent in some valley communities.

The social consequences of such a closure programme would be horrific. Already, because of unemployment, South Wales is experiencing increases in physical and mental illnesses, more suicides, and greater domestic tensions leading to the break-up of families, and domestic violence. Nowhere are social problems more acute than in the County of Mid-Glamorgan. Without doubt, this is one of the most deprived areas in Europe. It is the Welsh county with the highest population and yet the lowest rateable value. Life expectancy in the county's valley communities is much lower than in other parts of the country. Hospital waiting lists are the longest in Wales. The level of wages and the number of car owners are far below the national average. Moreover, the quality of housing and the housing amenities can only be described as appalling. In the Rhondda, for instance, 24.8 per cent of pensioners houses do not have a bath and over 30 per cent do not have an inside toilet. Here, as in the other valleys, the houses are owner-occupied. In row upon row, as their owners grow older and the buildings deteriorate, South Wales is getting Britain's first own-your-own slum.

Mid-Glamorgan, like other parts of South Wales, needs an urgent financial blood transfusion if it is to survive socially.

*　　*　　*　　*

Yet, despite everything, South Wales continues to hold its corner. Even with an insecure economic base the housing renovation goes on, the local councils fight ferociously − and with increasing acumen − for British and international companies to settle in South Wales. The sons and daughters of Japanese managers and technicians are the latest newcomers to be 'Taffyised' at the Comprehensive Schools. South Wales seven centres of Higher Education thrive even in the bitter climate of cuts. Its culture grows back like the grass over wasteland. And the collective determination of the people of South Wales remains a potent force.

The Miners' Strike of 1984/85 gave evidence of that. Throughout the whole of the dispute, the widespread and sustained support for the miners surprised everyone who does not know South Wales. The response was not the product of sophisticated planning well beforehand, neither was it a spasm of sympathy. It was the willing, tangible, collective reaction of a society which understands that the nature of the threat with which it is confronted requires concerted opposition.

The spirit and the system of South Wales will not die, because the people of South Wales will not let it die. The lessons of history are being learnt and the unquenchable resilience of its people will ensure that the 'sloughs of slavery' will be avoided. Throughout South Wales, there is a growing determination that the future shall be greater than the present or past.

BRISTOL AND AVON
Michael Colvin

Michael Colvin, now Member for the Hampshire constituency of Romsey and Waterside, was one of the Bristol Members — for Bristol North-West for four years 1978-83. But it is clear from his colourful account of this city of the Merchant Venturers that he is steeped in its past as well as in its present civic and economic life. What he has to say about Bath and various Gloucestershire and Somerset towns and villages, now absorbed in the unloved administrative novelty of Avon, (as well as his own Hampshire background, he was a member of the Andover Council from 1965-78 and then for two years of the Test Valley Council) make him a particularly well-qualified interpreter of the West Country. He was, in fact, Secretary of the West Country M.P.s for two years.

Michael Colvin is an Etonian who went to Sandhurst and later studied at the Royal Agricultural College at Cirencester. He is a man of many interests, among which aviation ranks high. He is the Chairman of Conservative Back-Bench Committees both on aviation and on Smaller Businesses. He has been Parliamentary Private Secretary to Ministers of State at the Foreign and Commonwealth Office since 1983.

My view of Avon, Bristol and Bath and the countryside around is primarily the fault of a wild Welshman. In 1973, driving me, a Hampshire born man, across the hills of Montgomery to look at forestry, he tipped us both over a precipice. The 300 feet drop broke a lot of bones, including my back in three places. The doctors said if they shook me I'd rattle.

Lying black and blue in Aberystwyth Hospital, I read a biography of Ian Macleod and decided that I also wanted to be a Member of Parliament. Eventually, after the Tories had been beaten in Bristol North West by 633 votes and urgently wanted a new candidate, I became a Bristolian by selection, adoption and, eventually, by election in 1979.

*   *   *   *

Bristol's story may span a thousand years, but Bath is more than twice as old. The threads of their history weave a tapestry in clashing colours, so no view of the area can avoid a strong historic perspective of the two neighbouring cities.

The area I view has little common identity, other than a desire to be different from your neighbours. Contrasts are sharp, and none more stark than those between Bristol and Bath.

Both cities stand astride the River Avon, surrounded by an immensely varied landscape.

To the west is the Severn Estuary with its forty-five feet tides. Move clockwise over the marsh and mudflats of the Vale of Berkley on to the southern Cotswolds. Then over the east-west communications axis of the M4 motorway, the Kennet and Avon Canal and Brunel's GWR railway, which bisects the area that is now the county of Avon — and used to be the dividing line between the counties of Gloucestershire and Somerset — into the Vale of Malmesbury. Climb west onto the Mendip Hills and finally descend to the Severn again at Weston-super-Mare, Bristol's seaside resort.

*   *   *   *

Travelling to Bristol today, for me, is motorway all the way. The M4 and then M5 to Avonmouth, or M32 to the city centre. Bath is still a cross-country journey over the Wiltshire Downs, past Waylands Smithy — and prehistoric Avebury, rival to Stonehenge; on through Devizes, wealthy in its cloth-making days, now a market town, and then the plunge down the steep decline to the fertile and sheltered Vale of Malmesbury, where the fields are never brown and the springs never dry. The country is absolutely different from the open cornfields of the Downs and Cotswolds. A world which seems to be constructed on a smaller and more luxurious scale. A rich mass of grass and the skeletal remains of the noble elm trees which once graced this land, ravaged by the Dutch Elm disease of the 1960s and 1970s.

Following the Kennet and Avon Canal, now being restored by General Sir Hugh Stockwell and his voluntary helpers, I reach Bradford-on-Avon, a sort of appetiser for nearby Bath. Compact, ancient and harmonious stone buildings, the most famous of which is also the smallest — the Bridge Chapel.

Travel north-west and you come to Calne, once famous for its pork pies, sausages and bacon. Then west again, to Chippenham and Castle Coombe — proclaimed the prettiest village in Britain which, in spite of being the setting for the *Doctor Dolittle* film, has withstood the tourist invasion.

You must cross the M4 motorway and touch the Southwolds, as the southern tip of the Cotswolds is called, to reach real olympian country with three Royal Homes — those of the Prince of Wales, Princess Anne and Prince Michael of Kent. And there are the great houses too like Dyrham, Doddington and Badminton, the home of the Dukes of Beaufort. The tenth Duke, who died in 1984, was 'Master' to his friends — and even his wife. He founded the Three Day Event at Badminton. First held in 1949 to improve our equestrian standards after the 1948 Olympic Games, it has grown into the most celebrated equestrian event in Britain.

Just north of Badminton, on the Tetbury road, lies the Westonbirt Arboretum, a 500-acre park run by the Forestry Commission, which contains one of the finest collections of temperate shrubs and trees in the world. There are some 17 miles of woodland paths to walk if you are feeling energetic.

A minor road opposite Westonbirt leads to Malmesbury with its partly ruined 12th century abbey church.

Half-way between the two is the Roman road called the Fosse Way, which once linked Bath with Ilchester to the south, and to the north, Cirencester, the capital of the Cotswolds — Corinium, as the Romans called it when it was the second largest town in Britain.

And so to Bath. Along country lanes, sometimes through their straightness betraying a Roman ancestry, but more often giving way to the wiggly convenience of generations of farmers; through places with names such as Upper Fosse Farm, Fosse Lodge, Fosse Gate, to Three Shire Stones where Gloucestershire, Somerset and Wiltshire used to meet on the west side of the beautiful St Catherine's Valley called ' incomparable' by Arthur Mee. Then down over Banner Down and the Mount, to join the A4 Bath road for the last couple of miles into the city.

*   *   *   *

I have been visiting Bath for years — always for pleasure — but that was why the city was built.

According to legend, it was King Lear's father, Bladud, who discovered the hot mineral springs and built the earliest Bath there in 863 BC.

Nearly a thousand years later, the Romans were as taken by the hot springs as Bladud. They called the place Aquae Sulis. Graced by beautiful temples, a forum and the system of baths, lined with lead from the nearby Mendip Hills, the place was transformed into a leading spa.

Bath with its Benedictine abbey became a monastery town and was granted a Charter in 1189. It became a pretty lively place, if Chaucer's Wyf of Bathe is anyone to go by. She excelled as a clothmaker, which was the city's chief industry, with Bath 'beaver' famous throughout England.

Bath's reputation as a spa grew slowly until by the start of the 18th century the city was a sink of iniquity, with charlatans and footpads milking her distinguished visitors of every penny they had. Then, in 1705, Richard 'Beau' Nash arrived as Assistant to the Master of Ceremonies. This latter gentleman met an untimely end in a duel over a card game, leaving Beau Nash in charge. He then transformed Bath into a social Mecca, and the father and son team of John and John Wood, architects of exceptional vision and skill, built houses for the fashionable – the Royal Crescent, Queen's Square, the Circus – and the Assembly Rooms and Parades.

Bath went up-market. Style and fashion were everything, yet city society became quaintly egalitarian, with aristocrats mixing with trade, their dress and conduct decreed by Nash – the undisputed King of Bath – until gambling was banned in 1745, thus depriving him of his livelihood. But not before Nash had organised the daily routine of self-indulgence for visitors to Bath.

Charles Dibdin writing in 1797 said: 'At Bath everything is superficial – At Bristol everything is grave. In Bath they live in fine houses and are poor – in Bristol in shabby ones and are rich. At careless Bath nothing is thought of but the present moment – at provident Bristol no step is taken but with a view to the advance of prosperity'.

In the Regency days, Brighton overtook Bath as the fashionable resort, and the city took on a more genteel character. The glamour and the glory was replaced by preaching and praying. Bath had become a place to which one should retire. Dr Oliver prospered with his biscuits, the antidote to rich foods.

Today, this Regency treasure attracts visitors from world wide. But besides its beauty and history, the Theatre Royal (built in 1805 the year of Trafalgar) and Music Festival, Bath has moved with the times. It has a University and shares a Diocesan Bishop with Wells. Baynton still binds the best books, and Sally Lunn's house, the oldest in Bath, is a must for tea. Bath is home for 80,000 people. They are locked in by nature's green hills and man's green belt, so urgent decisions need to be taken now on how, and where, Bath is to expand, bearing in mind the late Poet Laureate, John Betjeman's lines:

'Goodbye to old Bath! We who loved you are sorry they're carting you off by developers' lorry.'

There are contrasts which cause concern between the city centre with its Georgian affluence, and the less well off suburbs with their housing and transportation problems. Three quarters of jobs in Bath are in the service industries, half of these in the public sector – and only a handful in manufacturing, but the greenish tinged waters at a constant temperature of 49 degrees Centigrade constantly flow from the springs at the rate of half-a-million gallons a day, and continue to be good for rheumatism, gout, nervous disorders — and tourism.

*   *   *   *

A tourist visiting Bath — and there are many of them — contemplating a day out, would consider anything but Bristol.

They would rather go south through rusting Radstock with its disused mills, mines and Roman remains. And maybe even down the road to where the road signs say 'Beware of Lions' to see Longleat, home of the Marquis of Bath. Longleat House is one of England's most stately homes, preserved through the commercial sense of its owner. There you can soak up the ambience of early Renaissance architecture and treasures which include a Titian, letters from Queen Elizabeth I, a First Folio Shakespeare and a collection of Hitler memorabilia - and of course the Capability Brown landscape, now enlivened with roaring lions and thieving monkeys of the Safari Park.

I would then drive on to Shepton Mallet with a nostalgic glance at Warminster, where in the 1950s I spent many a cold night under military canvas fighting imaginary Red Armies.

On past Shepton Mallet lies Glastonbury, wreathed around with romantic legends. One is that it is the place to which St Joseph of Arimathea brought the legendary 'Holy Grail' — the chalice used at the Last Supper. Glastonbury is said to be the Avalon of Arthurian legend, and King Arthur and Queen Guinevere, whose remains were supposedly discovered nearby, were reburied in the presence of King Edward I in front of the High Altar in the Abbey — now a ruin.

The 525 feet Glastonbury Tor, crowned by a 14th century tower, overlooks the town. From there one can see Wells, one of England's smallest Cathedral cities and a mediaeval gem, in spite of the damage inflicted by the Puritans. In the moat around the Bishop's Palace the swans ring bells to announce their own mealtimes.

Close by Wells is Wookey Hole, the oldest known cave-dwelling in Britain, and the spectacular source of the River Axe which gushes from the Mendip Hills by way of the caves.

Climb north-west to Priddy and on to Cheddar, original home of the famous cheese, and put your car into low gear as you dive down the two mile long Cheddar Gorge, with huge limestone cliffs soaring 400 feet above you. Wind on westwards to Sedgemoor, the site of the last battle to be fought on English soil, and to Winsford, an Exmoor picture-book village, birthplace of Ernest Bevin — of whom more later. Drive north across the soggy, flat, green landscape with its rhyne (pronounced 'reen') ditches to Weston-super-Mare and Clevedon next door. This is Bristol's seaside, with the only stretch of sand in Avon

* * * *

In Roman times there was little west of Bath but the sea. The Romans journeyed further for two reasons only — to subdue the south-west and as traders who went nearer the Avon Estuary to its junction with the River Trym in order to establish a port at Seamills (Abona).

The Bristol area has given us a wealth of prehistoric material, but enough is known to establish the fact that during the Bronze and Iron Ages the site of the city was uninhabited. There was nothing there for the Romans to subdue and Bristol stands, like Rome, on seven hills, with the River Avon as her Tiber.

Anglo Saxon Briggstowe (the 'L' was added by the unique and dreadful 'Bristle' accent) or 'the Place of Assembly by the Bridge' near the confluence of the Avon with the River Frome from the north, grew into a town of importance. By the Middle Ages, its geographical advantages, exploited by the trading enterprise of its citizens, enabled it to outstrip its rival seaports long before the discovery of the New World opened up fresh horizons. It was already the key to the West Country and trade with Ireland; it boasted 2,300 inhabitants when mentioned in the Domesday Book.

Bristol received its Great Charter from Prince John in 1188, which freed the merchants of the borough and its suburbs from burdensome external control, and is regarded as the foundation stone of Bristol's liberties. This preferential treatment to which Bristolians became accustomed may explain their traditional disdain for the authority of Westminster. It was no doubt with his constituents in mind that Edmund Burke, when a Member of Parliament for Bristol said:

'To complain of the age we live in, to murmur at the present possessors of power, to lament the past, to conceive extravagant hopes for the future, are the common dispositions of the greatest part of mankind'

Bristolians do not like outside interference. In 1312 they staged their 'Great Rebellion' to resist the authority of Edward II's Constable and his alliance with 'the Fourteen', the oligarchy which ruled the city. Building walls to protect themselves from the garrison of the Norman castle (destroyed after the Civil War), Bristolians cut off its supplies and declared Bristol a Free State, only capitulating two years later when attacked by the King's forces by land and by sea.

This was no ordinary city: 'Leave us alone to get rich in peace' could have been its motto. In 1373 Bristol became a county in its own right, the first provincial town to achieve this status, having bought it from the financially pressed Edward III. Its boundaries stretched right out to the Flat and Steepholm Islands in the Severn Estuary (incongruously part of my constituency and the favoured tidal power line for the Severn Barrage, yet to be built after half-a-century of indecision). Bristolians were exempted from the control of the Gloucester and Somerset County Courts and their Sheriffs.

Although this 'Great Charter of Liberties' gave defined powers to the Common Council of the City, an elective body of forty, who were intended to act as Councillors to the Mayors, real power and patronage lay in the hands of the merchants' families – Mayors, Aldermen and later, the two Burgesses to be elected as Members of Parliament were chosen from, and by, this oligarchy.

This City Council status – an autonomous Council, or unitary authority, which could have been the prototype for the single tier of local government recommended by a Royal Commission for the rest of the U.K. in 1970 – was superseded after 600 years, in 1974, by the County of Avon, an abomination which cannot even boast a Cricket Club (W.G. Grace must have turned in his grave!) but which fitted the Westminster view of local government conformity.

Wealth is power and power brings with it responsibility. William Canynges, born in 1400, was a member of a wealthy family of merchants and cloth manufacturers who began the long tradition of Bristol philanthropy, inspired maybe as much by conscience brought on by the sinful sources of their wealth – drink, slaves and tobacco – as by pride in their city. Bristol merchants stayed put and ploughed their wealth back into Bristol, rather than taking themselves and their fortunes out of the city. Five times Mayor and twice Member of Parliament, Canynges' fleet of ten ships was the biggest in the land. He rebuilt St Mary Redcliffe Church, described by Queen Elizabeth I as 'the fairest, nobliest and goodliest parish church in all my Kingdom'. (She also said of the Bristol ladies: 'I never saw so ugly a collection of women as your city can assemble' – not a quote often used in Bristol!).

The tall ship which rides proudly on the seals and coat of arms of Bristol illustrates the city's successful commercial activity. Its trade across the Atlantic to Madeira, Iceland and then Greenland led, inevitably, to the link with North America.

In 1450, a remarkable venture launched from Bristol in search of the 'Isle of Brasylle', thought to lie to the west, ended in failure after two months' search in the Atlantic. But the die was cast and, inspired by this venture, Bristol merchants financed John Cabot's momentous voyage in 1497. This led to his discovery of the northern shores of the American continent, 'Land Newly Found'. He named it after local Bristol merchant, Richard Ameryke. (Supporters of Amerigo Vespucci may need to think again). It was not the expected Cathay – no silks or spices – just more fish and virgin land.

It was this pathfinding to new markets along the Atlantic coast of western Europe and North America which reinforced the foundation of Bristol's prosperity. In the 16th century Bristol became a Bishopric – suffragan to Bath and Wells – and was granted the golden unicorn supporters for their coat-of-arms and which now stand sentinel at each end of the new City House. In 1552 the Society of Merchant Venturers first obtained a Royal Charter giving it the right to exclude non-members from overseas trade, but this was a century in which the Merchant Venturers' main concern was to consolidate their existing monopoly rather than to venture further. Not for them the risky freebooting expeditions of the Elizabethan age. Three ships and a pinnace were all that sailed under Drake against the Spanish Armada.

The Bristolian venturing spirit of Captain James – of James Bay and Hudson Bay – also led to John Guy, a Bristol merchant, establishing the first settlement on the Avalon Peninsula. The name of Bristol appearing frequently on American maps is evidence of links with those colonies' mother city, and St Mary Redcliffe Church houses the memorial and armour of the most distinguished Bristolian of his age, Admiral Sir William Penn, who captured Jamaica for England in 1665 and whose Quaker son, William, founded Pennsylvania.

Then, twenty-five years after the Restoration, had Monmouth captured Bristol as a base, the wealth of the city might have launched his rebellion – and our nation – on a very different course.

*   *   *   *

Described by Daniel Defoe as the 'greatest, the richest, and the best port of trade in Great Britain, London only excepted ...' Bristol was not only an oceanic gateway, it also provided the commercial hub of the West Country with a thriving inland trade. Imports boomed and the city expanded fast. The population had doubled in the course of the 17th century to nearly 70,000 (still only one-tenth of London) and though commerce was still king, the city was beginning to establish manufacturing industries based on its trade. New sugar houses sprang up to handle increasing imports from the West Indies. Glass and printing were added to tobacco and pipe manufacture.

As a contemporary observer commented 'even the very clergy talk of nothing but trade and how to turn the penny' and they paid 'on the nail' literally. In Corn Street there still stands a row of bronze tables or 'nails' outside the Exchange, where farmers and merchants used to deal in corn − hence the expression

You can still turn the clock back to those days by having a drink in the Llandoger Trow pub on the city dockside, an inn immortalised by Robert Louis Stevenson as the haunt of Long John Silver and his parrot in *Treasure Island*

Bristol marked the start of the 18th century by obtaining an Act of Parliament to levy a 'Rate' to cover the cost of cleaning, paving and lighting her streets, because householders failed to do so, although it was a hundred years before John McAdam became the city's first General Surveyor and did the job properly by 'macadamising' the roads.

Set at the hub of a web of land and water communications, Bristol was without a rival as the capital of the west and the wealth which 18th century Bristol merchants and manufacturers brought to their city was reflected in the development of churches, colleges, schools and mansions which, though fine, nevertheless somehow lack the elegance of Georgian Bath nearby. John Betjeman, described Bristol as 'a city with a cathedral built like a railway station − and a railway station built like a cathedral'.

By 1774 British colonial history was approaching a crisis point. North America seethed with discontent at the imposition of taxes, not only to pay for the Seven Years War to beat the French in Canada, but also to restrain trade. Bristol merchants saw their prosperous trade with the colonies threatened and Edmund Burke, a politician of national repute and at the height of his powers on the opposition benches, was thought the man to defend their liberties − and their financial interests. His six years as one of their Members demonstrated to the merchants of Bristol that Burke was more concerned with the liberties of men generally than protecting the pockets of the Bristol establishment. In his speech to the electors of Bristol on 3rd November that year he said:

'Parliament is a deliberative assembly of one nation, with one interest, that of the whole; where, not local purposes, not local prejudices ought to guide, but the general good, resulting from the general reason of the whole. You chose a Member indeed; but when you have chosen him, he is not a Member of Bristol − but he is a Member of Parliament'.

Too big a man for 'that rascally city' he believed that the power to govern better rested in the hands of the representatives of the people, not delegates acting on mandates.

'Your representative owes you not his industry only, but his judgement, and he better instead of serving you if he sacrifices it to your opinion'.

Burke's definition of the 'representative' has stood the test of time, and Bristol eventually honoured his memory with a statue overlooking the docks.

*   *   *   *

The words Slaves, Sugar, Tobacco and Rum are writ large across the pages of Bristol's story and certainly Africa, the West Indies and America provided opportunities for making — and occasionally losing — fortunes. Much trade, however, was still elsewhere. Out of 485 ships arriving in 1787, it is recorded that 179 came from Europe and 161 from Ireland.

The previous year a young man arrived in Bristol to become one of the city's favourite sons. The Wills name is synonymous with tobacco and benefaction, and it is the young Henry Overton whom we must thank for bringing the family to Bristol. Alighting stiff and mud-bespattered from the Salisbury coach in 1786, H.O. was intent on making his fortune, but little imagined the mark his family would leave on this city.

His modest beginning in tobacco manufacturing in a shop in Mary-le-Port was timely. The House of Wills grew during the industrial revolution and H.O. ensured, through enlightened industrial relations, that the Luddite attitude to mechanical production was absent from his factories which used every possible device to improve production and efficiency. He regularly had four of his workmen to dinner and, as an ardent churchman, he insisted that his employees had been Sunday School members.

A hundred years later, the third generation made British industrial history by placing the following announcement on the factory notice boards:

'We have great pleasure in informing you that instead of the usual outing, we have decided to grant annually a week's holiday *with* a week's wages.'

The Will's legacy to Bristol includes the University and its playing fields, with many foundation scholarships, the Victoria Rooms, the Homeopathic Hospital, St Monica Home of Rest and the Art Gallery and Museum Extensions. Also, in 1890, Sir George Wills gave to the city all the woods on the south side of the Avon River, thereby preserving the gorge, spanned by the Clifton Suspension Bridge, as a beauty spot for all

·time. Nightingale Valley is rich in flora and fauna and boasts the unique Bristol Whitebeam tree.

The Wills certainly heeded John Wesley's dictum:

'Do all the good you can,
By all the means you can,
In all the ways you can,
In all the places you can,
At all the times you can,
To all the people you can,
As long as ever you can'

Wesley may have 'looked upon all the world as his parish' but the headquarters for his Methodists was in Bristol, to where he moved in 1740. His open air preaching started in Bristol in 1739. Soon the voluminous sermons were preached everywhere and by 1791, when Wesley died, Methodism had nearly 100,000 followers.

In spite of the arrival of Wills, Joseph Fry and his chocolate making machine and diversification into banking and insurance, Bristol's pre-eminence waned as the 18th century drew to a close.

Although six miles upstream, the anchorage on the Avon in Bristol suffered a forty-five feet difference between high and low tides, so docking was a hazardous business. As early as 1240 the first floating harbour or 'key' had been constructed, at a cost of £5,000, to prevent ships getting stranded or capsizing. 'Shipshape and Bristol fashion' meant that ships were built well enough to rest on the mud without breaking their backs. Then Bristol Dock Company built a bigger floating harbour and the heavy port dues charged to pay the cost slowed down the city's rate of growth.

Even the Bristol-built *S.S. Great Western* found its home port uneconomic. Rival ports developed in South Wales. Bristol replied with the controversial Avonmouth and Portishead docks, thus diluting the value of city trade. The textile industries of the south west declined and the slave trade was abolished, thus removing two props of the city's economy.

*   *   *   *

Bristol was therefore a less venturesome city by 1831 when the mob in the Reform Bill Riots got out of hand. The city fathers stood by and watched the Mansion House, the Bishop's Palace and the Customs House go up in flames. Charles Kingsley, then a schoolboy in Bristol, described the scene as being like Dante's Inferno.

The following year the great Reform Bill was passed abolishing the 'rotten' and 'pocket' boroughs, bringing the rest of the country more into line with Bristol with its two elected M.P.s (today there are five).

The same year the first successful company was formed to construct a railway from Bristol to London to rival the Bath road of Regency fame and the Kennet and Avon Canal. The directors of the Company appointed a twenty-seven year old genius as Chief Civil Engineer whose Clifton Suspension Bridge, hailed as 'the ornament of Bristol and the wonder of the age' had so impressed them.

Isambard Kingdom Brunel began work on the Great Western Railway in 1833. The 118-mile 'billiard table' stretch from Paddington took eight years to build with Brunel working up to twenty hours a day. 'If I ever go mad, I shall have the ghost of the railway walking before me', he wrote.

The GWR was the best and most profitable of Britain's railways and in 1985 celebrated its 150th anniversary – an occasion marked by John Harvey & Sons producing a special bottling of sherry, 'The Brunel Blend'.

When one of Brunel's directors was complaining of the railway line's excessive length from London to Bristol, he made the quiet retort: 'Why not make it still longer and have a steamboat to connect Bristol with New York and call it the Great Western?' The oak paddle-wheel steamer of 1,340 tons, immense for those days, was launched by Queen Victoria in Bristol in 1837 and was followed in 1843 by the first iron ocean-going, screw-propelled steamship in the world – the *S.S. Great Britain*. This vessel recently returned from her grave in the Falkland Islands to the dry dock in Hill's Yard, where she was built, and is now almost restored to her former glory.

* * * *

As the 20th century dawned, Bristol looked back on a hundred years of settled prosperity. Its population had increased five-fold to 328,000 and in the campaign for better welfare for those in need, the Liberals took control of the City Council for the first time and began to build council houses – at £400 each. It was a Labour Council which began selling them to their tenants in the 1970s.

The First World War brought new and acute problems – unemployment, high prices, great poverty and industrialised unrest. Then the political and industrial upheavals of the 1920s saw Bristol's first two Labour Members of Parliament returned – in 1923 – to support the Labour Government under Ramsay MacDonald. When the General Strike paralysed the city in 1926, Bristol provided one of the strike's chief organisers and perhaps the most famous of its several favourite (political) sons.

*   *   *   *

Ugly but jovial, Ernie Bevin was a self-made man of no education who rightly described himself as 'the best turn-up in a million'.

Born at Winsford in 1891, he left school at eleven and worked on a farm for sixpence a week. He then spent eleven years as a drayman in Bristol (two horses – not one) before entering politics at the age of thirty. In ten years he worked his way up the trade union ladder until, as national organiser of the Dockers Union, he became known as the 'Dockers' K.C.' because of the way he championed their cause.

He was nearly sixty when he became Minister of Labour in Churchill's 1940 wartime Coalition. He mobilised the industrial strength and manpower of the nation against Hitler through, in Bevin's words, 'the voluntary submission of a free people to discipline'.

After the War he became Foreign Secretary in Atlee's Labour Government, and can claim the credit for turning General George Marshall's speech on United States help for Europe into the Marshall Plan for reconstruction and for containing communism.

While distrusting Soviet Russia, Bevin was a great believer in negotiation rather than sterile confrontation; but also in the collective defence of democracy. For this purpose he negotiated the Treaty of Brussels in 1948 and next year the North Atlantic Security Treaty. This brought the United States and Western Europe into a defensive alliance (Nato) against possible attacks from the Soviet bloc. He failed, however, to devise a solution for the Palestine problem.

Ernest Bevin was a man of immense power and vision. He strove to improve the condition of working men and women and, having helped to win the war against Nazi tyranny, he went on to help restore battered Europe. Social and economic advance for workers was his achievement; the lasting peace in Europe his epitaph. Perhaps in sympathy with his refusal of all honours, Bristol has yet to erect his statue.

A contemporary of Bevin's who also looms large in my view of Bristol from Westminster is Sir Stafford Cripps. Scholar of distinction, lawyer, Red Cross truck driver and boss of an explosives factory in the First World War, he was Member of Parliament for Bristol East from 1931 until 1950, when ill-health compelled him to resign from office.

Some of his political ideas would suit today; he called for a strict fiscal policy to check inflation reinforced by a sense of moral responsibility and duty to the community. 'You must not expect any further advance in …. wage levels until we have been able to increase the productivity of our industries', he said. 'Democracy must be regarded as both a science and a religion, it must, like the individuals of which it is composed have a body and a spirit ....'. He practised what he preached and many Bristol churches have echoed to his words.

Cripps was succeeded in his constituency in 1950 by one of today's most controversial politicians – Anthony Wedgewood-Benn. In 1960 Benn's father died and he found himself – not a reluctant peer, but a persistent commoner. His three year battle to renounce his Viscountcy displayed courage, intellect and dedication. His principles triumphed over his privileges.

It was just after Labour were re-elected in 1966 that the new Britain 'forged in the white heat of a technological revolution' had Benn as its Minister of Technology, determined to make his department a catalyst of economic growth – 'to pick up and fertilize the points of growth in the economy' or, as seen by Conservatives, an instrument of intervention and creeping socialism.

The Upper Clyde Ship Builders crisis in 1969, the funding of the Rolls-Royce RB211 aero-engine and the Concorde supersonic airliner were all Benn miscalculations, where his socialist ideals – and sometimes constituency interests – came into conflict with commercial reality. Then the Conservative election victory in 1970 marked, so Benn thought, the end of the post-war consensus. Having once been in favour Tony Benn was now passionately against Britain joining the EEC. He fought and won the campaign for a referendum. With 'loss of sovereignty' as the main plank in his platform, he fought and lost the referendum itself.

At the Department of Energy Tony Benn found himself at odds with his cabinet over economic policy – particularly Government spending cuts; and in conflict with the massive oil companies whose co-operation was vital at the start of the North Sea oil era, and who described Benn's appointment as 'pouring trouble on oily waters. He saw his vote split by the Liberal/SDP Alliance candidate in 1983 and once more he was in the political wilderness, until the Chesterfield by-election enabled him to return to Parliament. Bristol was sorry to see him go and Conservative M.P.s were delighted to welcome him back. His constituency loved him, and the Tories love to hate him. He is good for politics.

Thus the only Labour M.P. in the south west to survive in 1983 was Michael Cocks, Member of Parliament for Bristol South. One of the shrewdest on the Labour benches, he is well-suited to the unenviable task of Chief Whip over a parliamentary party in turmoil. Cocks has also had to contend with attempts in Bristol to unseat him under Labour's annual 'reselection' procedures. Yet this staunch democrat, with a great sense of humour, the laugh to go with it and the appearance of an over-weight Sean Connery, should survive because he has the guile of James Bond, the constitution of an ox and the support of his city.

*   *   *   *

Having escaped the worst of the 19th and 20th century industrialisation, Bristol was devastated in the Second World War. The first of many blows fell on the night of the 24th November 1940, when large numbers of enemy bombers wrought great havoc on the city and its people. Over 3,000 homes were destroyed, including the narrow lanes with their tall, overhanging houses and the little churches in the centre of the city. During these air raids 1,299 people were killed and 3,300 injured.

In 1976 I found a plaque on Manhattan Island, erected in 1942 by the English Speaking Union of the USA and which commemorates the courage of the blitzed Bristolians with these words:

> 'Beneath the East River Drive of the city of New York lie stones, bricks and rubble from the bombed city of Bristol. Brought here in ballast from overseas, those fragments that were once homes testify, while men love freedom, to the resolution and fortitude of the people of Britain. They saw their homes struck down without warning. It was not their walls but their valour that kept them free'.

Aware of the loss of many buildings in the War — and afterwards by bulldozing in the name of planning — and realising almost at the eleventh hour how much this old city had to show the world of history, grandeur and architecture, Bristol has made a remarkable recovery.

Historic buildings are now being restored and the 3,000 acres of open space within the city boundary have been enhanced with over 20,000 trees to soften the ugliness of appalling post-war inner city redevelopment. Quaysides and docks — where once merchants brought ashore their produce from far off lands and ships' masts had stood, thick as pinewoods, among church spires and warehouses, taverns and tramcars — have now been restored and wait to be discovered down the lanes and cobbled streets.

A walk along King Street brings you to the Theatre Royal, home of the Bristol Old Vic, and the oldest in the country. When it opened in 1766 the prologue to the first play was written by the great David Garrick. Yes, history is everywhere — in museums and outside — and of an intoxicating nature at the Harvey's Wine Museum. You can sample wines at the World Wine Fair and Festival — but try Bristol's first; Harvey's famous Bristol Cream sherry — as a French lady did soon after Harveys was founded in 1796, saying: 'If that is Bristol Milk then this must be the Cream'.

The Wine Fair carries on a tradition, since Bristol has been renowned for its wine trade with France, Spain and Portugal for more than 700 years. It is held in Bristol's historic harbour. One of the most exciting tourist developments in any town and city. An area which was once responsible for generating Bristol's wealth and prosperity, the harbour is again achieving prominence, not through shipping and trade this time, but through the development of tourism and leisure activities — pedestrian routes, water bus services and other transport links — it has become Britain's first Urban Heritage Park.

Nine centuries of commercial shipping in the city centre has ended with the building of yet another controversial dock at Avonmouth. Again, this is not only to keep abreast of the times and cater for bigger ships, but also to say once more to central government, as the country's biggest municipally-owned port and the best sited for inland communications: 'We'll do it our way'. The Labour Government, bowing to pressure from the 'Welsh Mafia' of leading M.P.s like Jim Callaghan and Michael Foot, had tried to stop Bristol building it.

Bristol has learned and built on its history. To paraphrase Burke — 'A city without the means of some change, is without the means of its conservation'. The city has moved with the times and the inventiveness and enterprise of her people will ensure that she will ride high into the 21st century.

It was really the genius of Brunel that sparked off the engineering tradition which has helped to fund the metamorphosis of Bristol and which was continued by George White, who in 1909 recognised the significance of aeronautical developments, and in the year after Bleriot's first cross-Channel flight established the works at Filton that became the Bristol Aeroplane Company, then the British Aircraft Corporation, now British Aerospace.

Combined with Rolls-Royce aero-engine factories next door, the Filton Works provide the most comprehensive aerospace complex in the world, with a pedigree that includes such famous aircraft as the Boxkite, then the Bristol Fighter (The 'Brisfit') — as important in the First World War as the Spitfire and Hurricane were in the Second; the Bulldog, the Beaufighter, Blenheim and Beaufort of Second World War fame; the Brabazon and Britannia airliners of the post-war era; and today's Concorde, the world's first supersonic passenger aircraft.

The pace of technological advance accelerates. Bristol is now a micro-chip city reaping the harvest of the seeds of venture capitalism sown in the North Atlantic centuries ago — the Hewlett Packard Company is building its European base in the city.

*　　*　　*　　*

For centuries Bristolians have never found it necessary to promote their city. Bristol was no upstart like Manchester or Birmingham. They were shaped by history, while Bristol made history. Most of the city's traditional industries have continued to expand, but we are constantly reminded of those that have passed, like shipping and slavery. Outside the church I used to attend in Henbury there is a tombstone to a boy slave, 'Scipio Africanus', surmounted by a negro's head.

This has always been a city of business – and still is. Leisure was left to Bath. Understandably, there is no Bristolian tradition of culture. The boy poet, Chatterton, is the only wholly Bristol character who is remembered in this field. Before he died by his own hand in London in 1770 he said sarcastically: 'Lost to all hearing, elegance and sense, long had this famous city tolled her pence'.

Like Bath's 'two cities', Bristol has her contrasts. Social tensions, which have simmered beneath the surface for years since the influx of black workers in the 1950s, burst out in 1980 when the Black and White Club in the St Pauls area in the centre of the city was the scene, literally, of a conflagration, which was sparked off by insensitive policing of the area in seach of drugs.

St Pauls contains the kind of once handsome town houses and artisan terraces that, elsewhere, the middle classes would eagerly doll up, but it is now an area fallen to the level of a 'red light district'. The tidal wave of black frustration which engulfed the police on the night of the 2nd April 1980 came as a profound shock to everyone in authority – 'We thought we were doing so well', they said.

That such a thing could happen in elegant old Bristol, of all places, rivetted the minds of white do-gooders to the enormity of what might happen elsewhere. As a black Rastafarian said, as people swept up the mess: 'Now it's started, they'll be more'. He was not only voicing resentment at being decanted from school to the dole queue, but adding his ingrained hatred of the white betrayal and exploitation of Africa in the past, which struck near the bone in Bristol – home port of some noted exploiters of those lands. St Pauls was, itself, the merchants' patch.

The 'two cities' contrast – a city within a city – is borne out by recent surveys of housing in Bristol. The social and economic gap between St Pauls and Easton in the centre – and the rest of the city has widened over the last decade, and the City Fathers are worried.

There is a football analogy to the problem. St Pauls and Easton are in the area where the footballers wear the red of Bristol City, which was slipping from the First Division when I was in Bristol – just as Bristol Rovers, who wore blue and drew support from my north west area of the city, slipped to the Third. Both clubs face a shortage of finance, goals and fans. What is needed, in more ways than one, is Bristol United.

*   *   *   *

I have left Bristol in many different ways. By ship on the floodtide; by motorway from the city centre in a 'Bristol' car (built at the aircraft works); by Highspeed 125 train from Brunel's cathedral-like Temple Meads Station; by Concorde from Filton aerodrome; by hot-air balloon from Aston Park (almost); and by bicycle up one of the first cycle ways along the banks of the Avon that links the two cities that I have Viewed from Westminster.

Bristol was a fine city to represent and I agree with William Cobbett, who said of his Rural Ride in the west in 1830:

> 'Never shall I see another place to interest me, and so pleasing to me, as Bristol and its environs .... A good and solid and wealthy city: a people of plain and good manners; private virtue and public spirit united; no empty noise, no insolence, no flattery .... it surpasses all that I ever saw. A great commercial city in the midst of cornfields, meadows and woods, and the ships coming into the centre of it, miles from anything like sea, up a narrow river, and passing between two clefts of rock probably a hundred feet high; so that from the top of these clefts you look down upon the main-top gallant masts of lofty ships, that are gliding along!'

Cobbett was on Clifton Downs, overlooking the early workings on Brunel's Suspension Bridge across the Avon Gorge. He stood in the shadow of an old windmill, now the observatory. Enter there today, pay your 10p and ascend the winding stairs to a darkened room and gaze into the camera obscura. Watch Bristol revolve slowly before you, oblivious of your interest, impervious to your thoughts — and you will begin to share the sensation of representing Bristolians in Parliament!

DEVON AND CORNWALL
David Harris

David Harris was well-known as a journalist at the House of Commons, where he was for 18 years correspondent of the Daily Telegraph, *before his election as M.P. for St Ives in 1979. He is himself a Devonian and was at school at Mount Redford School, Exeter.*

In the European Parliament at Strasbourg he was the Conservative spokesman on regional policy, and, though in his essay he contrasts the ruggedness of Cornwall with the douceur of Devon, it is evident that the local authorities of both counties have a common interest in such regional advantages as can be gained from the EEC.

David Harris had himself been a member of the Greater London Council and Chairman of its Thamesmead Committee before the inter-city train from Paddington to Exeter and Penzance became his regular life-line. He is editor of the review European Conservatism *which he founded. He is 49.*

Like neighbours who have always lived next door to each other right at the end of the street, Devon and Cornwall have a lot in common, and yet are strikingly different. They are bound together by geography, history and economics. They are also joined by Brunel's masterpiece of a rail bridge across the Tamar and by a modern equivalent alongside. They share a four-mile-thick link of land in the north-east, a joint police force, regional television, and the widespread view of people in the *rest* of the country that their sole role in life is to provide a sort of national holiday camp.

But they are as much alike as cob and granite, thatch and slate, Saxon and Celt, church and chapel, wool and tin, rich red loam and thin grey soil. And whilst generalities are always dangerous and can be punctured by contrary examples, the overall impression is there to be seen – and, more importantly, to be felt.

Who could doubt, standing in the square at St Just, that one was in Cornwall. The granite buildings, the tiny fields and stone hedges stretching out to the Penwith Moors in one direction and Cape Cornwall in the other, often enshrouded in sea mist, with nearby mines (one alive and the rest all dead) – it is as Cornish a town as you could possibly find. The contrast with, say, Ottery St Mary sings out. The one epitomises Cornwall and the other captures the gentler characteristics of Devon.

Being the end of the land wedge, Cornwall is dominated by the sea. Its coastline is its glory, whether the rocky grandeur of the northern cliffs or the wooded inlets of the Helford and the Fal and the Fowey along the southern shore. The string of small fishing ports, such as Looe, Mevagissey, Cadgwith, Coverack, Porthleven, Mousehole, Sennen, St Ives, Padstow, Port Isaac and Boscastle, is what the tourist remembers – together with those long stretches of sandy beaches which have given Cornwall its tourist industry. The St Ives Parliamentary constituency has no fewer than five lifeboat stations within its boundaries. You are never far from the sea in Cornwall.

Devon has its fine coastline too, but it is the land, rather than the sea, which is the dominant feature. Devon is a much bigger county, a much more comfortable place, with attractive villages and towns which look as though they have lived peacefully through the centuries without having to fight for existence. Compared with those of its neighbour, the farms and the fields are larger, the soil deeper and richer. It is altogether a more prosperous place, less remote and easier going.

As for contrasts in temperament of their people, a politician who was born in Devon but who represents a Cornish seat (perhaps, surprisingly, there have been quite a few of us, including Isaac Foot) might be unwise to draw any conclusions except to recognise that roots, pride and independence are important. 'I'm Cornish, and proud of it,' is an almost matter-of-fact statement; hardly a boast, but more of an assertion of identity at a time when the forces of uniformity have to be fought even in this most distinctive corner of the land.

As a candidate, I once mentioned to a long serving Tory agent in Cornwall that I was replacing my French car with a British model. 'Good', he said, 'but you will be sure to get a Cornish number, won't you?' That was sound advice. But I did not need anyone to tell me when I became Euro-M.P. for Cornwall and Plymouth that while it was fine to wear my Devonshire Regiment tie at the Remembrance Sunday service on Plymouth Hoe in the morning, it was just as well to change it for a plain black one by the time I laid a poppy wreath on Truro's war memorial in the afternoon.

About the only factor which would forge the Cornish and the Devonians in a united uprising today would be the threat that they were being lumped together in some awful reorganisation of local government to form a Devon and Cornwall Regional Council. But, surely, no government would be daft enough to propose that. Or would it?

I am pretty sure that I was the first elected representative whose constituency spanned the Tamar when I went to the European Parliament in 1979. The decision of the Boundary Commission to put Cornwall and Plymouth together for that purpose was pretty controversial, but the arguments were as nothing compared with the row over an ill-fated proposal that there should be a sort of 'Greater Tamarside', based on Plymouth but taking in parts of south-east Cornwall for local government purposes. Quite rightly, it came to nothing.

*　　*　　*　　*

With about a quarter of a million people, Plymouth is by far the biggest centre of population. But, to its chagrin, it is not, and never has been, the county capital. The cathedral city of Exeter holds that title, and has reinforced its position not only by holding onto the seat of the County Council but also by having a university. Plymouth has to make do with a polytechnic − a very good one − and with being demoted from a County Borough to a District Council under the 1973 shake-up of local government. But it's the real centre of economic activity in the South-west, its prosperity still based largely, and perhaps dangerously, on the Devonport Dockyard and the Armed Forces.

Still, the city has had some success in broadening its economic base by attracting new, modern industries. High speed trains, a regional airline (Brymon) and good roads (although the M5 ends at Exeter, the A38 on to Plymouth is almost up to motorway standards) have combined to reduce Plymouth's main stumbling block, its distance from other large centres of population and from London in particular. Its enterprising City Council has not been slow to take advantage of the shrinkage in journey times, and has sold hard the natural attractions of the city, not least to overseas investors.

Indeed, they have been so successful that Plymouth was quite lucky not to lose its assisted area status under the 1984 review of regional policy. Increasingly, the city, as befits its merchant venturer past, is becoming plugged into the European Community, largely through Brittany Ferries with its well-established route to Roscoff, but also with its roll-on, roll-off ferry to Santander in northern Spain. Drake's port − the old buccaneer was once Mayor − is well placed to get some commercial advantage from Spain's entry to the EEC.

The tremendous improvement in communications is probably the biggest single change to affect the South-west since the Second World War. It has brought benefits to the whole of Devon, and, to a lesser extent, Cornwall. But here again, there is a world of difference between the two. While Devon is almost within easy reach – a two hour train journey – of London, Cornwall is still a long way off. The prosperity of the home counties and the M4 is seeping down the M5 so that Exeter is becoming an attractive location for dispersed offices. A large insurance company has already gone to nearby Clyst St Mary, while Plymouth is looking to the new industries.

*   *   *   *

Through being at the end of the peninsula, Cornwall has to struggle hard to overcome the distance factor. It is not just a question of miles. There is a deterioration in communications the further west one goes, so the disability of remoteness becomes compounded. The miles seem to get longer.

Take for instance the train from Paddington. The chief steward in the dining car has to get a move-on to feed a Taunton-bound passenger and give him his bill before the Golden Hind glides into Somerset's county town. Half an hour later, the train is at Exeter. Then the going becomes slower as the train takes an hour to cover the curving, scenic route to Plymouth, actually touching the coastline at Dawlish and Teignmouth, so that passengers have the red sandstone cliffs on the one side of the carriage and sea and sand on the other. In the winter storms, the waves crash over coaches.

But once it crosses over Brunel's bridge, opened in 1895, into Cornwall, then the train positively crawls. The High Speed 125 which took off from Paddington at 5.45 p.m. becomes an upgraded local train once it crosses the Tamar, the station stops become a litany – Saltash, Liskeard, Bodmin Parkway, Lostwithiel, Par, St Austell, Truro, Redruth, Camborne and Penzance. The bar and buffet have long since been closed, the carriages have only a residue of tired passengers and a lot of jettisoned newspapers and plastic coffee cups.

The train is just as much part of my life and my weekly routine as Question Time, constituency surgeries, hanging around for late night votes in the Commons, bed and breakfast in the Farmer's Club, and dealing with the ever growing tide of correspondence. Indeed, Paddington is where the South-west begins or ends. The train is also a meeting place and I can hardly remember making a journey without bumping into someone I knew.

Normally, there is a little group of Cornish M.P.s on the train up on Monday - David Penhaligon or David Mudd and, perhaps, Bob Hicks. We try to get on top of the letters, using our small tape machines, but usually gossip takes over for a lot of the journey.

Usually, the Cornish Members come back on the sleeper after a 10 o'clock vote on Thursday night so that we can be in our 'far west' constituencies on Friday. The stewards know us, automatically booking our normal early-morning calls as we check in at Paddington. I might open an eye at Exeter or Plymouth, but the day begins with a cup of instant coffee as the train passes the China Clay port of Par.

*   *   *   *

If the train takes a long time to get to Cornwall, the same is true for cars and lorries. For those choosing the shorter, northern route, the motorway is replaced beyond Exeter by the quirky delights of the A30. The road has been the subject of a running campaign with Cornish M.P.s joining forces with (most of) their Devonshire colleagues in a joint campaign to persuade Ministers (or their civil servants) that a dual carriageway is needed.

Most people — certainly those who control the government departments — seem to overlook the sheer length of the peninsula. They equate Bristol with the South-west because that is where their regional headquarters are housed. They just don't realise that Bristol is 200 miles from Penzance! Why, even Exeter is 121 miles from Penzance, and when a driver is setting out from that part of Cornwall to London he is about half way there in miles, and more so in terms of time, when he passes out of Devon.

That is why it is absolutely incomprehensible to us in Devon and Cornwall that successive British Governments have insisted on having, for their own statistical and departmental purposes, a meaningless South-west region based on Bristol. Goodness me, that city is almost part of the Midlands. Thankfully, we have broken down the Government's attitude a little in persuading it to send separate statistics for Devon and Cornwall to Brussels for European Regional Development Fund grant purposes. If we had not, we looked at one stage like losing European finance simply because the high unemployment figures in the west were 'diluted' by much lower figures for Somerset, Avon, Dorset, Gloucester and Wiltshire — which are included by Whitehall to form its own artificial region.

*   *   *   *

But do Devon and Cornwall form a natural sub-region. Well, they are frequently looked at together, whether by a Government Department or by the author of this chapter in this book. For all the reasons given earlier, they are natural partners but they will never form part of a natural whole. Of course, there is scope for co-operation. The sort of arrangement which works well is the Joint Committee of the two County Councils, which meets only once every six months in Plymouth to discuss matters of mutual interest and concern. The chair alternates between Cornwall and Devon, so as to emphasise that it is a body of co-equals, and Plymouth City Council provides the lunch. The two counties run a joint industrial development bureau, which tries to compete against the massive efforts of Scotland, Wales and some of the other regions in attracting foreign or national investment. It is a sensible, cheap, unbureaucratic set-up which preserves identities but which caters for shared interests.

Ordinary people are not terribly interested in institutional structures. They only get het up about them when changes are proposed. I don't suppose that there was great attachment to the old pattern of urban and district councils, but there was certainly antipathy to the new district councils of Peter Walker, not to mention the feelings against the South West Water Authority, which are still taking time to die down.

*   *   *   *

Still, the people of Cornwall and Devon don't much like change. Politically, this has been reflected in their basic allegiance to the Conservative and Liberal parties, with Labour only getting a look in at a few places. There have been just nine Labour M.P.s, and, naturally enough, most of those have sat for Plymouth, the big city. The first, J.J.H. Moses, a dockyard shipwright, Methodist lay preacher and a convert from the Liberal ranks, was elected to Plymouth Drake in 1929. The Socialist highpoint came in 1945 when Labour won all three Plymouth seats — a young chap called Michael Foot captured Devonport by defeating Hore-Belisha (of beacon fame) — and Cornwall had its first Socialist M.P. in Evelyn King at Penryn and Falmouth. But apart from Plymouth and the Falmouth, Penryn and Camborne areas, the only other seat ever to have gone Labour was Exeter when Gwyneth Dunwoody snatched it from the Conservatives in 1966. Her then husband, Dr John Dunwoody, sat for Falmouth and Camborne as a Labour M.P. at the same time.

Two of the nine Labour M.P.s who have represented Devon or Cornish seats, Evelyn King and David Owen, left the party. King re-entered Parliament later as the Conservative M.P. for South Dorset and Dr Owen left to help form the SDP. In tune with West Country moderation, David Owen's departure had nothing to do with left-wing extremism in the ranks of his constituency Labour party at Devonport. The Plymouth Socialists are moderates in the spectrum of today's Labour party, and there was no attempt to push him out and replace him by a Militant. In the 1983 General Election, the Conservatives held 14 of the 16 seats in Cornwall and Devon, with David Owen holding Devonport for the SDP and David Penhaligon retaining Truro for the Liberals. The nearest Socialist constituency was in Bristol.

The Liberals have always been the natural challengers to the Tories in the two counties, largely because of the non-conformist tradition, so it is not surprising that the Alliance pins some hope on the South-west. After all, in 1966, the Liberals held not only North Devon (Jeremy Thorpe's stronghold until his personal and political downfall) but also North Cornwall (John Pardoe's seat) and Bodmin (represented by Peter Bessell).

Another factor tied in with the moderation of South-west politics is the importance attached to being 'a good constituency M.P.'. Harold Hayman, who represented Falmouth and Camborne for Labour from 1950 until his death in 1966, not only managed to live down his younger reputation as being something of a firebrand, to such an extent that he became Hugh Gaitskell's Parliamentary Private Secretary but he held the seat largely on his 'he looks after us' reputation. For exactly the same reason, Falmouth and Camborne is not so much a Tory stronghold now as a David Mudd seat. Several other South-west members, including Peter Mills, David Penhaligon, Janet Fookes, and Robert Hicks, have built up personal support which goes over normal party allegiances.

The 'we vote for the man' tradition is particularly strong in Cornwall and it has only once voted to put a woman in Parliament — but strangely it has had two women M.P.s. Mrs Hilda Runciman won St Ives for the Liberals in a 1928 by-election. However she was really 'keeping the seat warm' for her husband, Walter Runciman, the former President of the Board of Trade. He was about to transfer from Swansea West to the Cornish seat at the General Election and to become, eventually, a Liberal National. He was duly elected for St Ives in 1929 and his wife went off — politically that is — to get beaten by just a few hundred votes at Tavistock. But for a brief time they were in the House together, they made the first ever husband and wife team of M.P.s at Westminster. During the last war, Mrs Beatrice Rathbone was returned unopposed for Bodmin after her husband, who had been elected as the M.P. in 1936, was killed while on active service with the RAF. But she did not stand in 1945.

Mrs Runciman apart, women have not done well on the few occasions that they have stood in Cornwall. The Equal Opportunities Commission must be much more pleased with Plymouth, which has something of an opposite tradition since Nancy Astor was elected for Sutton in 1919 and became the first woman M.P. to take her seat in the Commons. First Joan Vickers and now Janet Fookes have followed her lead, building up reputations not only for being always immaculately turned out but also for meticulous representation of constituents' interests.

Perhaps because of the importance attached to the constituency side of the job, the two counties have not produced many cabinet ministers in recent years. John Nott and David Owen are exceptions, and so was Derek Heathcoat-Amery, who got as far as being Chancellor of the Exchequer. Possibly his post-war Tiverton constituents were less demanding than they would be today. At an election meeting in one of his villages, the chairman asked for questions for the candidate after he had spoken. There was silence and a shuffling of feet until an old farmer asked: 'Yes, Mr Derek, when are you going to bring the hounds our way again?'

*　　*　　*　　*

Today there would be questions from constituent farmers about the CAP and milk quotas and unemployment. As in all rural parts of the country, agriculture has declined sharply as an employer as mechanisation has taken over down on the farm. Take the small East Devon parish of Combe Raleigh, for instance. In the 1950s it had sixteen farm labourers. By the 1980s, there were two, and one of these was part-time. Farming has become a family business in the narrow sense of the phrase. Yet agriculture is still one of the two pillars of the local economy, challenged only by tourism − if we leave out the biggest employer of all, the public service. Indeed, one of the paradoxes of Devon and Cornwall is that, despite all the unemployment and the drift of labour from the land, the area has never looked so well off. All those market towns, from Honiton to Helston, have had facelifts and supermarkets over the last twenty years, and car parking is as everywhere the big problem. True, many of the family shops have given way to the multiples and the building societies, and out of town hypermarkets are beginning to syphon off trade. Yet the cattle markets continue, and a lively town can just about hold its own.

The sudden introduction of milk quotas in 1984 brought agriculture up with a jolt. Not only is dairying the mainstay of farming in Devon and Cornwall, but Cornwall, in particular, has a lot of small farms which are completely dependent on the milk cheque. Perhaps those 50-acre holdings are an economic anachronism. It has been a mystery to me how people make a living off them even with the usual addition of a few rented acres and a 'Bed and Breakfast' sign by the farm gate in summer. I don't want to see them swept away, but how can the small man survive in this setting?

Well, we might see more part-time, small farmers on the continental or crofter model. The trouble is that there are not many other jobs about. Cornwall, at the beginning of 1985, had an unemployment rate of around 20 per cent and Devon one of over 14 per cent, compared with a national figure of 13.9 per cent of the workforce. Averages are deceptive, and the Devon figure masks very high unemployment in some places. Cornwall's fire brigade received 750 applications for six fireman's jobs paying only £7,000 a year, which says something both about the unemployment rate and the low incomes of the area.

But how long will the acceptance of unemployment last. And can more be done to bring it down. Time will answer the first question, but only an abject pessimist would reply 'no' to the second. Few people think that large scale firms can, or even should, be lured to the South-west by regional bribes. The future lies in having a lot of small and, hopefully, some medium-sized companies, most of them 'home grown' so that they have real roots in the area. There are signs that this is happening. The distance factor can be overcome by modern communications of the information technology kind rather than by road, rail and airline, although these are also important. Porthleven, with its little harbour near Helston, is the home of Curnow Shipping, a company which, among other activities, runs the sea link from Britain to St Helena. It finds that, thanks to telex and much lower overheads, it can function better in Cornwall than in London EC2 or EC3, and it could be the forerunner of several other businesses which 'opt out' but only from the high costs of life in the big cities. At the individual level, self-employment has grown rapidly in the South-west as people have taken their redundancy payments, often in other parts of the country, and have set up one man businesses.

Two areas where there is a need for increased public spending is on the A30, the main road into Cornwall, and on water and sewerage schemes. The upgrading of the A30 has not only been hampered by the Department of Transport's attitude mentioned earlier, but also by the conservationists, particularly the powerful Dartmoor lobby led by the formidable Lady Sayer.

The conservationists not only mounted an all-out campaign against the route of the Okehampton by-pass, but have also, over the years, played havoc with the reservoir building programme of the South West Water Authority. But the 1984 drought and the widespread water restrictions have probably weakened the anti-reservoir case. Most people seem to think that existing reservoirs fit well into the Dartmoor scene, and can actually enhance it given proper landscaping.

*   *   *   *

The population of Cornwall has grown significantly in recent years; it went up from 380,000 to 430,000 between 1971 and 1981. Devon has also had its increase.

A factor in the increase is middle-age migration. The executive who has had a golden handshake or who simply wants to take things a bit easier, even at the cost of being less well paid, has headed west. Some have taken over the village shop or a small hotel – and have found that the reality is not so idyllic as the dream. Others – probably the lucky ones – have reckoned that they can work from the South-west with pretty regular business trips to London or abroad. British Rail's 125s and Brymon's Dash 7 (flying from Newquay and Plymouth) seem to be carrying a growing number of 'consultants' up to town and make possible a split existence.

Of course, the other big element in the population growth is the influx of pensioners. Retirement is now a major industry, and perhaps the fastest growing one in the region. Many a hotelier has been quick to see the possibility of all-the-year-round occupancy – the dream of the trade – and has turned his property into a 'retirement home'. Indeed, some resorts are becoming worried at the trend as they see more and more hotels switching over.

*   *   *   *

Despite the rush into the retirement industry, tourism is still the lifeblood, along with farming, of the local economy. Yet the easy days of the 1960s and 1970s are over. The industry is highly susceptible to the movement of sterling, both from the standpoint of attracting overseas tourists and of competition with overseas holidays for British holidaymakers. Now the emphasis is on upgrading what is already there, as well as providing wet weather attractions for holidaymakers. From seal and bird sanctuaries to Exeter's maritime museum and the stately homes of the National Trust, there is plenty to see.

Self-catering is the fashion, and traditional seaside boarding houses are out.

A company which has increasingly diversified, particularly into the leisure business, is Cornwall's biggest single firm, English China Clays, or ECLP Ltd, as it is properly known. No group has done more for the economy of Cornwall in modern times, and its impact on the life of the St Austell area and beyond has been far bigger than pay packets and contracts. It is a major benefactor, and has played its part in fostering the cultural, educational, sporting and charitable life of Cornwall. Part of that life revolves around choirs, bands and rugby. The company has left its physical stamp on that part of Cornwall but it is accepted that if there were any proposals to remove the 'white Alps', the conservationists would probably demand that a preservation order be slapped on these gigantic spoil heaps.

Further west, beyond Truro, with its relatively modern (by Church of England standards) but traditional-style cathedral, is all that is left of the once mighty tin mining industry, at South Crofty, Pendarves, Wheal Jane, Mount Wellington and, not far from Land's End, Geevor. Only five mines – four if Pendarves is counted in with South Crofty – but, at the time of writing, it was an industry which was undergoing something of a limited renaissance with high tine prices (around £10,000 a ton) and earnings of over £20,000 a year for some miners. Exploration was going on in other parts too, particularly outside Callington, at the other end of the county, while tin is also being extracted from the sea bed and river valleys. But no-one expects mining to approach anything like its one time importance. After all, when John Wesley visited Cornwall on almost thirty missions, he was drawn not only because of the challenge posed by local mining communities but also because of the density of population. 'The common people are a very strange kind of being – half savage at best', was how one chronicler described them at the time. Hard as it is to imagine now, St Just, at the height of the mining boom was almost as big as Manchester at the time, while St Ives was supposed to be larger than Liverpool. Huge fortunes were being made not only by Cornwall's landed gentry but by some tough entrepreneurs who fought their way into the establishment. All that remains now are a few of the houses they built and the litter of tips and shafts, and those gaunt shells of engine houses which are an evocation of Cornwall – that and the chapels of the miners themselves.

The other great Cornish working heritage, fishing, has also seen better days although, despite all the difficulties, it is in sounder shape than the industry in many other parts of Britain. But what opportunities have been thrown away! Not, let me hasten to add, by the Cornish fishermen but by successive Governments in their failure to control the gross over-exploitation of stocks. The mackerel came in vast shoals during the 1970s and, with them, came the purse seiners, mainly from Scotland, and the factory ships. The over-fishing was little short of criminal, and the stocks disappeared as the local men predicted they would. The movement of the mackerel is a mystery, but no-one can believe that the sheer greed of the bulk catchers and wanton destruction of young fish did anything to conserve stocks.

A visitor to Falmouth, standing on Pendennis Head and looking out to sea, could see the fleet of Russian, Bulgarian, East German and Egyptian factory ships – 'the Klondykers' – in Carrick Roads on the left and in Falmouth Bay on the right. Their lights shone like two small towns and their machinery hummed as they processed fish for Africa or Communist countries throughout the night. Clearly the bonanza was not going to last long. And so it proved. By the time the EEC introduced a new Cornish mackerel 'box', a huge conservation zone in the western approaches inside which bulk catching was banned, the mackerel had almost disappeared.

Hopefully, a more stable and local industry can be built up, based on well-established ports like Brixham and Newlyn, and also on all those small boats which fish the bays from coves like Beer or Penberth, and from the small harbours and estuaries. The need is to have a well-balanced but mixed fleet supplying local processors, merchants and exporters. Food processing, packaging and marketing should be one of the growth industries of the South-west.

Just as the fishing boats could lead to the creation of more jobs on land so the growing of food should not be the end of the story as far as the West Country is concerned.

As they have always done in the past, the two counties are going to have to make a living from what is basically at hand. They need to capitalise more on their natural assets without ruining those resources, be they scenery or fish stocks. The challenge facing both neighbouring counties is how to increase activity without wrecking the environment. After the brief lull, the battles between the developers and the conservationists are likely to start again in earnest.

Why, not even those most westerly of locations, the Isles of Scilly — off, but not part of Cornwall — are immune; far from it. The planning pressures there are all the more intense because of the very smallness of the islands and the beauty which they encapsulate. Even on the main island, St Mary's, nothing can be done without having a visual or physical impact, so schemes like the designation of a rubbish tip are controversial to say the least. Yet not even the good islanders are prepared to be denied the modern things of life. Those on the four off-islands have just won their skillful campaign to have their homes linked by undersea cable to the oil-fired power station on St Mary's.

On the mainland, it is not so much a matter of catching up with the 20th century, for the electrification programme was all but completed in the countryside several years ago. It is more the retention of existing facilities as a rural rearguard action. Each village in North or Mid Devon wants to keep its subsidised bus service, even if it is poorly used, and its local shop and sub post office. The country copper is nearly an extinct species in spite of all the talk about community policing, and the remaining faithful have got used to sharing their vicar with two neighbouring parishes and to having 10.00 a.m. Communion only on the third Sunday in the month. The doctors are in group practices, and the fields are empty of workers. Many of the branch lines went with Beeching, their bridges leading to nowhere and their over-grown cuttings now well on the way to becoming objects of archaelogical interest. As the supermarket parks show, it is the age of the car — for those who can afford one.

Still, it is difficult to see how it could be otherwise. People want the charm of the countryside but the facilities of the town, Cornwall, at least, is no stranger to change. The walker up on deserted Caradon Hill can scarcely comprehend the population that lived there, not all that long ago, during the mining boom.

If the Duchy has had its tremendous upheavals and the next-door neighbour has experienced a more gentle transition down the centuries, then that again highlights the differences between the two. Whatever happens, Devon and Cornwall will be my part of the world. Viewed from Westminster, they are home and the true South-west.

CENTRAL SOUTHERN ENGLAND
Julian Critchley

Julian Critchley, writing about Berkshire, Hampshire, Oxfordshire, Buckinghamshire and Surrey, has the good fortune of describing life in an area where the unemployment figures are the lowest in the country. But the mushroom growth of population brings its own problems, such as the contention between builders and defenders of the countryside, in which he plays his part.

Precluded (or spared) by a little quirk of mischief from public office, Julian Critchley has a distinctive role particularly in the sphere of defence, having been prominent in organisations supporting NATO since the 1960s. Thus from 1968-70 he was President of the Atlantic Association of Young Political Leaders, Chairman of the Defence Committee of the Western Union from 1974-77, and a delegate also to the Council of Europe and the North Atlantic Assembly, of whose important report on Nuclear Weapons in Europe he was joint author with John Cartwright.

Julian Critchley is a prolific writer, both serious and playful, both of books (e.g. Westminster Blues) and newspaper articles. He has been the Member for Aldershot since 1970, and M.P. for Rochester 1959-64. In the Conservative Party he has been Chairman of the Bow Group and Chairman of the Media Committee and has been Vice-Chairman of the Defence Committee since 1976. He is 54.

T he five counties of the centre of Southern England have been going through a swift economic transformation. They are still a green and very pleasant land, thanks to the (normally) benign climate, the river valleys, the abundance of woods, rolling downs and good farmland. But superimposed upon this natural background, to which belong the surviving village and town communities with their history in stone and brick, there have come, in the last half century, two great waves of change. First came the organised overspill of London's population; then all the new firms and industries that have swarmed along and between the M4 and M3 motorways which radiate west and south-west from the capital.

These two developments interlock in what an optimistic tourist guide describes as 'the sunbelt of England'. The phenomenon can best be seen in places like Basingstoke and Andover in Hampshire, Bracknell in Berkshire and the ambitious New Town of Milton Keynes in Buckinghamshire. These small towns and villages, whose expansion was originally planned between the London County Council and the rural County Councils to accommodate the crowded Londoners, have themselves attracted the headquarters of big insurance and other corporations, multiple stores and new technical industries, all of which have relocated in order to take advantage of the lower rates, the office space and housing available.

All sorts of social changes have accompanied this phenomenal expansion of population in what had been previously small or medium sized towns, or even villages. Of course, it has its political consequences, which are generally favourable to the Labour Party as against the ingrained Conservative habit of the region. This is observable in Oxford and in the Southampton area. Elsewhere, with the increase of property-owning households, there is an opposite effect. This mushrooming of towns has been detrimental to the continuity of any civic sense, since local history and tradition are meaningless to the mass of newcomers. However, the valiant efforts of minority groups of the historically minded, some, like 'Thames Valley Heritage', supported by local businessmen, help to keep memory alive. Basingstoke now numbers 113,000 people, as against 26,000 a generation ago. Reading grew from 114,000 in 1951 to 139,000 in 1985. The most rapid growth before the Second World War was in Surrey, now filled up with Londoners. Since the War it has been in Buckinghamshire, because of the Los Angeles-like spread of Milton Keynes. This small county now has the fastest projected growth of any in England. For the 20 years 1981 to 2000, it is 27.6 per cent; that of Berkshire 19.8 per cent and of Oxfordshire 15 per cent. Surrey is not expected to grow any more; Hampshire to grow by 9.2 per cent. So much for statistics.

*　　*　　*　　*

One feature of life, especially in the northern parts of Surrey and Hampshire, the rest of Berkshire and the south of Buckinghamshire — and all the towns — is the great number of cars. One can see many streets of terraced houses with cars lined up by each pavement, while there are one or two in the garage of every suburban and country home. All this means people moving about constantly between home and work, and it is in marked contrast to the immobility of depressed areas in the North, where one is more likely to be tied to the place of heavy industry, which used to provide the employment. Now there is not just one 'commuter belt' inhabited by businessmen – civil servants and the staff of service industries whose daily round means railway journeys between home and London on the fast new electric and diesel trains. There are now several dozen commuter zones of the people who have made their homes within motoring distance of their place of work. In addition to those who commute to inner or outer London, about one sixth of the working population moves in this way between home and work at least five days a week. This adds heavily to the congestion of road traffic; and the problem of driving through and around the constantly expanding towns with their tangle of roundabouts is a headache, the more so when there is lack of co-ordination between those responsible for the flow of traffic and for road repairs. Reading is notorious for this.

Another troublesome consequence of the growth of population in these counties is a duel, which has been going on ever since the overspill from London started. It is a duel between the commercial and administrative proponents of urban expansion and those devoted to the conservation of the countryside and the *genius loci*. There were some 116,764 new houses built between 1980 and 1985 in these counties and these in addition to power stations, factories and industrial buildings of all kinds. Planning permission for all this has to be obtained from the local authorities. So in Berkshire, Hampshire and western Surrey the fight is on between the local groups, who want to save the countryside, residential areas and familiar aspects of their town or village, and the rich and powerful builders' consortiums, who want to weaken or destroy the County Council's right to withhold planning permission. The Department of the Environment is in the thick of the battle. The M.P.s for the constituencies concerned are, as a rule, on the side of the local authorities and are supported by a vigorous national lobby for the conservation of the countryside. In 1983 two draft Circulars from the Ministry to the local Councils, obliging them to give priority to the builders' demands, were withdrawn as a result of 100 Tory M.P.s, led by myself, signing an Early Day Motion in protest in the House of Commons. The County Councils, of course, favour necessary development, to which the Government is committed. Every county has to agree and abide by a structure for this purpose and nowadays there is a County Development Officer to promote it. His task is vitally important in areas of great road works such as those now under way in the south of Hampshire, for the linking of Southampton and Portsmouth in the M3 motorway network. In Milton Keynes, the problem of reconciling local and larger interests does not arise for the Corporation, because 55 per cent of the area of the New Town is still available for development.

The London and South East Regional Planning Conference is an organisation consisting of representatives of the GLC, the London Borough Councils and the County and District Councils of all the counties concerned. It is with this body that the Secretary of State for the Environment discusses the general strategy of development. It is here that the Counties' Structure Plans are reviewed and efforts made to conciliate the claims of conservation and new building. The present planning objective is to provide 460,000 extra dwellings in the Region as a whole (but this, of course, includes, say, 60,000 in Greater London) in the years 1990 to 2000. This is compared with the total of about 600,000 which seems likely in the 1980s, and the 750,000 which were built in the 1970s. The agreed objectives of the Conference include 'to conserve the countryside, the region's Green Belts and other valuable landscape areas', as well as making full use of urban land, 'revitalising' the older urban areas and supporting economic growth. But the increase of households contemplated is still sizeable; and there are still plenty of local battles ahead to protect villages from absorption, particularly in central Berkshire and north-east Hampshire.

*   *   *   *

These five counties have the lowest rates of unemployment in England, ranging from 7.38 per cent in Berkshire to 9.8 per cent in Hampshire, compared with 13.4 per cent in the United Kingdom as a whole.

Though the farms are prosperous and produced their share of the bumper harvest of 1984, no more than 33,500 people out of a total workforce of 1,900,000 earn their living in agriculture, forestry and fishing. That is because mechanisation, including electric milking, is so far advanced that only one or two workers are employed where there were a dozen or more, living and working on the farm thirty years ago.

On the outskirts of every village you will see groups of unlovely, uniform council houses. It is here that the dispossessed rural poor are to be found, the unemployed and ageing farm workers, for whom part-time gardening and odd jobs for the retired gentry and the new rich are about the only opening. In the Farnham area of Surrey, and in Hartley Wintney and Odiham in the neighbouring part of Hampshire for example, well-to-do retired Service officers and their wives abound. Hereabouts, as well as in the Chilterns, the Thames Valley and the Berkshire countryside, live executives of the new computer and electronics firms whose work is in Reading, Farnborough, or Bracknell. It is they who occupy not only the attractive new properties, but also the tarted-up village houses and farm cottages, some even thatched, with their pretty gardens and pastel-painted front doors.

There is a great variety of employment in these parts, including many manufacturing firms of medium size, which account for about a quarter of the workforce. Road and house building is a constant activity and occupies as many people as transport and communication; distribution and catering employ three times as many. The west bank of Southampton Water is a long strip of advanced technology, in which Esso predominates with its oil refinery at May 1985 figures. Comparable figures for Surrey are not available because much of it is in the London area. Fawley, together with the new power station between there and Calshot, and the International Synthetic Rubber Company. Farnborough, home of the Royal Aircraft Establishment, is a centre of the defence industry. The nuclear work of the Ministry of Defence at Aldermaston, the Harwell research centre in Berkshire and the huge Joint European Torus at Culham in Oxfordshire employ a large number of civil servants. But with the exception of the great motor-making complex of British Leyland at Cowley, and to some extent labour in the Southampton and Portsmouth docks, there is little of the nature of mass employment involving a confrontation of trade unions and management. Far the most numerous openings for employment in the towns are in what is called 'service industries', meaning for the most part office work. They account for 65.4 per cent of all jobs, and this is most evident in the newly expanded towns. For instance, IBM occupies the bulk of Basingstoke's office space and the Sun Life of Canada insurance company has also made that town its headquarters in England, as has the Diners Club charge card organisation in Farnborough.

What is more characteristic of the many enterprises in electronics and computers is not the number but the quality of the young men and women for whom openings are now available. It is university graduates who are in demand and others who have already had some technical training. Thus we find the Milton Keynes Development Corporation involved with the Local Education Authority in the Technical/Vocational Education Initiative, whose object is to increase the amount of technical and commercial-orientated education in the 14 to 16 age group. Here is a typical advertisement, from *The Times*, October 29, 1984, designed to attract the ambitious:

MONSANTO
The World's largest producer of high grade silicon wafers
for the electronics industry is establishing a £35 million European
manufacturing and research facility in Milton Keynes.
Over 100 people will be recruited shortly to staff the site's
new production, technical service and research departments.

There are those who believe that high technology development in this part of the world is likely very soon, with the help of Oxford University as it tries to catch up with Cambridge. There, 325 successful high technology companies have been started and large businesses are moving into the Cambridge Science Park. Oxford has as yet few such companies – about 50 – but the University Industry Committee is committed to promoting them, and the Clarendon Laboratory is a power-house of the new sciences. The Oxford Instrument Group shows the practical advantage of starting a high technology business near the University. Martin Wood, working in the laboratory, founded this company in the traditional garden shed and disused slaughter-house. Today it has five factories, employing 275 people in the city and 490 in the county. This is useful because unemployment in Oxford at 11.5 per cent is higher than in the rest of the region. But it is uncertain how far these new inventions can make a real impact on unemployment, for their staff is generally so small. Oxford Lasers, for instance, another product of the University, has a staff of 20 with six laser physics doctorates, helping to research new forms of cancer therapy. Only when the technology of these new units can be used by larger concerns can they have any appreciable social effect.

This has happened on an impressive scale in what is described, in imitation American journalese, as Britain's 'Silicon Gulch', namely the strip of country along the M4 motorway in which so many new technology industries are clustered, reaching from London to Newport and beyond. They are also scattered more loosely in other parts of England and Scotland, but Reading seems to be the principal centre. Here, 20,000 people are employed by high technology firms; 57 of these businesses have been established since 1980 in Berkshire, having chosen the Reading/Bracknell areas as their base in the United Kingdom. They include big American British concerns such as Racal, Digital Equipment, Hewlett Packard, Honeywell and Sperry Gyroscope. Newbury has 700 people employed by 24 new companies and is said to have a higher ratio of microchips to people than anywhere else in Britain, and probably Europe. Maidenhead and Henley are also in the business, some of the firms having pleasant riverside premises. The Farnborough area too is home to many of them.

If you ask any of the prosperous executives of these large and small enterprises why they set up shop in these parts, they will probably say, because it is a nice place to live, near London and near Heathrow Airport. This concentration of high technology is certainly of growing value to the national economy but, for lack of millionaire entrepreneurs it is never likely to be of the same scale as California's 'Silicon Valley'. Nor, saving Surrey's pardon, is there here the equivalent of the great Universities of

Berkeley and Stanford, who inspire and reinforce the technical development of the whole San Francisco Bay area. Inmos, the one volume chip manufacturer in Britain, which has cost £100 million so far and is still short of cash, owed its foundation to an American entrepreneur. The whole development is, however, a great asset to Britain today and, though it can never hope to replace the massive employment of the old labour-intensive industries, it offers increasing opportunities of interesting and well paid jobs as the educational system adapts to it.

This adaptation is, of course, an important preoccupation of the governing bodies of the three modern universities of this region, Reading, Southampton and Surrey with their many thousands of students, more perhaps than it is of Oxford with its venerable framework of studies. It is a question of extending their opportunities for training in electronics, computer systems and the relevant technologies, without detriment to the existing academic disciplines, their international relations which are well-developed, and, in the case of Reading, its world-wide reputation for agriculture.

* * * *

Yes, this part of Southern England *is* a nice place to live. There is an abundance of areas of natural beauty; the waterways for instance. The Thames is a treasure shared by four of these five counties. Rising in the Cotswolds, it winds its way to Oxford, soon becoming the boundary between Oxfordshire and Berkshire till, between Henley and Marlow, Buckinghamshire succeeds to Oxfordshire, and soon after reaching Windsor, Surrey to Berkshire. The wave of the new technological revolution sweeping from London westward into the Thames Valley has not so far spoilt the beauty of its wooded banks, the fascination of its weirs and locks and beautiful old bridges. As the river sweeps around the west and south of the Chiltern range from Wallingford to Cliveden, the beech woods are first a mass of green and then the gold of autumn.

The other big river in these parts is the Ouse, flowing eastward from its source near Banbury through the north of the Vale of Aylesbury and Bedfordshire towards the Wash. It has no need of locks like the Thames but, as William Cowper wrote two centuries ago, flows:

slow-winding through the level plain
of spacious meads, with cattle sprinkled over

This is still a rich farming area, despite Milton Keynes and all that.

In Hampshire, it is the valley of the Test, the best trout stream in

England with salmon on its lower reaches, which is almost a world of its own, running from north to south through a string of beautiful villages and small towns. It flows, as does the Itchen, into Southampton Water. At the mouth of the Itchen, in the Solent and in the small creeks and harbours round the coast to Lymington there is nowadays a great fleet of yachts.

There has been a steady growth latterly of waterways enjoyment. The Thames is so full of motor cruisers in the summer – the days of skiff and punt are over – that it takes an hour or more to get through a lock. Families hire the cruisers from the many boat builders located between Kingston and Oxford and live on them for their holiday. Canoeing clubs for boys abound. The tributaries of the great river, the Kennet and Lodden also attract the smaller motor craft, up to Hungerford, for instance. There has been much progress hereabouts, as in other parts of the country with the work of clearing the old canals with voluntary labour and getting their handworked locks into working order. So, gaily painted narrow canal barges have now joined the white motor boats. Marinas for small yachts have also sprouted in the lakes formed by the large scale extraction of gravel for road building along the Thames, Lodden and Kennet.

There are quite a number of national sporting events in those Southern counties too; the Oxford and Cambridge Boat Race and the Henley Regatta are the main contributions of the Thames to the annual calendar, but there is also a host of other regattas. Then come the Derby and the Ascot and Newbury Race Meetings, with the racing stables which provide the main industry of Lambourn and the Berkshire Downs where once grazed the huge flocks of sheep. All these sporting events draw great crowds, with tennis at Wimbledon, the culmination of the summer sports season, most of all.

Of cricket, it would be impious to write without special mention of Hampshire, the birthplace of the game. Is it still our national game. At any rate it is the most distinctive. While even in the Netherlands there are cricket clubs, it is in almost all the countries – African, Asian, Australian and Caribbean – which used, not so long ago, to belong to the British Empire, that cricket remains a national institution. And American baseball, played with an implement not unlike the 18th century English bat, is, of course, a derivative of it. There is some dispute about where in Hampshire the game originated, but certainly at Hambledon, on Broad Halfpenny Downs, near Petersfield, cricket was already the centre of attraction by the 1770s. What a contrast it is to compare the televised Test Matches, that money and the media have made the gladiatorial shows watched by millions today, with the freshness of a contemporary account:

There was high feasting held on Broad Halfpenny during the solemnity of one of our great matches. Oh! It was a heart-stirring sight to witness the multitude forming a complete and dense circle round that noble green. Half the County would be present and all their hearts with us. Little Hampshire against all England was a proud thought for the Hampshire men.

Thus John Nyren, writing of his boyhood in *Cricketers of my Time* [quoted by Noreen O'Dell in her *Portrait of Hampshire*].

*   *   *   *

There is no doubt that the physical attraction of the South country, as well as the warmer climate and the opportunities of good employment, draw many people from the North. Yet I know of no signs of clannishness in the new industries and settlements between the original population, Northerners and the Londoners. As I have said, newcomers know nothing of local history, nor indeed do many of the products of public education, as they are taught none of it. But a natural pride in one's present home does often extend to its old buildings of interest. Thus it is evident that the recent efforts of Local Authorities to restrict the rapacity of developers by preserving, at least the house fronts of 17th, 18th or 19th century buildings in the towns is generally approved.

There is a great wealth of beautiful old country churches in these counties, many of them with Norman features. One generally finds both church and churchyard lovingly cared for, though congregations are sparse, except for marriages and funerals. The vitality of the Church of England parish in a town or large village seems to depend very much upon the parson's character. Free Church numbers are reduced, but one can find some very active Baptist and Methodist communities. The Catholic churches, generally built for smaller congregations, seem to be packed on Sundays. The Quakers, small in number, keep up their old Meeting Houses, of which William Penn's at Jordans near Beaconsfield, is the most famous and a place of pilgrimage for Pennsylvanians.

Of all the great English churches, the Cathedral at Winchester, the old capital, has pride of place; and the mediaeval and 18th century colleges and university buildings at Oxford remain for those of us who went to that university the heart of England – even if some women are nowadays members of the men's colleges and undergraduates call themselves students. But while Oxford, along with Stratford-upon-Avon, is part of the regular American tourist route, there is no doubt that for foreign tourists and natives alike it is Windsor which heads the list. Berkshire is the Royal County and has something of a proprietary interest in the Royal

Family; but Windsor Safari Park, with its dolphins, elephants, lions, and even parrots on roller-skates, has a total of visitors that is creeping up to that of the hundreds of thousands who visit the State Apartments in the Castle, St George's Chapel and Queen Mary's Dolls' House. Windsor Great Park is a wide area of woodland, open to the public, and there are several other great estates in these parts, such as the Park of Blenheim Palace, Vanbrugh's monstrously great tribute to Marlborough's victories over Louis XIV, and the much more modest tribute to Wellington's over Napoleon at Stratfield Saye in Hampshire. Here, alongside of the home estate and its farms, the present Duke of Wellington has opened the Wellington Country Park, a popular area for picnics, riding and boating and a centre for demonstrating the crafts and products of the country.

But if we are to judge from the reports of the English Tourist Board it is the wide open spaces that have the greatest appeal to Londoners, townsfolk and visitors. The New Forest in the south-west of Hampshire is the largest of these areas, and one in which most of the wild life of the country, with its woods and moorlands, has survived. Ponies, deer and cattle move freely, often to the peril of motorists. But it is the high open downland of the Box Hill Country Park in central Surrey which accounted in 1984 for a million tourist visits.

*   *   *   *

It is the fact that nearly every family seems to have its car which permits this great mobility, especially at weekends, and accounts for many social changes. For example, the middle aged 'old boy' of any of the big public schools, which are clustered in these counties – Eton or Winchester, Wellington, Charterhouse or Stowe – who visits his old school on a Saturday afternoon or Sunday is surprised to find hardly any boys in residence. They have all gone off to stay with their families or relations for the weekend. I cannot say how far this is the practice with other Headmasters' Conference schools, such as Bradfield or Douai and at the girls' boarding schools, but it is evidently widespread. These counties – and it is evidence, I suppose, of the number of well-to-do and well-educated families – are particularly well off not only in boarding schools, but also in the surviving grammar schools and those which, like Abingdon, had till lately that status. Among these, Guildford's Royal Grammar School, which chose to go independent, stands high. The two Reading Grammar Schools, Reading School for boys and Kendrick School for girls, have also good academic records. It is thanks jointly to Margaret Thatcher, when she was Minister for Education and Science, and, the two county councils, that they were able to retain their status in the face of a long standing Labour campaign in local politics. But here we enter the sphere of scholastic politics in which there is no need to be entangled in describing life in these counties. Indeed, there are very many excellent comprehensive schools, and, to judge from the number of 'A' level examination passes, the *sine qua non* nowadays of admission to Oxford or Cambridge, which their Sixth Forms produce, there is little to choose academically between them and the independent schools.

* * * *

The problem of law and order is uncomplicated in these counties by those collective feuds between strikers and non-strikers, pickets and their opponents and their families which characterise industrial disputes in the North and elsewhere. Nor is there any substantial racial tension of the sort that pits black and Asian youths against the police in some of the depressed city areas – an attack on members of the Thames Valley Police at High Wycombe in August 1983 was an exception. The general prosperity of the region is, no doubt, one reason for this. Another reason must be that the not very numerous West Indians and Asian Muslims are well integrated into the community. So the tasks of the police, difficult as they are, are concerned with the normal protection of life and property, the prevention of crime, by education and vigilance, and the bringing of malefactors to justice. The conflicts between police and demonstrators which were the favourite topics of the media from 1982 to 1984 were looked upon by nearly all those who inhabit the neighbourhoods of Greenham Common and Upper Heyford as the consequence of outsiders' interference. There is a general relief that they have apparently fizzled out. Of this more anon.

Looking at the reports of the Chief Constables of the Thames Valley, which includes Berkshire, Buckinghamshire and Oxfordshire, and those of Hampshire and Surrey as a whole, one is struck by the lack of any outstanding differences between them – except, of course, for the impact of the nuclear disarmament controversy in Berkshire. There is, overall, an increase in the total number of reported crimes (a 'crime' being anything from petty theft to murder), for the Thames Valley, 6.9 per cent in 1984, for Hampshire and the Isle of Wight, 6.5 per cent, for Surrey, 2.5 per cent. I should say that this is little more than wrong-doing keeping pace with the increase of population. There has been a decrease of juvenile offences in the Thames Valley and of burglary in Surrey; there, says the Chief Constable, most of the burglars come from London. There has been an increase of 9 per cent in road injuries in Hampshire, which can no doubt be accounted for by the great road extensions in the south of the county. Hunt saboteurs are in evidence in Surrey and Hampshire. But when all is said, the level of violence, including attacks on women and muggings, and house-breaking – often amateur – by youngsters are depressingly common. Football hooliganism is not unknown, but has not erupted on a major scale in these counties. More attention has been given everywhere to the prevention of crime. The Thames Valley Police have given priority to their Schools Involvement Programmes and have found plenty of welcome and encouragement from teachers and pupils.

The motor bike is, of course, the status symbol of the teenager. While the majority of motor cyclists cause no trouble, except for the noise, the covens of Hells Angels, with their free use of knives, guns and daggers, give rise periodically to murderous fights with which the police have to cope. The killing of two 'Road Rats' at a party of the Windsor Chapter at Cookham in September 1983 and the discovery of two other dead bodies of Hells Angels in Salsey Forest earlier in the year, led to trials for murder. We even have a Hells Angels Chapter in 'high-tech' prosperous Farnham.

A more serious social evil is the drug traffic. The drug squads of all three police authorities have been busy tracking down the dealers, and also giving lectures to various groups, including Sixth Formers, on the danger of taking drugs. There is a lot of heroin in the Aldershot and Farnborough areas, and a joint Surrey/Hampshire drug squad hunted and arrested several heroin dealers there. For the Thames Valley Police, heroin addiction has also been a cause of anxiety, particularly in the Oxford area. There, the arrest and imprisonment of the main dealer, and then of his successor is reported to have stemmed the supply of the drug in the three counties; 681 offences of drug abuse were dealt with in 1983 compared to 1,093 in 1982.

Such, together with an exceptionally heavy job of traffic control, and a contribution to the care of the Royal Family (since Windsor is within the Thames Valley area), are examples of the routine duties of the police in this part of the world.

*   *   *   *

But it is as the battleground between the forces of Law and Order and the militant pacifism that the Thames Valley Police area became famous between 1981 and 1984. The Women's Peace Movement has camped outside the Main Gate of RAF Greenham Common since September 1981; and the Campaign for Nuclear Disarmament organised a number of large demonstrations and marches focussed on Greenham Common between June 1982 and December 1983. Of the two bodies, both of which aimed at preventing the deployment of cruise missiles, in accordance with the European nuclear defence plans of NATO, it is the former which has been throughout the more violent and responsible for more damage. This is in contrast to the prior consultation, which has taken place on several occasions between the CND and police authorities on traffic control.

The largest CND event in 1983 was the 'human chain' of 40,000 people linking arms along the roads between ROF Burghfield, AWRE Aldermaston and RAF Greenham Common. The main problem for the police was to maintain, as they did, a system for routing the cars and some 600 to 700 coaches without blocking roads and villages for miles around. The human chain and the subsequent festival at Padworth Common turned out to be a peaceful operation. 'The demonstrators had the opportunity to make their point', writes the Chief Constable, 'and mass arrests were not necessary — in fact not one person was arrested'.

It was a very different matter with the 'Wild Women' during the summer of 1983, but, though there was great publicity for their attacks on the perimeter fence and gates of Greenham Common, the numbers involved were in fact insignificant.

The most concerted attack on the base was made on October 29th, in view of the build up of media speculation about the arrival of the first cruise missiles at Greenham Common. In the event, no more than 400 militant protesters arrived, but they were armed for their purpose. They cut the tensioning wire of the chain link fence — nine miles of it — in hundreds of places and pushed down lengths of it. In all, 179 people were arrested, almost all for criminal damage or being equipped to commit it. Over 130 pairs of bolt-croppers were seized.

From then on during November, as the huge Galaxy aircraft were delivering the cruise missiles and equipment, the siege of Greenham Common continued until a final demonstration of more than 20,000 people on Sunday, December 11th, 1983. More of the fence was pushed down by sheer weight of numbers. There were many personal attacks on policemen, 30 of whom were injured. In total, 745 people were arrested in 1983; Newbury Magistrates Court was kept busy with two sittings a week and a number of women were sent to prison for refusing to stop interrupting court proceedings.

The temper of the protesting crowds at Greenham, as in Germany, became more and more openly hostile to NATO and to the United States, as distinct from the moral tone of the original anti-nuclear movement. This became even more evident in the campaign to stop the operation of the US Air Force at the RAF base at Upper Heyford, which has also been an affliction of the Thames Valley Police. Fortunately, this was on a smaller scale than Greenham.

The feelings of American servicemen can be imagined. As for the sentiments of the majority of people living thereabouts, Newbury and western Berkshire, they are inevitably angry at the disturbance which the disarmament agitation has brought into their life, and sickened by the squalor of so many of the more permanent protesters.

I have included this summary of the political turbulence which invaded parts of Berkshire and Oxfordshire during the 1980s not because it affected most of the people living in these counties, but because of its relevance to the controversy about nuclear armaments which has loomed large in the television and press reports of the Western World and the Soviet Union. As I have suggested, I doubt whether the agitation will have much influence upon the political life of the constituencies concerned. Only the next General Election will show the result of the local Labour Parties' adoption of unilateralism as a legacy of it.

*   *   *   *

Differences between local interests and the central Government are more likely to arouse public feeling. Among such issues at the moment, it is the future of Milton Keynes which stands out. Those involved in its administration and economic expansion believe that this largest, and most successful, British experiment in social engineering is in danger of serious disorganisation if the original idea persists of winding up the Development Corporation in 1989.

What should be the permanent form of what is already called a 'city' remains to be seen; but the immense variety of undertakings which the Corporation has stimulated would be in disarray if they were simply handed over to local authorities. The Government's desire to reduce the funding of the Corporation by the Department of the Environment comes, I believe, from the Prime Minister's pre-occupation with spending money rather on revitalising the old city centres, than on New Towns initiated by the former Administration — and of which Milton Keynes is the most eminent example. I hope, in any case, that this most encouraging of British experiments in constructive development will not be jeopardised.

LONDON
John Cartwright

John Cartwright is the spokesman for the SDP on the environment. He joined the SDP/Liberal Alliance in 1981 having been elected as Labour M.P. for Woolwich in 1979; he was then for two years Chairman of the Defence Group of the Parliamentary Labour Party. He is very knowledgeable in matters of defence and is a member of the North Atlantic Assembly. Together with Julian Critchley, also a British Member of that body, he produced in 1983, the Report on Nuclear Weapons in Europe which the Assembly adopted. This report, dealing in particular with the much-debated subject of the cruise-missile deployments of NATO, was especially well received by the United States Senate.

John Cartwright was born in 1933 and was educated at Woking County Grammar School, and was an Executive Civil Servant for three years. It was as a Director of the Royal Arsenal Cooperative Society that he gained his economic expertise. He was Chairman of the National Union of Labour Organisers in 1969-70, Leader of Greenwich Borough Council from 1971 to 1974 and has been Vice President of the Association of Metropolitan Authorities since that year. He is also a Trustee of the National Maritime Museum.

Most of the many millions of visitors to London see only a tiny fraction of the capital's varied life. For them London is a mixture of Big Ben, Buckingham Palace, Oxford Street and Madame Tussauds.

Their time is spent in the bright lights of the West End, never venturing further east than the Tower of London. The city they see is full of smart shops, plush hotels and expensive night spots. It presents a glitteringly successful image but without quite the friendly relaxed style of the past. Periodic bomb scares, security checks and wailing police sirens all hint at potential danger not dream't of in happier days.

Yet London has much more to offer than its highly publicised and much frequented tourist attractions. Dating back to Roman times, the City of London crams into its square mile all the nation's leading financial and commercial institutions, and in a combination of ambitious glass-fronted towers and more solid, self-confident, Victorian buildings.

Wren's churches provide an occasional oasis of calm amidst the solid mass of traffic and the surging tides of office workers.

Just beyond the City lies the East End. Traditionally the home of the genuine cockney, born within the sound of Bow Bells, the East End has seen massive re-building during the post-war years. Homes which survived Hitler's bombs proved no match for local council bulldozers. Tower blocks have mushroomed where narrow streets of back to back houses used to huddle together.

London's docks, for generations the dominant factor in East End life, lie empty and unused. Buildings which once housed thousands of workers now stand as derelict monuments to industrial change. Only a few swans glide gracefully across vast stretches of water which were once filled by vessels from the four corners of the world.

The River Thames has been a vital part of London's life from its very earliest days. The Romans set up their original city to take advantage of tidal flows and a safe crossing. For centuries afterwards, the Thames provided a broad highway on which much of London's prosperity was founded.

Today the river lies largely unused except for pleasure craft and summer disco-outings. But it still forms a major barrier dividing the city. Despite all the bridges and the tunnels, Londoners remain obstinately reluctant to cross the river except for essential trips to and from work.

Another essential element in the London kaleidoscope is the presence of villages engulfed but somehow preserved as the city sprawled ever wider. Places like Dulwich and Blackheath in the south and Hampstead in the north have retained their rural flavour despite the onward march of modern building.

All round the outer suburbs are pleasant, comfortable, communities with tree lined streets, neat gardens and desirable semis. These provide the havens to which the fortunate Londoners can retreat after a 'hard day in the office'.

Like many of the city's elected representatives I cannot claim to be a genuine Londoner. Politics brought me to the south-east London borough of Woolwich at the age of 29.

I can still recall the sense of community in the Woolwich of those days. It felt like a genuine town in its own right and not an anonymous part of a vast city. London has always been a collection of such communities with strong local loyalties, but the upheavals of the past twenty years have done much to undermine this local identity in many parts of the capital.

The revolution in London's government in the early 1960s played some part in this change. Small, comfortable boroughs were swallowed up in much larger and inevitably more impersonal local authorities.

The boundaries of London itself were pushed out to engulf virtually all of Middlesex, together with large parts of Essex, Kent and Surrey. The old London County Council with its well understood responsibility for personal services like health, housing and welfare, was replaced by the vastly bigger Greater London Council with a much less clearly defined 'strategic' role.

I arrived in London just in time for the funeral of the old system and the birth of the new. It has taken years for many Londoners to come to terms with their new Council and some have still not succeeded. Now they face further changes with the scrapping of the GLC and its replacement by a more shadowy network of joint boards and Government appointed bodies.

I suspect that few London residents had more than a vague idea of the GLC's powers and responsibilities. Yet they do seem to feel that their city is more than a patchwork quilt of thirty-three individual local councils and that it does need some overall elected body to speak for London and its inhabitants. Despite the obvious differences between, say Hampstead and Hackney, people do think of themselves as Londoners. They are likely to go on doing so whether or not they have an overall London Council to represent them.

But the changes of the past twenty years have not just been in London's administrative machines. Powerful natural forces have also been at work. Arguably the most dramatic has been the continued flight of population from the city.

When the first census was taken in 1801 there were just 1.1 million people living in what is now Greater London. That population grew by leaps and bounds to a peak of over 8.5 million just before the Second World War.

Since the War's end, the process has gone into reverse, producing huge population losses in the late 1960s and early 1970s. Between 1971 and 1981, one in every ten Londoners packed up and left. As a result, the population of Inner London is now lower than at any time since 1841. Even in Outer London, which has seen substantial new house building, population is now down to the level of 1931.

Migration reached a peak of 117,000 people a year in the early 1970s but has since slowed to around 50,000 a year. Although some of this was a planned removal to the ring of new and expanded towns around London, many more people simply left under their own steam for what seemed to them a more attractive environment.

A 1970 survey suggested that London's housing problem was one of the main reasons for the exodus. The rapid disappearance of industrial jobs and the declining quality of life in many, high-stress, inner areas also persuaded many families to seek greener pastures beyond the city limits.

Some planners have always believed that such a fall in London's population was the only way of tackling the chronic overcrowding in the inner areas, the transport problems and the urban decay. A slimmed-down London would, in their view, become a much more pleasant place in which to live. Whatever the truth of that theory, the decline in population has not been accompanied by any obvious environmental improvements. Indeed some would argue that it has made things worse.

It has certainly left London with a less balanced population. Central London remains a magnet for young people, attracted by the glamour, the bright lights and job prospects. This aggravates the housing problems of the central areas where the supply of bedsitting room accommodation and affordable private rented flats is drying up. The growth of commuting beyond the Greater London area has also added to the city's transport problems and fuelled the demand for more road building.

It is also true that those who leave London are much more likely to be the professional or managerial people rather than manual workers. Those most likely to stay are the unskilled and semi-skilled workers who are most vulnerable to unemployment. The various ethnic minorities have also been less involved in the migration. Indeed, they have tended to take over housing in the run-down inner city areas vacated by their more fortunate former neighbours. However, there are now some signs that the more successful families from the New Commonwealth and Pakistan are following the pattern of previous immigrants by moving out to the suburbs.

The overall impact of population changes means that Greater London is aging more rapidly than the rest of the country with relatively fewer children and more retired people. The impact of all these changes is a severe threat to London's economic health with a growing proportion of its citizens retired, unemployed or in low wage jobs.

Just as damaging to London as the haemorrhaging of its population have been severe job losses, particularly in manufacturing industry.

There has always been a tendency to see unemployment in Britain as a problem limited to Scotland, Wales and the old industrial areas of Northern England. Yet, over recent years, more people have been drawing unemployment benefit in London than in Scotland and twice as many as in Wales.

London may be thought of as a capital city, a great commercial and financial centre and a major provider of tourist and leisure opportunities. But it used to be an important industrial centre. In 1951, 36 per cent of its working population had jobs in manufacturing industry. Over the following thirty years that proportion has been halved. Since 1961,

London's population has dropped by 17 per cent but the number of industrial jobs has declined by no less than 51 per cent. That is a far more dramatic fall than has occurred across Britain as a whole, or in other large British cities. The painful results can be seen in the dole queues and in empty, desolate factory buildings.

The impact has been particularly severe in some parts of London. The riverside based heavy engineering on which south-east London traditionally depended, has been virtually wiped out. When the AEI plant closed at Woolwich in the 1960s, some 6,000 jobs disappeared at a stroke. Closures like these have forced Londoners to travel further afield in search of work.

Few of London's job losses have resulted from the efforts of successive Governments to re-locate firms in traditionally hard-pressed areas of the country. Far more have been caused by firms simply shutting down or severely cutting their work force. Employers point to a variety of reasons for the massive decline in London's industry.

Substantial increases in local rates are often the final blow which sends an ailing business over the edge. The determination of local Councils to move small firms out of cheap back-street sites and into purpose-built factories at much higher rents has also killed off many jobs. The hampering effects of clogged roads and skill shortages have also played their part in persuading some employers to switch to green field sites in the more attractive parts of the South East.

During the relatively prosperous 1960s, this trend was offset by the growth of jobs in the service sector, in national and local government and in general office work. But the growth of offices slowed down in the 1970s and has now been reversed as the high cost of operating in London has forced more firms to move routine work to less expensive parts of the country.

Now the introduction of new technology even threatens some of the remaining clerical and secretarial jobs in London offices on which women have particularly depended. At the same time, Government plans to cut jobs in the Civil Service and in local government will have a major impact on a city in which the public sector provided 29 per cent of all jobs at the end of the 1970s.

The growth of unemployment has aggravated the divisions between London's rich and poor. One Londoner in every five now depends on state benefits. Wealthy West End diners will spend on one meal as much money as an unemployed East End family will have on which to live for a whole week. In some of the hardest hit parts of Inner London, unemployment levels are as bad as in any of the depressed areas of Wales, Scotland and Northern England.

Some London boroughs have tried to ease the problems by creating new jobs, but have made little impression on the rising tide of losses. Indeed, some boroughs are caught in a classic inner city vicious spiral. They levy high rates in an attempt to combat the effects of unemployment, but these high rate levels simply discourage businesses and make the job situation even worse.

The abrupt departure of manufacturing industry may have released more land for housing, but neither this trend nor the fall in population has done much to reduce the chronic housing shortage that has bedevilled London throughout the post-war years.

Overall, the capital's existing housing is sliding downhill towards slumdom. Nearly one home in four is officially unfit for use, lacking modern amenities or in need of major repairs. Nearly half the houses let by London's private landlords are below acceptable modern standards. Many of these problems are quite simply from the age of London's housing stock. One out of every three homes in Inner London was built before 1919 and many have now reached a point where substantial spending is vital in order to bring them back up to a reasonable standard.

Furthermore, the problems are not confined to the private sector. Some of the post-war council housing – particularly the system built flats of the 1960s – are showing serious faults. Design problems combined with the tenants' inability to pay high heating bills have produced appalling problems. Some families are forced to live in flats dripping with condensation and covered with foul-smelling mould growth.

The reduction in the money being invested in housing has also meant that fewer rented homes are being built. The number of new houses and flats started by London's local Councils fell from 24,620 in 1975 to only 5,465 in 1983. This is bad news for the many thousands of London families who are unable to buy a home of their own. It means that they will have to go on living with parents or in-laws, waiting their turn in an ever-lengthening queue.

The more fortunate can take advantage of low-cost starter homes for first time buyers that are being built in many parts of London. This is only the latest round in the dramatic growth of home ownership over the past twenty-five years. As recently as 1961, only 36 per cent of Londoners owned their own homes. By 1981 the figure had passed 50 per cent and is still rising today. In contrast, private landlords are on the way out. They were letting 43 per cent of London's homes in 1961. Twenty years later their share was below 20 per cent and still falling.

But these overall figures conceal startling differences between inner and outer London. Only one in four of inner Londoners are home owners, compared to two out of every three in the outer boroughs. In contrast, council housing is much more a way of life in the inner areas, where 43 per cent are council tenants compared to only 23 per cent in outer London. Indeed in some inner London areas, council tenants represent well over half the electorate.

The 'right to buy' revolution giving council tenants the power to buy their homes from unwilling councils has had only limited effect on this situation. About 8 percent of London's council housing has been sold since 1978, yet the overwhelming majority of sales have been of desirable houses complete with gardens. Few tenants have shown much interest in buying flats or maisonettes in the high density estates and more would have been happy to buy if they could have moved their home to a better environment. The graffiti-covered walls, broken windows, vandalised lifts, the smell of urine and the general air of neglect and decay which characterise so many inner London council estates does little to encourage pride of ownership.

Yet when despairing councils have sold off blocks of flats which they were quite unable to let, imaginative private developers have been able to transform them into attractive and much sought after homes for sale. Unfortunately, local councils appear not to have either the expertise or the resources to perform a similar miracle.

The most heart-rending feature of the London housing scene is the number of families with nowhere to live. They turn up at M.P.s' constituency surgeries desperately trying to find help. In 1984, nearly 25,000 families were officially accepted as homeless by the London borough councils — most of them in the hard pressed inner areas. Almost one third of all England's homeless families are concentrated in Greater London. The lack of available houses and flats means that many of them are forced to spend lengthy spells in hostels or hotels which provide no more than 'bed and breakfast'. A new problem has been the number of single Londoners with nowhere to live and who cannot look to local councils for help; some 20,000 are now estimated to be homeless or living in poor quality, temporary accommodation. Nor is this only a central London problem, as even in suburban areas there are homeless young people constantly on the move, sleeping on the floors of friends' homes or living rough.

*   *   *   *

Transport has always been vital to the life of London. The growth of railways in the 19th century lead to the widespread development of the suburbs. As land in or near the centre became increasingly attractive for commerce and industry, more and more people started to live outside the city and to travel in to work every day. Over the past 150 years, the distances which workers have been prepared to travel to get to and from their jobs, particularly those in professional and managerial jobs, has grown steadily. Daily commuting now occurs from areas as far flung as Southampton, Bristol and Birmingham.

London's transport is thus dominated by the commuters and their needs. Nearly three quarters of all British Rail journeys in London and the South-East are commuter trips. In 1983, some 383,000 commuters used British Rail every day; 339,000 travelled by tube train and 97,000 used London Transport bus services. A further 211,000 depended on some form of private transport. That adds up to a tidal flow of well over a million people travelling in and out of London every day, mainly in the morning and evening peak periods.

Travel problems are a major talking point for Londoners, who regularly exchange 'horror stories' about traffic jams, cancelled trains and rush hour buses that seem always to travel in pairs. Perhaps that is why the balance between the capital's public and private transport dominated the political scene after the GLC took over London Transport in 1969. The debate about the relative merits of the bus and Underground network and the road system was caricatured as an argument between high-fare, low-subsidy, low-rate pro-car Conservatives and low-fare, high-subsidy, high-rate anti-car Socialists. This battle reached its climax in 1981, with the election of the left wing Ken Livingstone regime at County Hall.

The central plank of the Labour manifesto had been a pledge to cut London Transport fares by an average of 32 percent. The cost of £228 million was to be borne by London's ratepayers. This so incensed some of them that it was successfully challenged in the courts, although it finally went ahead in a modified form.

One of the basic objections came from south-east Londoners unable to use the Underground system yet expected to subsidise the fares of those who could. This demonstrates one of the integral problems of London's rail system. British Rail's commuter services are concentrated in the south and east, while most of those travelling from the north and west can use the Underground. The obvious solution was to link the two. That was one of the reasons given by Ministers for their 1984 decision to take back responsibility for London Transport from the GLC and to place it, once again, under the supervision of Whitehall. However, there is no doubt that Conservative exasperation with the political priorities of a Labour administration at County Hall played a major part in the decision.

Although London Transport's 1983 fare reductions reduced private car journeys into central London by some 40,000 vehicles (or 15 per cent) in the peak morning periods, traffic congestion in central London in particular continues to be a major headache. Car ownership has grown roughly in line with the rest of Britain and threatens to bring the central areas to a grinding halt. In the 1960s, London planners thought they had the answer with an ambitious programme of urban motorways. There were to be two ringways inside London together with the planned M25 outer orbital motorway beyond the London boundary. These roads would carry traffic around the city and link up with a number of radial routes for vehicles heading into and out of central London.

The project would have cost more than Concorde or the Channel Tunnel and threatened the homes of some 100,000 Londoners. Not surprisingly, the plan provoked enormous opposition. After Labour took control of the GLC in 1973, the whole idea was formally scrapped and no one at County Hall has since dared to propose any major new examination of London's strategic road system.

Nevertheless London's main arteries regularly become clogged with the sheer volume of vehicles trying to get in and out. The noise, fumes and sheer frustration involved have encouraged the Government to look again at some of the worst 'black spots' such as the so-called South Circular Road, which is really no more than a straggling collection of village high streets. In the meantime, the River Thames, which offers a great broad highway into the centre of the city for both goods and people alike, remains criminally under-used.

*   *   *   *

The solution to many of London's planning, housing and industrial problems requires open space and the chance to start again from scratch. The Docklands Development Area offers just that chance. Once the container revolution drove the Port of London down river to Tilbury, the 8.5 square miles of London's docks became the biggest urban redevelopment opportunity in the whole of Europe.

The first ideas put forward by consultants in 1971 laid great stress on leisure schemes such as golf courses, marinas and even a safari park. These were rejected, as being frivolous, by the local authorities who saw the empty areas as a heaven sent chance to solve their employment and housing problems. Their priorities were traditional council housing and more factories, both of which figured prominently in the masterplan produced by the Docklands Joint Committee in 1977.

However, progress was so slow that the Government's patience finally ran out. In 1981, Environment Secretary Michael Heseltine established a Docklands Development Corporation with sweeping powers to 'get things moving'. Vice-Chairman Bob Mellish, a former Labour Cabinet Minister, set the tone: 'We don't just pass resolutions here', he said, 'we get on with things'. The Corporation's approach has been directed much more by market forces than by overall planning considerations but it has produced results. Over 2,000 houses have already been built, with a further 7,000 planned by 1990. Approximately 5,000 jobs have been attracted into the Docklands area with more on the way.

However, the Corporation is not universally admired. Its ability to ride rough shod over the views of local councils is very much resented. There are charges that many of the new starter homes for first time buyers are beyond the reach of long-established Dockland families. Critics also claim that new firms moving into the area bring their own staff with them and provide only menial jobs like catering, portering and baggage handling for local people.

The sheer size and scale of the Docklands redevelopment has dwarfed an earlier and rather less successful attempt to use a sudden land windfall to solve London's pressing housing problems. The closure of the Royal Ordnance Factory at Woolwich Arsenal in 1965 released a large area of marshland. Combined with the neighbouring Erith Marshes, this was developed as the Thamesmead New Town.

Originally planned by the GLC to house 60,000 people — two thirds in council owned property and the rest in owner occupied homes — Thamesmead was to be a town of the 21st century rising dramatically from the Thames-side mud. It was to have a range of schools, shops, leisure activities and local employment.

Pedestrians and vehicles would be kept apart but there would be a garage for every home. A system of lakes and canals would drain the marshland and the development would be based on separate neighbourhoods all linked to the town centre.

In fact, the dreams turned into something of a nightmare. Soil pollution, building problems, changes of GLC policy and reductions in public spending all combined to slow down the pace of development to a crawl. The Government's decision to build a prison near the town centre has not helped, while the lack of local jobs has forced many Thamesmead residents to travel long distances to and from work.

The abolition of the GLC will leave Thamesmead as a potential orphan searching for adoptive parents. Whether it is taken in by the two local boroughs of Greenwich and Bexley, or by some independent trust, the remaining unused land is to be sold off for private enterprise housing. This will make it much more difficult to achieve the original exciting concept of Thamesmead as a pioneering new town inside London's boundaries.

*   *   *   *

London's criminal underworld has provided the inspiration for countless films, novels, TV documentaries and newspaper exposures. But the organised gangs which flourished in the East End and in south London no longer seem to dominate London's criminal fraternity. In their place has emerged a much larger army of petty criminals, with a more individual and opportunist approach to their calling.

The result has been a dramatic increase in the 'bread and butter' crimes, of housebreaking, theft and vandalism. In 1983, the Metropolitan Police recorded over 659,000 offences, almost double the number of ten years earlier; and the overall trend looks like continuing upwards.

Since the mid-1970s, robbery has increased by an average of 16 percent every year; burglary by 8 percent; and theft and the handling of stolen goods by 6 per cent. Even more worrying has been the growth in the use of violence against individuals. These attacks have risen by an average of 7 per cent every year since 1973.

Such figures have had a profound effect on most Londoners. Those who have not actually suffered break-ins themselves know of friends, workmates or neighbours whose homes have been ransacked – sometimes more than once. Some surveys suggest that as many as half the people of London are afraid to venture out at night for fear of being attacked. This may be an exaggeration, but it is certainly true that the elderly feel particularly threatened by what they see as an increasingly violent society.

London's crime seems to be dominated by young people. In 1983, for example, three quarters of all those arrested were under the age of 30. The 17-20 age group accounted for a quarter of all arrests and those under 17 for another 21 per cent. It is hardly surprising that the Police seem to welcome the projected decline of the 10-20 age group in London's population.

Unemployment is clearly one reason for young people turning to crime. Another is the growth of drug abuse. In the past hard drugs were either not available or well beyond the means of ordinary youngsters. Today they are both easy to get hold of and comparatively cheap. This has produced a whole new market for the pushers, particularly among unemployed young people bored with life in London's anonymous council estates.

The growth of drug taking has, in its turn, fuelled other crimes as addicts are forced into theft or burglary in order to pay for their habit. Parents, teachers and community leaders have all reacted strongly against this new threat and are starting to work with the Police in an effort to stop the drug menace before it takes root among young Londoners.

Faced with a rising level of crime, the Metropolitan Police is now giving top priority to securing maximum co-operation from the public. Formal consultative committees have been set up in many of the boroughs. These provide a forum in which ordinary people can influence the objectives and the performance of their local force. The difficulty of catching those responsible for petty theft, robbery and mugging has also forced the Police to place much greater emphasis on the prevention rather than detection of crime.

Crime prevention panels are one expression of this change but the most obvious has been the development of neighbourhood watch schemes. These encourage local residents to keep their eyes open for suspicious activity in their area and to alert the Police at the first sign of trouble. Predictably such schemes have taken off more rapidly in the better-off, owner-occupied, areas than in the council estates where crime is at its worst and people are most at risk. Nevertheless, the concept of neighbourhood watch has generated a good deal of interest and enthusiasm and done something to forge closer links between Londoners and their Police.

*   *   *   *

Shorter working hours, longer holidays and unemployment have all combined to give today's Londoners more free time than had their parents. Leisure is now big business, but one which has seen massive changes over the post-war period. Soccer and the cinema no longer have the same appeal. Football teams which regularly drew crowds of 50,000 now scrape by on barely one tenth of that figure. Cinema attendance in London in 1984 was only a quarter of what it had been as recently as 1966.

The changing style of London leisure can be seen in the shopping centres. Young people sporting 'ghetto blasters' or personal stereos stroll past video shops and sports boutiques that were undreamt of even five years ago. But one feature has remained constant − London's pre-eminent position as a national and international artistic and cultural centre. This is a major attraction for the visitors who helped to produce the record 10 million attendances notched up by the Society of West End Theatres in 1984. Yet London's role as a cultural centre is mainly restricted to the West End − just as its role as a financial centre is mainly restricted to the City. Outside the central area, the number of theatres, art galleries or concert halls is limited. The Theatre Royal at Stratford in the East End and the Fairfield Halls at Croydon are the exception rather than the rule. Like visitors from the provinces and from overseas, Londoners tend to make the pilgrimage to the West End for their cultural night out.

The continuing flow of overseas tourists, cameras clicking and guide books in hand, is one of the few bright spots on London's otherwise gloomy economic horizon. Four out of every five visitors to Britain spend several nights – and considerable sums of money – in the capital. The national Government seized on this potential bonanza in the late 1960s with cash grants to encourage more hotel building. This helped to achieve an explosion of 25,000 extra bedrooms over a four-year period. That investment has clearly paid off. Over 8 million overseas tourists visit London every year spending almost £2,500 million in the process. They make about a tenth of all Underground train trips and contribute around 40 percent of London theatre takings. Their favourite spots remain the tried and trusted attractions typified in the Tower of London, the British Museum, Buckingham Palace and Big Ben. However, strenuous efforts are being made to lure them away from central London. Greenwich, with the spectacular architecture of the National Maritime Museum, the Royal Observatory, and the Royal Naval College, has always had a particular appeal; but its less glamorous neighbour, Woolwich, now has something to show off. The Thames flood barrier, officially opened by Her Majesty the Queen in May 1984, has been hailed as the 'eighth wonder of the world'. Built in order to protect the city from the threat of disastrous flooding, the barrier spans a third of a mile across the Thames. Its ten massive steel gates swing up from the river bed when danger threatens. Its nine stainless steel clad piers rise from the grey river like a huge set of capped teeth. The tourist potential of such an extraordinary sight and such a remarkable technological feat was recognised from the start and facilities have been provided to cope with up to half a million visitors a year.

But this welcoming attitude to tourism is not universal. Some Londoners clearly resent the numbers of foreign visitors who throng the West End, fill the restaurants and shops and take over the traditional attractions during the height of the summer. Others point to the fact that tourist-related employment in hotels, catering and shops tends to be low paid and beyond the reach of trade union organisation. Nevertheless, for good or ill, London is likely to remain heavily dependant on the interest of overseas visitors and, more important, on their Dollars, their Deutschmarks and Yen.

*   *   *   *

Ever since the days of Dick Whittington, and probably before, London has been attracting ambitious people from all parts of the United Kingdom seeking fame, fortune or just a reasonable living. Unrest and repression in Europe also generated successive waves of refugees seeking a chance to live their lives in peace and freedom.

During the affluent 1960s, London attracted a very different type of immigrant. Workers from the New Commonwealth, brought from sunnier climes to run vital public services, put down roots and gradually became a part of London's cosmopolitan scene. Some of these new immigrants settled in East London following in the footsteps of pre-war European groups fleeing from persecution. Others set up home in more solid, settled areas of south and west London unused to strangers and their foreign ways.

Once the pioneers had established themselves, the ties of nation, culture and language attracted new arrivals, solidifying neighbourhoods into Caribbean, Bengali, Indian or Pakistani communities. The concentration of these black and brown Londoners in some of the city's toughest areas has always left them vulnerable to attack. Popular support for the National Front and other overtly racialist parties has declined somewhat from the worryingly high levels of the 1970s but windows are still smashed in black homes and 'Pakky bashing' still goes on.

Unemployment has hit black youngsters particularly hard and their conviction that the whole system is stacked against them occasionally boils over into violent protest. The Brixton riots of 1981 in south London revealed just how wide the gulf had become between the machinery of the State and a deprived and despairing black community.

The enterprise and skill of Asian businessmen, on the other hand, have enabled them to carve out a growing share of London's commercial life. Patel and Singh are now familiar names above corner groceries, off-licences, sub-post offices and even supermarkets. Hard work and a reputation for service to the public have brought their rewards and enabled many families to move up-market away from the ghetto and into the suburbs.

The varied backgrounds of the new Londoners, following on past waves of immigrants from Ireland, Central and Eastern Europe, has enriched the cultural life of the capital. Events like the Notting Hill Carnival and the celebration of Hindu, Moslem and Sikh religious festivals have brought new life and colour to some previously staid parts of the city. Politically the ethnic vote has been closely but not enthusiastically identified with Labour. However, activists are now setting up separate black sections in a number of London constituencies in a deliberate attempt to mobilise the black vote for socialism.

The political map of London predictably reflects the social divisions between working class inner areas and the more affluent outer boroughs. The old London County Council area, now contained within the twelve inner boroughs, has for generations been Labour's traditional heartland. In good years as many as 10 inner London Councils are Labour controlled. Only once since its establishment has the Inner London Education Authority slipped from Labour's grasp.

Outer London, on the other hand, has a much more varied political pedigree. It includes rock solid Labour East End areas like Newham and Barking, together with high Tory Boroughs like Bromley and Barnet and more evenly balanced areas like Brent and Ealing. But the predominant political feeling in Outer London is Conservative. Even in its best years Labour has failed to win a majority of the twenty outer boroughs.

The election of Greater London councillors has produced much more even contests. Control of County Hall has swung backwards and forwards at almost every election, with Labour and Conservatives enjoying an almost equal share of the Council's twenty-one years of life.

The social changes which hit London during the 1970s and 1980s have had a profound effect on the capital's Labour Party. The departure of heavy industry robbed it of the skilled craftsmen who traditionally supplied its local leaders and activists. The influx of young, well-educated and articulate teachers, lecturers and social workers shifted the centre of gravity to the Left. The seven-day a week dedication of these newcomers made it comparatively simple for them to achieve control of ageing constituency organisations and the London Regional Committee.

The next step was to win seats on local authorities and to gain control of traditional mainstream Labour Boroughs like Southwark, Hackney, Greenwich, Lewisham and Haringey. This turned London into one of the main battlegrounds between Tory Ministers and Left Wing Labour Councils. The one exception is Richmond, where a strong Liberal-lead performance in the 1982 election was turned into eventual Alliance control of the Council through subsequent by-election victories.

London's polarised politics made it difficult for the Alliance to break through in the 1983 general election. Although achieving best results in outer London, where it polled only 2,400 fewer votes than Labour, its only two successes came in the archetypal south London Labour strongholds of Bermondsey and Woolwich. However, both probably owed more to particular local circumstances and to sustained community campaigning than to any national political appeal.

Whilst not succeeding themselves, Alliance candidates undoubtably helped to cut Labour down to holding only 26 of London's 84 Parliamentary constituencies. Even in its inner city citadel, Labour's strength was reduced to 15 of the 29 seats. However, this overwhelming Conservative domination may not last. Since 1983, London politics have been dominated by the planned abolition of the GLC. There is no doubt that this issue has re-kindled Labour support and that the Government's case has been overwhelmed by a skilful and well funded public relations campaign masterminded from County Hall.

*   *   *   *

Thus we seem to end back where we began. For most people the mere mention of London conjures up exciting images of success. The West End's luxury hotels, department stores and smart eating places; the world wide influence of the City's financial and commercial institutions; the capital's historic role as the seat of Parliament and Government − all combine to convey the impression that London's streets really are paved with gold. Even the neat, well-tended semi's and the tree-lined avenues of the suburbs exude an air of comfortable security.

This image of prosperity and well being makes it difficult to persuade national Governments that London has serious problems and that they are getting worse. Cuts in public spending programmes will do nothing to shorten the dole queues, sweep away the decaying housing or clean up the vandalised council estates that characterise the deprived inner core of London.

Abolishing London's admittedly imperfect strategic authority will make things worse. Thirty-three boroughs with differing interests and sharply contrasting political attitudes will not find it easy to agree on overall solutions to promote new jobs, modernise outdated transport links and improve the quality of life. The more affluent outer boroughs have never shown much enthusiasm for helping their harder pressed inner neighbours and the absence of an overall London authority is likely to encourage this isolationism.

Yet, the problems of inner city decline cannot be bottled up indefinitely. If they are not faced soon, they may well spill over into more fortunate neighbourhoods. Ministers have decided that strategy will be decided, not by an elected London body, but by Whitehall and Westminster. Given the track record of national Government, the chances of arresting London's decline do not look good.

THE SOUTH EAST
Teddy Taylor

A distinguishing feature of Teddy Taylor's contribution is his description of the contrast which he found on moving from Glasgow to Southend. This contrast is between the tradition of the extended family, which cushions the effects of domestic differences in Scotland, and the many broken families which occur in the affluent society of South East England.

Edward Taylor is 49. He was educated at Glasgow High School and University. He is a journalist and a company director. He was M.P. for Glasgow, Cathcart, from 1964 to 1979 and is now Member for Southend East. He has been Under Secretary of State (Development) for Scotland, but resigned in 1971 because he was opposed to the Government's policy on British membership of the EEC. He was Chief Opposition Spokesman on Scotland from 1977 to 1979. He was a member of the Select Committee on the Environment and Vice Chairman of the Committee of Conservative backbenchers on trade and consumer affairs.

It was in 1980, after a fiercely contested by-election in Southend on Sea, that I became the M.P. for the east part of that delightful town on the Thames Estuary and moved house, with the family, from Scotland to my new constituency. I hope that it is the fact of my relatively recent arrival in the South East that enables me to identify some of the special features of this most significant area of the kingdom in a way which long term residents cannot.

Perhaps one of the most interesting features about the commuter parts of the South East is that an M.P. coming from Scotland is not so unique and astonishing as he might be, say, in rural Cornwall or Shropshire where residents are said not to be 'accepted' until the third generation. In the Sunday lunchtime 'drinks parties' (a decidedly strong feature of commuter towns) it is far from unusual to find a host of people who have come from 'somewhere else'. Many who have made their home in this part of the country evidently come to the South East in search of promotion and prosperity.

The South East is generally accepted as consisting of the counties of Kent, Essex and East Sussex. These three counties share the common feature of having a coastline facing the Continent of Europe. They are also so close to London that many of their residents travel daily to work there.

Despite their proximity to the capital and its suburban expansion, each of the three counties has an abundance of good agricultural land. Both sides of the Thames Estuary are among the flattest areas in England. Certainly the South East is about the most prosperous part of the United Kingdom, with the high living standards, high property values and affluent lifestyle of a significant portion of the population which goes with such prosperity — exclusive golf clubs, massive sailing clubs, bulging private schools and an abundance of expensive restaurants.

In fact the term 'South East' has, in recent times, become almost a term of political abuse and criticism on the part of politicians and local councils in other regions who argue consistently that the prosperity of the mini-region in the South East should somehow be curtailed as a means of spreading development throughout the nation.

I mention 'recent times' because historically speaking and up till the mid-1930s, the economic strength of Britain was based in the Midlands and areas like the Clyde and Mersey. Then, beginning with the great depression of the early 1930s, there was a steady drift of population away from the areas hitherto dominated by the obsolete heavy industry to the southern counties. Since then its prosperity has increased steadily and *despite* rather than because of government endeavours and planning, which have in fact been concentrated on aiding development elsewhere via regional development cash and other measures.

No, the expansion of the South East has been the natural consequence of economic trends and this tends to mean that great areas of it are covered with modern housing estates from which armies of young fathers pour out to catch the 7.45 am trains to London.

*   *   *   *

So what are the special features of life in the South — the kind of things which as an immigrant Scot I find have hit me firmly between the eyes.

First, there is an astonishing and well-organised resistance to change. In the North, if 'the authorities' decided that it was the right thing to press ahead with a motorway development, most people seemed to accept it. Authority was, generally, not questioned and the appropriate steps were taken to re-house tenants, compensate property owners — and send in the bulldozers. By comparison, in the South East, even a proposal to extend a grass verge produces the normal response of the local residents in holding coffee mornings in the Church Hall to fight the plans through to the High Court. The basic ingredient of the difference is, I believe, twofold; the high incidence of costly, owner-occupied property (which makes residents fight with fury against anything which might affect their property values) and the highly articulate nature of a community which includes, in the area I know best, a high proportion of civil servants, professional people and leaders of the City's financial community.

On the more positive side, a real joy in the South East is the total absence of tribal or sectarian bigotry. Although church goers are not unduly more prevalent in the North, it would be wrong to ignore the major part which prejudice still plays in communities. For example, and from experience, in some parts of the West of Scotland, where owner-occupied estates adjoin council areas, vandalism and other social evils are invariably laid at the door of the 'tribe' in the council scheme. Likewise, there is still a deep belief in some areas that decisions on jobs, contracts, and even house allocations are made not on merits but on sectarian grounds. Conversely, the Scots have probably made Asian immigrants more welcome than any other part of Britain, but time alone will tell whether this is because of traditional hospitality or because the size of the 'tribe' is small. By comparison, religious denominations in the South East are basically harmonious. I think it is true, in general, that a South East father would regard the financial and mental stability of the young man his daughter intended to marry as more significant than the religious denomination to which he belonged. It must also be said that the South East makes it infinitely easier for people to move up and down the scales of social class. The heavy incidence of owner-occupation, and the higher number of well-paid jobs available, makes it possible for young people to move from humble terrace house to bungalow, to semi-detached — and then to the ultimate detached four bedroom property with a view of the sea or golf course — much more easily than in the North, where it can be most difficult to break through the class barriers.

On the negative side, it must be recorded that family break-up and the absence of extended families to support those with problems does create a great deal of unhappiness in the South East. In the North (at least when I left it in 1980), a family break-up and a divorce were still regarded as unusual and tragic events which would at least justify the perpetrators being pointed out by local gossips as objects of special interest. By comparison, I find that most of the invitations which I receive are addressed to 'Mr Taylor, M.P. and partner' because Secretaries of Clubs and neighbourly hosts clearly have a major task in keeping up-to-date with the latest details of those falling at the hurdles of the marriage stakes. In many of the local schools I visit, the teachers say that about half the youngsters come from broken homes or from homes where there is at least a degree of marital or non-marital disorganisation.

This absence of the 'extended family' in the South East may indeed be partly responsible for the higher incidence of marriage break-up. When the children become impossible in the North, when father has a bout of drinking or other anti-social activity, when boredom becomes chronic, when illnesses and depressions which afflict, there is always the sister-in-law, the granny or the multitude of cousins who can step in to take some of the strain. Granny can, for example, take over the children for a few days until the crisis fades away or the sister-in-law can 'move in' to provide the basis for reconciliation and recovery.

But for many of the young marrieds in the South East, granny may be in Cardiff, the sister may be in Newcastle, and the friendly neighbours may have moved away last month to Sevenoaks as a consequence of the husband's promotion. It is my belief that the lack of an extended family, readily available to provide help, is a major cause of sadness, misery and potential family collapse in the prosperous South of England.

I think it is also fair to make the broad generalisation that people in the South East tend to overspend their incomes in a way which would be unthinkable in the North. One of the reasons is the pressure of a competitive society. It is not a question of 'keeping up with the Jones's' — it is something more compelling and subtle. If you don't provide your child with a BMX bicycle when the other local children have one, there is a strong sentiment that you are letting your child down. Likewise in some areas, it is almost taken by some as to be a sign of showing inadequate appreciation of your wife if you cannot provide her with a small car of her own to take the children to the Cubs, the dancing class or the Girl Guide's Disco. And because optimism is high, because promotion prospects are more readily available, people are more willing to take on the most horrendous financial burdens through bank loans, second mortgages, credit cards and all the other financial facilities of a competitive society. When I was in my Glasgow 'surgery' for constituents, a financial crisis was regarded as when the Gas Board were pressing for payment of a £92 bill. In the South East, a financial crisis is more likely to be the problem of paying interest on a £4,000 loan from a finance company, taken on in happier days to pay for an extension to the bungalow and to provide room for the new baby. The pattern was made clear to me by a local bank manager, who told me that a normal young married couple tended to get deeper and deeper into debt until the age of around 43 when there was usually a legacy from an elderly relative to put things right. However, if the elderly relative lives to be over 80, or the expected promotion does not come or worse still the husband's employer goes into receivership then the crisis comes with a terrible crunch.

There are, of course, many other special features. People in the North tend to give generously at the door to the Salvation Army ladies when they call with little envelopes. The South East is hugely committed to charities, often astonishingly obscure. Indeed, I have attended many functions to raise funds for the relief of the social consequences of diseases, social maladies and injustices of whose existence I was previously unaware.

The roads are also a remarkable reflection of the difference in life styles. In the North, public expenditure programmes designed to relieve poverty have created a situation in which roads are built in anticipation of traffic increases, many of which just do not emerge. But in the South, the incidence of car ownership and the scarcity of public funds result in a situation in which motorists can never be certain of reaching any particular place at any particular time. Road congestion is an endemic feature of the affluent South East. Even the brilliant new motorways become horrific disaster areas of chronic traffic chaos if a lorry breaks down or if one of the lanes is being repaired.

Many of the women in the South of England are in a situation whereby a large proportion of them are employed in jobs — many of them rather menial — as a means of providing the extra family income to provide opportunities for their children. Ambition for children is an important feature of the lifestyle which is not restricted to education as a means of the child bettering himself. It is not unusual, for example, for a housewife to take on a job in a depressing factory, doctors surgery, or even a school kitchen, in order that her young son can pay a subscription to a golf club or go with his school for a skiing trip to Switzerland.

*   *   *   *

Features of the social scene must not however be allowed to dominate any exposition of the South East. The areas as well as the people are fascinating and interesting. Indeed it would be wrong to regard the South East as an area with common features in any except the social sense, for each county has a character and history of its own.

Essex, which is the most northerly of the three regional counties, lies directly east of London. Its prosperity can be gauged by the fact that more people now live in Essex than in any county outside the built-up metropolitan areas. It is a county of real contrasts; of rolling countryside and riverside marshlands, of farmlands and forests, of busy harbours and quiet anchorages, and of seaside resorts. It has inland centres of commerce and communications, contrasting ancient and historic towns, thrustful new concrete centres of population, magnificent motorways and narrow country lanes.

There is no place in a study such as this, of social and economic conditions today, as seen from Westminster, to record in full and thus still less do justice to, the history of these three counties, from Roman times onward. Of all the invasions of the south eastern corner of England from across the North Sea and the Channel there is one at least — the Norman — which is embedded in the popular memory. The East Sussex County Council issues its publicity handbook under the title *The 1066 County*.

The Essex County Council came into being in 1889, but after a short while East Ham (in East London) and Southend on Sea broke away to form self-governing boroughs. However their independence was short lived; in 1965 East Ham was absorbed by London and in 1974 Southend on Sea became part of the County of Essex.

In Southend there is still a sense of grievance about the loss of its 'independence' and of its right to run its own police and education services, although its great Pier — the longest in the world — remain under the control of the Borough Council. While the majority of Essex residents work within the county, the fact that more than half the county's railway stations are within one hour's journey of London means that an estimated 20 per cent of the population travel daily to work in London. While the pressures of high cost and local rates in London have resulted in a significant transfer of office work from the capital to the county, the number of commuters still remains high.

However, quite apart from office work, Essex has a significant number of major industrial and commercial firms operating within its boundaries. The giant Marconi Electronics firm employs about 20,000 people; Ford has a major investment at Dagenham; and other household names like Standard Telephones and Mobil have big establishments in the county. In Southend are the headquarters of the giant Access Credit Card Company and the Customs and Excise Office dealing with VAT.

Leisure is an important industry and the so-called 'sunshine coast' is within easy travelling distance of London. There, fishing, with no major port, is still widespread with many smaller ports specialising in shellfish. And of, course, oysters are a traditional speciality of Colchester.

With the superb recreational facilities in the county provided by the National Trust and Nature Conservancy Council, and with the remarkable cultural and artistic facilities throughout the county, Essex is an area of thrustful prosperity allied with a determination of its inhabitants to preserve a beauty and tranquility which stems from its historic past.

*   *   *   *

Kent is much the same size as Essex but faces it across the Thames Estuary. In consequence, travel from Essex to Kent was far from easy until the situation was transformed with the building of the Dartford Tunnel, and the consequent elimination of the London detour.

The Tunnel is now part of the new M25 Motorway which will encircle London and, within Kent, the M25 is linked to a network of post-war motorways. As a result, heavy transport from the North can travel by motorway through the Tunnel and on to the busy channel port of Dover.

Being the closest county to the Continent, Kent has served through history as the gateway to Europe. This link could be more direct if the Channel Tunnel were ever to be realised. This visionary idea, first considered in 1802, has been twice embarked upon and twice abandoned. It was opposed in the past by those who thought it might provide a facility for a French army of occupation to march into England when nobody was looking. Later, it was opposed by those who considered that French rats would bring disease into the British Isles. It is still even opposed by some, even though it has been agreed to proceed − and inevitably, the Dover Harbour Board still see it as an unwelcome source of unfair and possibly subsidised competition.

When the Romans invaded Britain in 55 BC, they built their famous Watling Street all the way from Dover to London in a straight line, a magnificent technical achievement. A world famous feature of Kent is the castle crowned huge white chalk cliffs of Dover, a sight which was said to uplift the spirits of pilots returning to base from sorties in the Second World War. Nowadays there are probably more heavy lorries pounding along the network of motorways which cross the county than in any other part of the country and the constant flow of vessels and hovercraft coming into Dover bring with them the trade from Europe. And the network of electric lines which make up much of British Rail's Southern Region carry thousands of commuters to and from work in London.

Above all, Kent can still claim to be the orchard of England, and yet unlike some other Home Counties, seems able to contain its substantial economic vitality without disrupting the charm and elegance of its towns. None of the towns are particularly large; even Canterbury is only a medium-sized city. Maidstone, Gravesend, Gillingham, Rochester and Chatham are all towns which have avoided becoming urban sprawls, and the seaside towns of Thanet and Folkestone are moderate in size by comparison with the huge resorts elsewhere. Tunbridge Wells retains the elegant distinction of an 18th century spa. Its rise to fame stems from the 17th century discovery of the Chalybeate Spring with its claim to great health giving qualities. And it certainly did no harm when King Charles I's Queen, Henrietta Maria, came to the borough in 1630 to recover from the birth of her son — and so the town became Royal Tunbridge Wells.

*   *   *   *

Sussex, which lies east of Kent is separated from the Greater London Area by the intervening county of Surrey. It has a long and rather thin shape with an 80-mile coastline with, historically, rather poor communication from east to west.

It lies just below the network of motorways surrounding London and of those linking the Kent ports to the capital. Its geographic features have resulted in it being divided for administrative purposes between East and West Sussex and the population of just under one-and-a-half million is divided equally between the two parts.

Whilst Gatwick Airport can be regarded as the most noteworthy modern feature of West Sussex, the site of the Battle of Hastings is regarded by many as the most famous historical feature of East Sussex.

The population of East Sussex is concentrated largely on a number of relatively large towns on the coast, the largest of which is Brighton and adjacent Hove with a combined population of about 250,000. Inland, however, the towns and villages are small and rather sleepy. The coastal resorts have a certain solidarity and grandeur not displayed in some of their more flighty and superficial counterparts in other parts of the South East; and one is much less likely to meet motor cyclists covered with tattoos or girls with hats displaying the 'kiss me quick' motif in Eastbourne than in, say, Clacton or Frinton.

Brighton itself has some handsome 18th century buildings surviving on its sea front and the famous Royal Pavilion which was a costly and extravagant seaside palace built for the Prince Regent, who became King George IV. It has been described as the most fantastic palace in Europe and was used not only as a royal residence but also as a home for the Prince Regent's treasures and works of art.

However, it would be wrong to regard Brighton as simply an elegant tourist resort or conference centre. It is a centre of enterprise and commerce with one of the highest concentrations of new and growth industries and activities in the South East. It is the place where in 1984, Irish terrorists endeavoured to blow up the British Cabinet who were staying at the Grand Hotel on the occasion of the Conservative Party Conference. But it is not only the resorts that attract visitors. Tourism is a huge industry in Sussex with East Sussex having about 3,000,000 holidaying each year, and of which over 400,000 are from overseas.

Inland, East Sussex has its own glories, particularly its Downs and woodland. The county contains the world famous Glynebourne Opera House, set amidst the beautiful South Downs. Lovely Sheffield Park is famous for its house and gardens and contains the delightful Bluebell Railway, a magnet for steam train enthusiasts from far and wide.

*   *   *   *

Thus, the South East of England is not a 'region' in any of the obvious senses which other parts of the Kingdom can be so classified. There is no identifiable South East accent and it is doubtful if residents of Brighton or of Eastbourne feel any more linked culturally or socially to the people of Dover or Southend on Sea.

But what does unite the area is that it has enjoyed the fruits of prosperity in recent years without the planning nightmares which were created by the earlier upsurges in activity in the Midlands or Merseyside. While being a vigorous area for new development, it still provides a haven of peace and tranquility which enriches the lifestyle of a multitude of people who earn their living in the busy and giant city of London.

Index